£1-95

The 30s Family Knitting Book

SPECIAL RUG-MAKING SECTION *Inside*

WOMAN and HOME

6D OCT 1935

THE NEWEST AUTUMN KNITTING INSIDE

A MAGAZINE OF DELIGHTFUL SUGGESTIONS

The 30s Family Knitting Book

Introduced & edited
by JANE WALLER

Duckworth

This book is dedicated to
Leo and Norah with love.

First published in 1981 by
Gerald Duckworth & Co. Ltd.
The Old Piano Factory,
43 Gloucester Crescent, London N.W.1.

ISBN 0 7156 1601 3

British Library Cataloguing in Publication Data

30's family knitting book.
  1. Knitting—Patterns
  I. Waller, Jane
  746.43′2   TT820

  ISBN 0-7156-1601-3

Printed in Great Britain by
Redwood Burn Ltd., Trowbridge, Wiltshire.

*To give complete accuracy, the patterns in this book have
been photographed straight from the original magazines.
The publishers hope that the authenticity of the lay-out and
designs will compensate for any unavoidable imperfections
in the reproduction.*

The Thirties Family Knitting Book provides a selection of patterns for every member of the family. Apart from the 'fashionable lady's jumper', there are garments for toddlers, teenagers, babies, boys, grannies and grandpas, and a few outsize sweaters. Advice on needles and wools is provided for every pattern. Knitters are advised to use the 'modern equivalent' needle-size chart provided and should read the following notes before starting a pattern.

1. ALWAYS knit a tension strip and change the needle size up or down accordingly, especially if you are using a thicker wool. Otherwise your garment won't have the same measurements as those given in the pattern. Personal knitting styles vary from very loose to very tight.

2. Modern wools being generally heavier than their pre-war equivalents, you will find that a ball won't go so far. Probably more wool will be needed today than is suggested in the pattern: roughly one ounce ball will be the equivalent of a 50 gramme ball. The fashionable style in the early Thirties was for sweaters to have a high waist. If you prefer a longer body, again you will need more wool.

3. Use pure wool if possible. This gives the right springiness and texture for an authentic Thirties look. Hand-wash your woollens in warm water and dry them flat on a towel or paper. A little olive oil added to the rinsing water will feed back oil into the wool.

4. Keep to the fine-ply wools and thin needles. These are what give the Thirties jumpers their essential quality. The garments may take longer to knit and require more patience, but the knitter will be well rewarded by the result and be justly proud of its fine appearance. The closely-knit stitches will keep their shape and last longer. Defying all changes in fashion, these garments will become 'woolly favourites' and look well for many years—even after they have had to be darned.

In 1930 appeared a jumper with an entirely new line which was designed to accentuate the qualities the Thirties woman required to suit her new image. It had to be soft and feminine, elegant and alluring, and show all the natural curves of the body. With its low floppy cowl necklines or a trembling bow set on the front, it was not afraid to emphasise the bust, and by tucking the jumper into the skirt, the wearer rediscovered the waist. The long tubular sweater of the Twenties which deliberately disguised the waist and flattened the chest vanished altogether. By 1932, the angular charms of the 'big' boyish flapper who only showed her ankles and knees were already out of date. The Thirties woman wanted to look tall, slim and graceful. Her skirts clung tightly and fell almost to her ankles. Her jumper had its waist set higher than normal to give the impression of longer legs. The shoulders were artificially widened with capes or puffed sleeves, giving an illusion of slender hips and waist. These garments were knitted in a loose bloused effect, with lacy stitches and in pale pastel shades, since these looked well with the newly-fashionable curled hair and a prettily made-up face. The choice of crepes, cottons and fine-ply wools lent further softness to the profile.

Preface

The era of the Charleston was left behind. The Thirties woman preferred to glide across the ballroom in her long fishtail gown to the strains of the big band. Perhaps beneath her dress she wore her knitted 'slimline undies', fashioned in the finest two-ply wool and knitted on the thinnest of needles to keep that alluring slim silhouette.

Women were now sexy, feminine and charged with mystery . . . and they demanded a different kind of man. The 'gay young man' of the Twenties had been too much of a gad-about. During the Depression the Thirties woman looked for a responsible adult, a dependable bread-winner—a good father to her child, a man she could lean on and trust. In the late Twenties, Jazz patterns and bold Jaquard designs on men's woollen garments had reflected the rather effeminate mood of the times. Fair Isles and bright garish colours were displayed on the vee-necked pullovers of every young man. By 1932, the masculine man reserved his knitted canary-coloured waistcoat for sport. He replaced it with a sober plain-coloured vee-necked classic which, instead of a pattern, had a textured stitch as part of the design. More often a knitted grey waistcoat replaced the one made of cloth in the grey flannel outfit which had become almost a uniform for the office man. The Prince of Wales, leader in men's fashion, chose to wear a new sleeveless slipover with a low rounded neck and sleeves. Men of taste all immediately chose to do the same.

The Thirties woman admired her new strong, fatherly man and strove with him to protect their ideal—the safety of a small home of their own, the security of a regular job and the care of children. As the effects of the Depression made themselves felt, she was thrown increasingly upon her own devices. It was often a case of mend-or-make-do. She knitted her own dresses, and made 'hubby's' pullover and serviceable sweaters for the children at school. And all the instructions came to her in the weekly women's magazines, together with advice on what wools and colours to choose.

Baby, the magazines said, should have his layette shorter, with fewer garments than had been thought necessary in the Twenties. 'Warmth without weight and freedom for the limbs'* was the aim. Though simplicity was still the keynote, the Thirties baby was allowed to display a frill or two. All garments should be of even thickness and weight: pink for a girl and blue for a boy. Baby's shawl and pram blanket were to be 'a porous cover of pure new wool'. Now that it was considered 'natural' for a child to get dirty, the toddler had a comfortable knitted two-piece suit with a chequered border—the same design for a girl and a boy. But after this stage, a little girl was expected to look very much like her mother.

* Quotations are from the fashion magazines of the time.

5

She should wear a knitted pastel frock with frills, and her hair should be encouraged to curl. A little boy should have short trousers with a crease down the front, like his father's long ones, and his pullover should be a 'miniature edition' of Dad's. Later, at school, where a child actively disliked appearing different from his fellows, 'a wise mother will watch how the other children in the neighbourhood are dressed and, as far as she can, try to have her children similarly attired'. They would need a plain pullover, and the girl a knitted pinafore dress with matching knickers to wear with her uniform school blouse.

As for her own sweater, the Thirties woman found that through her knitting skills she could vary the monotony of mass-produced clothes by adding character and 'a touch of individuality' to her apparel. Magazines began to offer exciting original styles to suit every occasion and competed to publish more appealing patterns than their rivals. By the mid-Thirties the craze for knitting was at its height. The economic situation had improved. Botany, angora, Astrakhan and Shetland wools were available, and the accessibility of dyes produced a wide variety of subtle colours and shades. The 'working girl' knitted striped outfits and 'sets' of smartly-matching skirt, scarf, jumper, gloves, handbag and hat to wear at the office. For the cinema a two-toned sweater was the right thing, and for a party or afternoon tea there were jumpers with capes and dainty buttons, ruffles and frills, puffed sleeves and bows, all looking charming and demure. These jumpers were often given special names—the 'Beatrice jumper', 'Sunray-neck', or even the 'dash about town'. Soon every knitting stitch possible had been invented or rediscovered. Knitters vied with one another to produce the most complicated stitch-work and elegant styles. Whole suits, skirts, jackets and dresses were knitted without difficulty. There seemed nothing that couldn't be made on the needles.

Throughout the Thirties a healthy complexion and physically fit body were what everybody wanted. Lesiure hours not spent at the cinema, on the dance floor or listening to the radio were used to pursue an active outdoor sport. Each activity demanded its own type of woolly. A white one for cricket or the cruise was still *de rigueur*, (though for tennis a small band of red or blue was allowed at the neck and hem), but for every other sport a bright colour was considered a good antidote to work. A pullover incorporating the new lightweight zip-fastener was good for cycling, a patterned vee-neck sweater for golf. Hiking was all the rage in the early Thirties. Suddenly people realised that you could be warm, without wearing several layers of garments, so hikers only needed a sweater over an airtex vest. This was light and warm and allowed the air to circulate freely. In 1933 it wasn't unusual to see a man and woman walking along hand-in-hand both wearing one of the new polo-neck sweaters in a basket-weave stitch. In summer there was a variety of cool knitted open-stitched sweaters for women in cotton, crepe, linen or fine wool. These could 'breathe' and were easily washed. They appeared in shades of pastel or white.

The family holiday by the sea became more feasible, especially from 1938 onward when 'holidays with pay' arrived. Swimwear in the new unshrinkable cottons and wools was knitted by mother for all the family, sometimes with a clever motif of a sea-horse in the design. The craze for sunbathing brought with it a range of daring low-backed suits for women, trunks with no top at all for men, and sizzling red-and-black-striped suits for the children.

As the decade wore on the mood in clothing reflected political unrest and threats of approaching war. The Prince of Wales had abdicated, and his brother, George VI, was conservative in his taste. Clothes became more formal and restrained, and severer lines appeared. Colours darkened, materials gained weight, and a tailored look was thought desirable. Women attached buckles, pockets, collars and cuffs to their knitted suits and pullovers. The waistline dropped to its normal position and was secured there with a belt. The aim was to look chic and smart. Buttons were decorative as well as functional; with brooches, pins and clips, they fastened themselves on to pockets or helped to secure a scarf around the neck. Knitted motifs and monograms appeared on the chest. Uplift for the bust was important, and the hair was shortened and swept upwards over the nape of the neck: a woman looked mature and ready for whatever might occur. The top-heavy fashion was still evident. Shoulders were wide and firm, acquiring padding to give strength to their outline. Sleeves were puffed into bishop or leg-o'-mutton styles, or were long and fitted to the cuff. Hems were raised, and hidden pleats or inset godets gave ease of movement to a skirt. Dresses acquired flared panels and were knitted tightly over hips and waist. A twin-set of matching pullover and cardigan was ideal. Taking her cue from the two Royal Princesses, every little girl chose to wear a red knitted twin-set with a kilt. Granny, however, preferred the comfort of a matronly cardigan in a neat effective stitch, and Grandpa liked to relax in a fawn, grey or brown cardigan with a pocket for his pipe.

A strange invasion from the continent in the form of 'folk' art was filtering through knitwear, producing tiny woollen coloured motifs of flowers, trees and peasants. Knitted smocked blouses had knitted 'bobbles' as draw-strings through their necks. Fair Isles with horses, soldiers and trains were created for little boys, and there was 'nothing so pretty or in such good taste as a little hand embroidery on a child's knitted frock'.

The father of the family chose a heavy overcoat, which was belted, with a pleat behind. The new range of thick 'double-knit' wools proved useful, for his wife could knit 'chunky' pullovers in a dark colour with a cable-stitch pattern, which looked masculine and strong. Or she could make him a heavy Shetland wool sweater in the popular style with rugged raglan sleeves. The cloth waistcoat returned to fashion, but if a man still preferred a knitted one, he chose a slipover which was quieter, and which relied for its effect on a variety of neat-looking stitches in the way of bars, honeycombs, small intricate ribs and wavy lines. In the country he wore the tough-looking zip-fastened 'lumber' jacket in a knitted dark-green moss stitch. Styles began to arrive from abroad. The Continent produced a pullover with a fashionable shawl collar which either buttoned on the left side or was zipped down the front. Colours were plain and dark. From the States, a slipover with a small stand-up collar became fashionable.

But in September 1939 knitting fashions came to an abrupt end. Patriotic knitters turned their skills to balaclavas, scarves, warm woolly blankets, service jumpers and gloves—if, that is, they had any spare wool and any spare time. . . .

Notes
on working from the patterns

Yarn Requirements

ozs.	Grams	25g	50g
1	28.35	2	1
2	56.70	3	2
3	85.05	4	2
4	113.40	5	3
5	141.75	6	3
6	170.10	7	4
7	198.45	8	4
8	226.80	10	5
9	255.15	11	6
10	283.50	12	6
11	311.85	13	7
12	340.20	14	7
13	368.55	15	8
14	396.90	16	8
15	425.25	17	9
16	453.60	19	10
17	481.95	20	10
18	510.30	21	11
19	538.65	22	11
20	567.00	23	12
21	585.35	24	12

25g = 0.8818342 oz.

Knitting Pin Metrication

English	Metric	English	Metric
14	2mm	5	5½mm
13	2¼mm	4	6mm
12	2¾mm	3	6½mm
11	3mm	2	7mm
10	3¼mm	1	7½mm
9	3¾mm	0	8mm
8	4mm	00	9mm
7	4½mm	000	10mm
6	5mm		

Crochet Hook Sizes

International Standard Sizes	Old Wool Sizes	Old Cotton Sizes	American Sizes
0.60	—	7	14 Boye
0.75	—	6½	12 Boye
1.00	—	5½	10 Boye
1.25	—	4½	—
1.50	16	3½	7 Boye
1.75	15	2½	4 Boye
2.00	14	1½	1 Boye or B Bernat
2.50	12	0	0 Boye or D Bernat
3.00	10	3/0	F Bernat
3.50	9	—	G Bernat
4.00	8	—	H Bernat
4.50	7	—	I Bernat
5.00	6	—	J Bernat
5.50	5	—	I Boye
6.00	4	—	J Boye
7.00	2	—	K Boye

Suggested Yarns

Page		Needles
9	Any standard Double Knitting Yarn	3¼mm & 4mm
10	Sirdar Country Style Double Knitting	3mm & 3¾mm
12	Any standard 4ply yarn	2¾mm & 3¼mm
13	Patons Beehive 4ply	3mm
15	Templetons H. & O. Shetland Lace	3mm & 4mm
17	Any standard 4ply yarn	2¾mm & 3¼mm
18	Any 4ply Baby Yarn	5½mm
20	Sirdar Wash 'n' Wear Crepe 4ply	2¾mm & 3¼mm
21	Sunbeam Sceptre Double Double	5mm & 6mm
22	Any standard 4ply yarn	2¾mm & 3¼mm
24	Sirdar Majestic 4ply	Ditto
26	Sirdar Majestic Double Knitting	3mm & 3¾mm
27	Patons Beehive OR Trident 4ply	2¾mm & 3¼mm
28	Ditto	
29	Sirdar Country Style 4ply	2¾mm & 3mm
31	Wendy Peter Pan Darling 3ply	2¼mm & 2¾mm
32	Any Double Knitting in a suitable mixture and 4ply Crepe in black	3mm & 3¾mm
36	Any standard 4ply	2¾mm & 3¼mm
38	Ditto	
39	Patons Fuzzy Wuzzy Angora	3mm & 3¾mm
40	Templeton's Glenayr Double Knitting	3¼mm & 4mm
42	Sirdar Sportswool	3¾mm & 4½mm
43	Sirdar Majestic 4ply	2¾mm & 3¼mm
44	Twilleys Stalite of Crysette	3mm & 3¾mm
46	Ditto	
48	Sirdar Wash 'n' Wear Crepe 4ply	2¾mm & 3¼mm
51	Any 4ply in suitable mixture colours	Ditto
52	Sunbeam 3ply or Jaegar 3ply	2¼mm & 3¼mm
54	Ditto	
57	Any 4ply suitable mixture colours	2¾mm & 3¼mm
60	Patons Beehive 4ply	Ditto
63	Any standard 4ply	2¾mm & 3¼mm
64	Sunbeam 3ply OR Jaeger 3ply	2¼mm & 2¾mm
65	Any standard Double Knitting	3mm & 3¾mm
66	Patons Beehive 4ply	2¾mm & 3¼mm
68	Sunbeam Sceptre Double Double OR Robin Double Double	4½mm & 5½mm
70	Any standard 4ply	2¾mm & 3¼mm
73	Any standard 4ply OR a fine cotton such as Twilleys Lysbet	2¾mm & 3¼mm
74	Any flecked Double Knitting	3mm & 3¾mm
76	Sirdar Country Style Double Knitting	Ditto
78	Any standard Baby 4ply— Wendy, Patons etc.	3mm & 3¾mm
79	Any Double Double such as Robin Crackerjack	5mm & 6mm
81	Templeton's Glenayr 4ply	2¾mm & 3¼mm
82	Sirdar Country Style Double Knitting	3mm & 3¾mm
83	An Aran weight such as Wendy Machine Washable Aran	3¾mm & 4½mm
85	Any standard 4ply	2¾mm & 3¼mm
86	Ditto	
89	Hayfield Sirius Double Knitting	3¼mm & 4mm
90	Phildar Menottes	Ditto
91	Useful pullover with V-neck—any 4ply	3¾mm & 2¾mm
93	Sunbeam 3ply or Jaeger 3ply	2¼mm & 3mm

CHECK YOUR TENSION

Work a sample 3" square, before starting on the garment. If the tension count in the pattern is, say, 8 stitches to the inch, count 8 stitches and mark them off with pins. If the distance between the pins is exactly 1", your tension is correct. If the distance is more, the stitches are too loose – try a smaller needle size; if it is less, they are too tight – try a larger needle size. A more attractive garment is produced if the knitting is kept fairly tight and even.

You can often use tension to alter the size of a garment without altering the pattern. For a garment one size larger, use needles one size larger, giving less stitches to the inch. For a garment two sizes larger, use needles two sizes larger.

GOOD MAKE-UP
makes all the difference

1. PINNING—Lay each piece wrong side up on an ironing pad. Place an 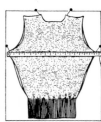 inch tape across the bust-line (A) and pin out to the right width. Do the same lengthways, (B), measuring from shoulder to lower edge. Pin all round the edges with plenty of pins about ½ inch

A. PINNING ACROSS

apart, (C). Pin the inside edge of ribbing.

B. PINNING LENGTHWAYS

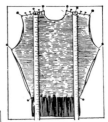

C. PINNING AROUND

2. PRESSING—Press each pinned piece. Dab the iron lightly up and down—don't rub. Use a warm iron and damp cloth unless instructed otherwise.

3. SEAMING—For tailored garments use a back-stitch seam, (D). Place pieces together, right side to right side and pin along, (E), matching row for row. Make a small stitch and insert needle about ¼ inch along seam. Draw needle through. Insert needle into end of last stitch and bring it out ¼ inch along seam

D. BACKSTITCH SEAM

again. Continue until seam is finished. For underwear and baby things, use a lace-up seam, (F). Place pieces together, right side to right side; with a finger between, seam corresponding ridges, matching row for row. Lock seam by stitching twice into one stitch every 6th ridge. Press all seams.

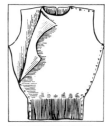

E. PINNING TOGETHER

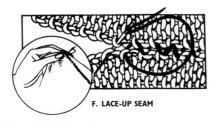

F. LACE-UP SEAM

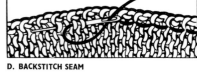

A KNITTED "TUCK-IN"

One Of The Neatest Jumpers You Could Ever Wish To See!

HEMLINES have been lowered, waists have been raised, and the tuck-in blouse has become one of our favourites—the knitted tuck-in being the newest and most popular of all.

ABBREVIATIONS : K., knit plain ; p., purl ; inc., increase ; dec., decrease ; st., stitch ; s.s. stocking stitch (that is k. on the right side of the work and p. on the back) ; tog., together.

MATERIALS : Five 2-oz balls of " Peacock " 3-ply Fingering in beige and one ball of dark brown ; a pair of No. 7 bone needles for the main part and No. 10 needles for the waist ribbing.

SIZE AND TENSION : Worked at a tension of 5½ st to the inch in width the following measurements are attained after light pressing. all round bust, 42 inches ; from shoulder to hem, 21 inches ; length of underarm seam without brown cuff, 21 inches.

TO WORK.—Using the beige wool and the No. 10 needles cast on 106 st., and k. one row plain, working into the back of the st.

Work 25 rows of single rib (that is k. 1 and p. 1 alternately).

Change to No. 7 needles and do 56 rows of s.s. On the next row, which is a k. one, k. the first st., inc. 1, by picking up the thread before the next st. with the left-hand needle, and k. into the back of this thread ; k. to within the last st., inc. 1 as before, then k. last st.

Inc. in this way every 6th row until 4 st. have been added at each end of the needle. Work two rows more.

THE FRONT OPENING.—K. 57 st. and pass the remaining half on a spare needle or stitch-holder and leave these for the working of the right front. On the needle with the first 57 st. cast on 16 st. for the rever facing. Work 5 rows more across all these st., when the underarm will be reached. Cast off 4 st at the beginning of the next 3 plain knitted rows and dec. 1 st at the beginning of each of the next 6 plain knitted rows. From here continue straight up until 36 rows can be counted at the neck edge.

Beginning at the shoulder end, k. 27, cast off 24 st., k. remaining st. to end, then cast off 1 st. at the beginning of each k. row until there is only 1 st. left, making a little point. Draw end of wool through this st. and fasten off securely.

Now go back to neck edge and p. back to shoulder. Work s.s. until there are 14 rows worked after the cast off neck st.

TO SHAPE THE SHOULDER.—P. to within 8 st of the end of the row, k. back. P. to within 16 st of the end and k. back. P to within 24 st. of end and k. back P. across all st. K. back and cast off on the wrong side.

THE LEFT FRONT —Begin at the middle of the neck where the st. were left on the first row of front opening. Cast on 16 st. for the rever facing, then k. plain to end of row. Work this front exactly like the left front, but remember that the shaping will be on reverse rows. The armhole st. will be cast off at the beginning of p. rows instead of k rows, and the rest of the shaping will follow suit.

THE BACK.—Work exactly the same as the front up to the underarm. The armhole shaping is exactly the same as on front, but it must be carried out at both ends of needle as there is no front opening. Cast off 4 st. at the beginning of each of the next 6 rows, after which dec. 1 st. at the beginning of each of the next 12 rows.

Now k. straight on all these st. until there are 4 rows less than on this part of the front.

BACK SHOULDERS.—K. 44, turn, cast off 10 st. and p. to shoulder. K. to neck, turn, and cast off 5 st. and p. back. K. 29 st. to neck. Cast off 2 st., p. to within 8 st. of end, turn and k. back to neck ; p. to within 16 st. of end, turn and k. back. P. across all st., and when you come to the little gap made by the turn, pick up the thread that lies between the st., twist it and put it on the left-hand needle and p. it tog. with the next st. to be worked. This will close the gap. Now cast off all the st.

For second shoulder begin at centre of neck, casting off the first 5 st., then k to armhole, p. back. Cast off 2 st. and k. to end ; p. back 27 st., k. to within 8 st. of end and continue to shape like first shoulder and cast off.

THE SLEEVES.—Begin at the shoulder end by casting on 48 st., then continue in s.s. casting on 2 st. at the beginning of the next 12 rows, after which cast on 3 st. at the beginning of the next 4 rows, making 84 st. altogether. Now dec. once at the beginning and end of every 6th row, inside the edge st., until the st. are reduced to 52. Continue straight down for 2 inches, or length required, less 1½ inches, which is finished in single rib of k. 1 and p. 1, then cast off.

THE COLLAR.—Using No. 7 needles and dark brown wool, cast on 29 st. and work moss-st., that is k. 1 and p. 1 alternately

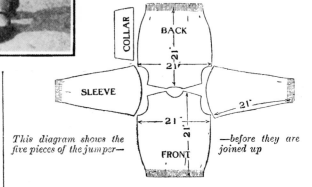

This diagram shows the five pieces of the jumper— *—before they are joined up*

on each row so that a k. st. comes over a p. st. and vice versa on each row. Continue for the length required, measuring from the front corner where the rever turns back to the corresponding corner on opposite side of neck, stretching the collar a little when measuring.

THE CUFFS.—Cast on 13 st. and work moss-st. the length required to go round the end of sleeve.

TO MAKE UP THE JUMPER.—Press all s.s. on the wrong side, putting a slightly damp cloth over the knitting. Turn back the revers and sew neatly along the top edge. Sew up the shoulder seam Tack sleeves in on wrong side, putting the centre of the cast-on st. to the shoulder line of the jumper when it is folded over—that is 4 rows down the front from joining of shoulders. Sew from this point down each side. Now sew up side and sleeve seam in one continuous line. Sew the moss-st. cuff on the right-hand side of sleeve, as it is afterwards turned over. Sew collar on right side of jumper, taking up one thread of collar with one on neck edge to make a neat seam. Now press all these seams

Fit on the jumper, turn back the collar and top of rever in desired position, pin before taking off tack and press well in this position.

BEWITCHING—with Its Lacy Scarf

A Soft Bow Tied Loosely Gives a Graceful Finish to a Jumper of Alluring Charm.

Here is a light-weight but cosy jumper, with an open-work scarf for neck trimming.

ABBREVIATIONS :

K., knit plain ; p., purl ; st., stitch or stitches ; tog., together.

MATERIALS :

For the jumper, 5 ounces of "Sirdar" Crochet Wool and 2½ ounces of the same wool for the scarf ; a pair of bone needles No. 8 and No. 11 for the jumper, and No. 9 and No. 11 for the scarf.

TENSION AND MEASUREMENTS :

The jumper illustrated was worked at a tension of 6 st. to the inch in width with the No. 8 needles, which produced the following measurements after pressing : round bust, 37 inches ; length from shoulder to lower edge, 18 inches. The scarf is 60 inches long and 7 inches wide.

The Jumper

Begin at the back and, using No. 11 needles, cast on 108 st. Work k. 2 and p. 2 rib for 20 rows.

Change to No. 8 needles and begin the fancy pattern.

1st row : With right side facing, k. plain.

2nd row: K. 2, * p. 2, k. 2 ; repeat from * to end of row.

3rd row : As 1st row.

4th row : P. 2, * k. 2, p. 2 ; repeat from * to end of row.

Note that on even rows "k. 2" always occurs over "p. 2" on the last even row, and vice versa. This will act as a guide in keeping the pattern correct when the shaping begins.

Repeat these 4 pattern rows 15 times more, when the underarm will be reached.

To Shape the Armhole

Cast off 2 st. at the beginning of each of the next 8 rows, then work 2 tog. at the beginning of each of the next 8 rows, leaving 84 st. Work 24 rows in pattern without shaping.

THE SHOULDERS · With the right side facing, k. 32 for first shoulder, and slip these st. on a spare needle. Cast off 20 st. for the middle of the neck, k. 32 for the right shoulder.

Working on the last set of st., cast off 2 st. at the neck end of every alternate row for 5 times, then work 2 tog. at the beginning of every alternate row (neck end) for 4 times. This leaves 18 st. Cast off.

For left shoulder, join to neck end of the spare needle st. and work as given.

When the evening is chill, after tennis, how cosy it would be to slip into this little jumper and tie the open-work scarf into a soft bow.

The Front

Work as directed for the back until the armhole shaping is finished and 84 st. are left. Now work 8 rows in pattern. Work the shoulders as given for the back until there are 18 st. left. Work 20 rows in pattern and cast off.

The Sleeves

With No. 11 needles cast on 76 st. and rib 14 rows. With No. 8 needles work 12 rows in pattern.

To shape the top of the sleeves cast off 4 st. at the beginning of each of the next 2 rows, then cast off 2 st. at the beginning of every row until 24 remain. Cast off the remainder.

Work the second sleeve in the same manner.

The Neck-Band

With right side of jumper facing, and using No. 11 needles, pick up and k. 104 st. on the front neck-edge. Rib 13 rows and cast off rather tightly.

Pick up and k. 72 st. on the back neck-edge and rib 13 rows. Cast off rather tightly.

To Make Up

First press all well, except the ribbing, with a damp cloth over the work. Sew shoulder seams and press. Sew sleeves to armholes and press, then sew sleeve and side seam in one continuous line. Press these seams.

Fine cord elastic can be threaded through the back of the stitches on the neck-edge, also on the upper edge of waist rib, to prevent stretching in wear.

The Scarf

With No. 9 needles, cast on 40 st., and do not work into the back of these. K. 18 rows.

Change to No. 11 needles and work in the following pattern :

1st row : K. 1, * make 2 by winding the wool twice round the right-hand needle, k. 1 ; repeat from * to the end of the row.

2nd row : K. 1, * drop the 2 made st. on last row, k. 1 ; repeat from * to the end of the row.

K. 2 rows plain.

Repeat from the 1st row 90 times more, then work the 1st and 2nd row again.

Change to No. 9 needles and k. 17 rows. Cast off.

Darn in any ends and press with a damp cloth over the knitting.

Demure Sophistication is the Subtle Effect Given by this Simple Jumper and Scarf. Here is no Characterless Shape, but a Line of Definite Appeal !

It is just as charming worn with a tweed skirt as it is with a summer outfit.

A WOOLLY FOR PREFERENCE—AND HERE IS OUR CHOICE !

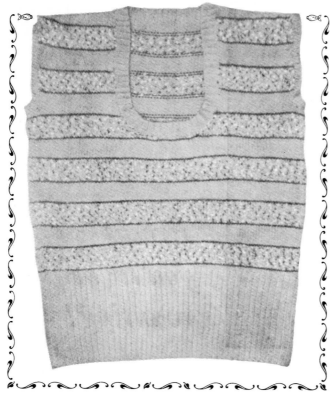

A Lady's Attractive Pullover

By

D. Whitley

For this cosy and attractive pullover you will require :

5 oz. of " Golden Eagle " merino 4-ply wool in plain saxe blue.

2 oz. of " Golden Eagle " Pastelprint merino 4-ply wool in blended shades.

½ oz. of " Golden Eagle " merino 4-ply wool in black.

1 pair No. 9 Milward's coloured "Archerite" needles and 1 pair No. 12.

Measurements.—Shoulder to bottom, 23 in. Round under-arm, 36 in.

Directions for Making the Front.— On No. 12 needles cast on 176 stitches in plain blue, and knit in ribs of 2 plain, 2 purl (knitting first row into the backs of the stitches to give firm edge) for 6 in. Then changing to No. 9 needles knit as follows :—On plain row : Knit 2 together 3 times, knit 1 : repeat this to the end of the row. (Knit the odd stitch plain.) You should now have 101 stitches on your needle. Purl 1 row. The remainder of the front is knitted in stocking-stitch ribs as follows :—1 row black, 10 rows blended, 1 row black, 10 rows plain blue. Continue in this manner until the work measures 14 in. altogether.

On the next plain row knit as follows :—Knit 39, cast off next 23 stitches, and knit the remaining 39. The work is now divided into two for the shoulders, continue on the piece of work to which the wool is attached, and knit to centre. Now knit 2 together, knit to end of row and back, repeating the last two rows until you have 34 stitches.

On the outside cast off 6 stitches to form part of the armhole, leaving 28 stitches. Continue in stocking stitch for 7 in., ending them at centre, then knit 21, reverse knitting and knit back the same 21. Knit 14, reverse knitting and knit back the same 14. Knit 7, reverse knitting and knit back the same 7. Cast off, and knit the other side to correspond.

Press the piece of work you have just finished with a hot iron over a damp cloth. On the right side of the work knit up (in plain) on No. 12 needles the stitches round the neck from shoulder to shoulder. (Approximately 14 stitches to each rib and 24 at the bottom.) Knit in ribs of 2 plain, 2 purl, for 9 rows. Cast off fairly tightly.

Directions for Making the Back

On the No. 12 needles cast on 160 stitches, using the plain blue wool. Knit in ribs of 2 plain, 2 purl, as at the front for 6 in. Change to the No. 9 needles and on the plain row knit as follows :—Knit 2 together twice, knit 1. Repeat to the end of the row—reducing your stitches to 96. Purl 1 row.

Knit in the fancy ribs as at the front until you reach the armholes, and then knit 2 rows, casting off 5 stitches at the beginning of each row, to form part of the armholes. You should now have 86 stitches on which to work 7 in. stocking stitch.

Do a further 8 rows of stocking stitch, casting off 7 stitches at the beginning of each row, leaving 30 stitches. On the right side of the work, with the No. 12 needles, knit a plain row, making an extra stitch in every 3rd stitch, bringing your stitches up to 40. Now do 9 rows of 2 plain, 2 purl, and cast off.

When you have worked both back and front of the pullover it should be thoroughly pressed with a hot iron over a damp cloth. Sew the shoulder seams together, and press.

Knit up in plain on the right side of the work approximately 112 stitches round the armhole, using the No. 12 needles. Do 4 rows in 2 plain, 2 purl, cast off, and press, sew side seams together, pressing these also thoroughly.

A Novel " Quick Change "

Two triangles of white piqué or silk, when buttoned to the front of a plain dress to look like revers, will completely alter the look of the dress.

Coloured revers can be substituted for a change when the others are soiled. Black buttons from wrist to elbow on the sleeve matching the rever buttons will bring them into line.

A PULL-OVER HE'LL APPRECIATE

designed by
Finella

Hubby will be only too pleased to discard his waistcoat and instead "sport" the comfortable garment his little wife has knitted for him. As you can guess from the photograph, the design is simplicity itself.

ABBREVIATIONS
K., knit; p., purl; st., stitch; in., inch.

MATERIALS
12 ozs. of 4-ply "Beehive" Scotch fingering in a tweed mixture, one small button, a small piece of material for the pocket lining, a set of No. 10 knitting needles with points at both ends and a pair of No. 10 knitting pins.

MEASUREMENTS
Length from the top of the shoulder—22 ins.

Width all round—36 ins.

Length of sleeve and shoulder from neck—31 ins.

Length of sleeve seam—21 ins.

TENSION
8 sts. to 1 in. in width.

THE *Back*.—Begin at the lower edge by casting on 142 sts., then work in k. 1, p. 1 rib for a depth of 3 ins., working into the backs of the sts. on the first row.

Change to stocking-st. and continue quite straight in this till the work measures a depth of 14 ins. from the beginning.

Now shape the armholes by casting off 3 sts. at the beginning of the next 6 rows, then 2 sts. at the beginning of each of the following 6 rows, then by decreasing next to the edge st. at both ends of the needle on each of the next 4 knit rows. 104 sts. remain on the needle.

Work quite straight for a depth of 5 ins., then shape the neck and shoulders.

1st row: Knit to within 7 sts. of the end, turn.

2nd row: Purl to within 7 sts. of the end, turn.

3rd row: Knit to within 14 sts. of the end, turn.

4th row: Purl to within 14 sts. of the end, turn.

5th row: Knit across 26 sts., cast off 24, then knit to within 22 sts. of the end, turn.

6th row: Purl to neck.

7th row: Cast off 10 sts. and work across the remainder.

8th row: Cast off.

9th row: Join the wool to the neck edge of the opposite side and purl to within 22 sts. of the end, turn.

10th row: Knit to neck.

11th row: Cast off 10 sts. and purl across the remainder.

12th row: Cast off.

The Front.—Work this in exactly the same way as for the back to within 16 rows of the armholes, i.e. for about 12 ins.

On the next row k. 28 sts., cast off 30 sts., and complete the row.

Now, using a spare pair of needles, cast on 30 sts. and work 6 rows in the ribbing. On the next row, work in the ribbing over 13 sts., cast off 4 sts. and complete the row in the ribbing.

On the following row, work along to the cast off sts., then cast on 4 sts. over those cast off, and complete the row. Work 5 more rows in the ribbing.

Take up the front, purl along to the cast off sts., then across the sts. of the pocket flap just made, and complete the row.

Now work across all sts. to within 8 rows of the armholes.

On the next row knit 71 sts., turn. On the next row, work back to the side edge.

Continue on these sts., passing the sts. of the opposite side to a safety-pin.

Now decrease next to the edge st. on the neck edge on the next and every following 3rd row till there are 22 decreases on this edge.

At the same time, when the side edge is the same depth as that of the back to the armhole, shape the armhole by casting off 3 sts. at the beginning of each of the next 3 knit rows, then 2 sts. at the beginning of each of the next 3 knit rows, and complete the shaping by decreasing on this edge on each of the next 4 knit rows.

Now keep the armhole edge straight and continue with the front shaping till this is completed. There will now be 30 sts. on the needle.

Work straight on these sts. till the armhole edge is 6 rows deeper than that of the back, then shape the shoulder.

1st row: Working from the front edge, work to within 7 sts. of the end, turn.

2nd row: Work back to front.

3rd row: Work to within 14 sts. of the end, turn.

4th row: As for the 2nd row.

5th row: Work to within 22 sts. of the end, turn.

6th row: As for the 2nd row.

7th row: Work across all sts.

8th row: Cast off.

Join the wool to the front edge of the opposite side and complete this side to match the first.

Sew the shoulders of the back and front together.

The Sleeves.—Begin at the shoulder-line by casting on 32 sts. Knit into the backs of these sts. and cast on 2 sts. at the end of the row.

On the following row, purl into the backs of the 2 cast on sts., purl the remainder and cast on 2 sts. at the end of the row.

Continue casting on 2 sts. at the end of every row till there are 120 sts. on the needle.

Work 7 rows straight, then on the next and every following 8th row, decrease next to the edge st. at both ends of the needle till 80 sts. remain. Purl the next row.

Change to k. 1, p. 1 rib, work a depth of 3½ ins., then cast off.

Work the second sleeve in the same way.

The Neck.—Using the set of needles, pick up and knit through every st., and the edge of every row round the neck.

Work a depth of 1¼ ins. in k. 1, p. 1 rib, decreasing on every row on each side of the V point at the centre-front of the neck. Cast off.

TO COMPLETE THE GARMENT
SEW the tops of the sleeves into the armholes.

Press out the work on the wrong, then on the right side with a hot iron over a damp cloth.

Make a small pocket with the material and sew to the pocket edges. Fold the flap down and sew the button in position.

Sew up the side and sleeve seams.

Press all seams well on the wrong side.

THE END

The Sweetest Thing in Capes!

Knitted in three harmonious colours !

Will This One Do?

**You Will Love Yourself
In This Pretty Jumper**

To Work : Begin at the main part of the back above the ribbed waistband, and cast on 109 sts. with coral wool and No. 8 needles. Work the first 3 rows in s.s., beginning with a k. row.

Next 3 Rows : Work in m.s., beginning with k. 1.

Repeat these 6 rows 10 times more, when the armhole will be reached.

To Shape the Armhole : Cast off 3 sts. at the beginning of each of the next 2 rows, then cast off 1 at the beginning of the following 14 rows. There are now 89 sts., on which work 35 rows straight, when the shoulder line will be reached.

Next Row : (4th row of pattern) Work 37 sts. and slip these on a spare needle for the left back shoulder, cast off 15 for the centre of neck, work 37 sts. for second shoulder.

Right Back Shoulder : Work in pattern, casting off 7 sts. at the beginning of alternate rows (armhole end); also cast off 3 sts. at the beginning of alternate rows (neck end) until all are worked off.

ISN'T it a delightful little jumper ? So light and pretty for the summer, because it is worked in the finest wool and on medium size needles.

The shoulder cape just covers the top of the arms, to prevent them from getting scorched in the sun.

MATERIALS : Use "Greenock" 2-ply Super-Fingering wool, in the following proportion : two ounces of coral, shade No. 251 ; and one ounce each of grey, shade No. 83, and light oatmeal, shade No. 141 (this wool can only be obtained at the Scotch Wool & Hosiery Stores). You need a pair of No. 11 and a pair of No. 8 long bone knitting-needles, and a spare needle ; also three small silver buttons.

ABBREVIATIONS : K., knit ; p., purl ; tog., together ; inc., increase ; st., stitch ; s.s., stocking-stitch (k. on the right side and p. back) ; m.s., moss-stitch (k. 1, p. 1 alternately, and on successive rows a k. must always come over a p., and vice versa).

TENSION AND MEASUREMENTS : Worked at a tension of 13 sts. to 2 inches in width, the following measurements are attained after light pressing : round bust at under-arms, 34 inches ; length from shoulder to waist, 18 inches

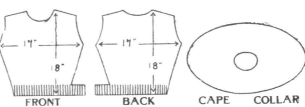

FRONT   BACK   CAPE COLLAR

This diagram will help you with the shaping.

LEFT BACK SHOULDER : Join the wool to the neck end and work 1 row, then work as given for right back shoulder.

THE FRONT · Work as given for the back until there are 89 sts. after shaping the armhole, then work 21 rows straight, when the front neck line will be reached.

NEXT ROW : P. 37 and slip on a spare needle for the right front shoulder, cast off 15, p. 37 for left front shoulder.

LEFT FRONT SHOULDER : Continue in pattern, casting off 2 sts. at the beginning of every alternate row (neck end)

Continued overleaf

WILL THIS ONE DO?

Instructions Continued From Previous Page

4 times, after which work 2 tog. at the beginning of alternate rows, at the same end, for 4 times. There are now 25 sts., on which work 6 rows in pattern, then cast off 6 sts. at the beginning of every alternate row (armhole end) until all are worked off.

RIGHT FRONT SHOULDER : Join the wool to the neck end and work 1 row, then follow the directions for the left front shoulder.

THE WAIST-BAND : First sew the back and front tog. at the right side-seam. With grey wool and No. 11 needles, cast on 35 sts. ; then, with the same needle, pick up and k. 100 sts. from the cast-on edge of the back, also 100 sts. from the front edge. Then cast on 35 sts. more, when there will be 270 sts. on the same needle. Rib 5 rows in grey, then with coral wool k. 1 row and rib 12 rows. With grey wool, p. 1 row and rib 5 rows. Cast off loosely.

Now press the whole piece with a damp cloth over the knitting, taking care not to press the ribbing. Sew up the other side-seam, leaving about 1 inch open at the waist, and press.

THE ARMHOLES : Holding the work with the right side facing, and using No. 11 needles and coral wool, pick up and k. 85 sts. round the armhole. Work 3 rows of m.s. and cast off loosely. Work the second armhole in the same manner.

Sew the shoulder seams on the wrong side and press.

THE CAPE COLLAR

FOR the edge of the back, cast on 39 sts. with oatmeal wool and No. 8 needles. P. 1 row. Now repeat the 6 pattern rows, casting on 6 sts. at the beginning of each of the next 4 rows (63) ; then cast on 4 at the beginning of each of the next 8 rows (95), cast on 2 at the beginning of the following 16 rows (127), cast on 1 st. at the beginning of the next 16 rows. There are now 143 sts. K. 1 row.

NEXT ROW : (4th row of pattern) Work 64 and slip these on a spare needle for the left shoulder, cast off 15, work 64 for the right shoulder.

RIGHT SHOULDER : Continue in pattern, casting off 3 at the beginning of alternate rows (neck end) 3 times (55 sts. on).

Work 16 rows, ending with a p. row (k. row on left shoulder).

Continue in pattern, casting off 1 st. at the beginning of the next row and every following alternate row (armhole end) ; also inc. 1 at the beginning of alternate rows (neck end) until 9 rows are worked (5 decreases at arm end and 4 incs. at neck). Now cast on 2 sts. at the beginning of alternate rows (neck end) 3 times, and also keep the arm decreases for 3 times more. There are now 57 sts., ending with the 5th pattern row (6th row on left shoulder). Cut the wool and slip these sts. on a spare needle.

LEFT SHOULDER : Join the wool to the neck end and work 1 row, then follow the right shoulder directions until 57 sts. are on the row, ending with the 6th pattern row. Cast on 15 sts. at the neck end, then work the 57 right shoulder sts. on the same needle (129 sts.). Repeat the 6 pattern rows, casting off 2 sts. at the beginning of each of the next 16 rows ; then cast off 4 sts. at the beginning of each of the following 8 rows. Now cast off 6 sts. at the beginning of 4 rows. Cast off the remaining 41 sts.

THE COLLAR EDGE : First mark the centre of the shoulder fold at each side ; then, on the front half with No. 8 needles and grey wool, pick up and k. 205 sts., with right side of work facing. K. 3 rows more in grey, then 4 rows coral, 3 rows grey, and cast off. Work the same on the back half and sew the edges together, then press the collar.

Now place the collar in position on the jumper, the shaped edges on both necks fitting exactly. Mark the shoulder lines, and for the front pick up and k. 74 sts. with the No. 11 needles and oatmeal wool, and with the right side of the collar facing. Take up two threads with each st., one from the jumper neck and one from the collar. Rib 5 rows and cast off.

At the back of the neck, pick up and k. 40 sts. in a similar way, rib 5 rows and cast off. Sew the neck ends together at the shoulders. Press the neck edge without stretching, and sew the three buttons in the front.

First Steps

must be taken in this Charming Little Knitted Frock

Here is a delicious frock to delight the heart of Miss Two-Years-Old. Mothers, aunts and big sisters will be getting out their knitting-needles without delay, for no one could possibly resist making this adorable garment if there is a baby girl anywhere waiting to wear it.

MATERIALS REQUIRED : *3 ozs. of Golden Eagle Merino Wool in any pastel shade ; 1 yard of ribbon to match ; three small pearl buttons ; a pair of No. 9 knitting needles ; a Stratnoid crochet-hook, No. 11.*

MEASUREMENTS : *After pressing, the length is 17 inches ; measurement round (under the arms) 20 inches ; underarm seam of sleeve, 3 inches.*

TENSION : *After pressing, 7 stitches make 1 inch in width and 9 rows make 1 inch in depth.*

ABBREVIATIONS : *st., stitch ; k., knit plain ; p., purl ; m. 1, make a st. by winding wool over needle ; inc., increase in the next st. by knitting two sts. into one st. ; s., slip ; p.s.s.o., pass slipped st. over last knitted st. ; tog., together ; st.-st., stocking-stitch, which is k. one row, p. one row.*

TO KNIT : Commence at the lower edge of the front by casting on 111 sts. K. two rows, then commence the pattern.

1st pattern row : S. 1, k. 2 tog., k. 3, *, m. 1, k. 3, s. 1, k. 2 tog., p.s.s.o., k. 3. Repeat from * till 6 sts. remain, m. 1, k. 3, s. 1, k. 1, p.s.s.o., k. 1.

2nd pattern row : S. 1, p. 4, * m. 1, p. 8. Repeat from * till 6 sts. remain, m. 1, p. 6.

Repeat these two rows until 80 rows are worked in the pattern, and the skirt is about 10½ inches long.

Next row : This is the 83rd row. S. 1, k. 2 tog., k. 6, * s. 1, k. 2 tog., p.s.s.o., k. 6. Repeat from * till 3 sts. remain, s. 1, k. 1, p.s.s.o., k. 1 (87 sts.).

Please turn to page 18

*T*his little frock is knitted in such a pretty pattern, and the collar, sleeves and hem are all finished with a charming Vandyked edge.

FIRST STEPS

84th row : * P. 2 tog., p. 2. Repeat from * to the end of the row (65 sts.).

85th row : * K. 2, m. 1, k. 2 tog. Repeat from * to the end of the row.

86th and all even number rows : P.

87th row : K.

89th row : K. 31, m. 1, s. 1, k. 2 tog., p.s.s.o., m. 1, k. 31.

91st row : K. 29, k. 2 tog., m. 1, k. 3, m. 1, k. 2 tog., k. 29.

93rd row : As 89th.

95th row : Cast off 3, k. 19 (the st. on the needle, after casting off 3 counts as the first of the 19) m. 1, s. 1, k. 2 tog., p.s.s.o., m. 1, k. 15, m. 1, s. 1, k. 2 tog., p.s.s.o., m. 1, k. 22.

96th row : Cast off 3, p. to the end. (59 sts.)

97th row : K. 2 tog., k. 15, k. 2 tog., m. 1, k. 3, m. 1, k. 2 tog., k. 11, k. 2 tog., m. 1, k. 3, m. 1, k. 2 tog., k. 15, k. 2 tog. (57 sts.)

99th row : K. 2. tog., k. 16, m. 1, s. 1, k. 2 tog., p.s.s.o. m. 1, k. 15, m. 1, s. 1, k. 2 tog., p.s.s.o., m. 1, k. 16, k. 2 tog. (55 sts.)

101st row : K. 7, m. 1, s. 1, k. 2 tog., p.s.s.o. m. 1, k. 35, m. 1, s. 1, k. 2 tog., p.s.s.o., m. 1, k. 7.

103rd row : K. 5, k. 2 tog., m. 1, k. 3, m. 1, k. 2 tog., k. 31, k. 2 tog., m. 1, k. 3, m. 1, k. 2 tog., k. 5.

105th row : As the 101st.

106-112th rows : St.-st.

113th-117th rows : As 101st-105th rows.

118th row : P.

119th row : K. 15 for left-shoulder, cast off 25, for the neck, place the left shoulder sts. on a holder, k. the remaining 15 sts. for the right shoulder.

Work 14 rows of st.-st. for the right shoulder.

Next row : P. to the end, cast on 14 sts.

Work another 26 rows of st.-st.

Next row : K. till 2 sts. remain, inc. in next st., k. 1.

Next row : P.

Repeat the last two rows twice more.

Next row : K. to the end, cast on 3 (35 sts.) Work 9 rows of st.-st.

Next row : * K. 2, m. 1, k. 2 tog. Repeat from * to the end of the row.

Next row : P. Cast off.

Return to the 15 sts. on the holder for the left shoulder and p. one row. Work 14 rows of st.-st., then finish this side of the back to correspond, with the right side, but cast on 16 sts. at the neck edge (after the 14 rows of st.-st.) instead of 14.

THE BACK OF THE SKIRT. Cast on 111 sts. and work as for the front until the 80 pattern rows are completed. Cast off.

SLEEVES. Cast on 57 sts.

K. one row, p. one row, then repeat the two pattern rows twice.

7th row : S. 1, k. 2 tog., * k. 6, s. 1, k. 2 tog., p.s.s.o. Repeat from * till 3 sts. remain, s. 1, k. 1, p.s.s.o., k. 1 (45 sts.)

8th row : * P 2, p. 2 tog. Repeat from * to the end of the row. (34 sts.)

9th row : K.

10th row : P.

11th row : Inc. in alternate sts. to make the number 51. Three rows st.-st.

15th row : As 11th, to make the number of sts. 76.

Work 10 rows in st.-st.

At the beginning of each of the next 12 rows cast off 5 sts.

Cast off the remaining 16 sts. Make the second sleeve.

THE COLLAR. Cast on 75 sts. and work the first 7 rows as for the sleeve.

8th row : P. Cast off.

To MAKE THE DRESS. Press the work with a warm iron under a damp [cloth. Join the back of the skirt to the bodice, so that the left side of the back overlaps the right side for half an inch. Sew the side seams and the sleeve seams. Place the sleeves in the armholes so that the fullness is at the top. Sew the collar to the neck.

Work double-crochet up the back and round the neck, and make three loops for buttonholes and sew the buttons in place. Run the ribbon through the holes at the waist and tie the bow in front, at the left side. Press the seams.

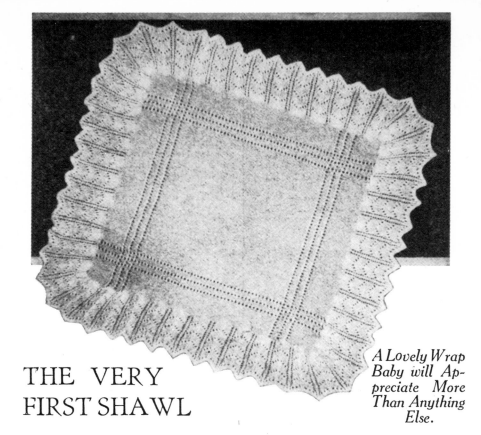

THE VERY FIRST SHAWL

A Lovely Wrap Baby will Appreciate More Than Anything Else.

To make this shawl, the square centre is worked first and the border is worked on each of the four sides separately, and is afterwards sewn up at each corner. The centre is plain knitting with some open rows made to form a pattern, but if preferred the whole centre can be plain knitting, just working the same number of rows as if the open pattern were worked : a warmer shawl is the result.

Materials

NINE balls of " Greenock " Sun-wool and a pair of long bone knitting needles No. 5.

Size and Tension

WORKING at a tension of 4 st. to the inch in width on the plain knitting a shawl measuring 60 inches square will result.

ABBREVIATIONS :—K., knit plain ; p., purl ; tog., together ; m., make (by bringing the wool to the front of the needle so that it passes over it when knitting the next st.) ; sl., slip ; st., stitch. Directions in brackets are worked the number of times stated immediately after the brackets.

To Work

FOR the centre cast on 135 st. and k. 4 rows.

1st pattern row : K. 16, (m. 1, k. 2 tog., k. 2) 3 times, k. 82, (m. 1, k. 2 tog., k. 2) 3 times, k. 13.

K. 3 rows.

Repeat these 4 rows 6 times more.

2nd pattern row : K. 2, * m. 1, k. 2 tog., repeat from * until within 1 st. of the end, k. 1.

* K. 3 rows ; work 1st pattern row ; k. 3 rows ; work 2nd pattern row ; repeat from * once more.

K. 3 rows.

Work 1st pattern row and k. 3 rows.

Repeat last 4 rows 41 times more.

* Work 2nd pattern row ; k. 3 rows ; work 1st pattern row ; k. 3 rows ; repeat from * once more.

Work 2nd pattern row, k. 3 rows.

Work 1st pattern row, k. 3 rows.

Repeat last 4 rows 6 times more, which completes the centre.

One quarter of the border is now worked on these stitches, but before the fancy pattern is begun, the st. must be increased thus : (K. 1 into the front and 1 into the back of next st.) 32 times, k. 1(this makes 65 st. on right-hand needle). * K. into front and back of next st., k. 1 ; repeat from * 34 times more, k. into front and back of the remaining 32 st., when there should be 234 altogether.

P. 1 row.

The Fancy Pattern

1st row : * Sl. 1, k. 1, pass the sl.st. over, k. 6, m. 1, k. 2, m. 1, k. 6, k. 2 tog. ; repeat from * to end of row.

2nd row : All purl.

Repeat these two rows twice more, then purl a row and knit a row.

9th row : * Sl. 1, k. 1, pass the sl.st. over, (m. 1, k. 2 tog.) 3 times, m. 1, k. 2, (m. 1, k. 2 tog.) 4 times. Repeat from * to end of row.

10th row : K. plain.

Repeat these 10 rows 3 times more, then k. 4 plain rows and coast off loosely.

Now on the opposite side of the shawl, which is the cast-on edge, pick up 135 st., and repeat the border.

At each side edge pick up 135 st. (1 st. to each ridge of knitting), and repeat the border. Sew the border together at each corner.

Spread the shawl out and press lightly, putting a thin cloth over the knitting. The points on the border may be stretched a little and pressed a little heavier.

NOW STRIPES ARE SMART

Two Delightful Designs.   Directions for knitting this set on page 20

Now Stripes are Smart

AS cheerful as the spring days is this three-colour striped jumper, with its jaunty little cap to match, and it is all plain and purl in bands or ribs, so there is no fancy pattern to worry the beginner.

MATERIALS : Use 4 ounces of Sirdar Crochet Wool in orange shade, 2 ounces in chocolate brown and 2 ounces in white, and there will be enough left to work the little cap. A pair of bone knitting needles No. 10 and No. 12.

ABBREVIATIONS : K., knit plain, p., purl ; st., stitch, tog., together . s.s., stocking-stitch (k. on the right side and p. back).

TENSION AND MEASUREMENTS : Worked at a tension of 15 sts. to 2 inches in width, the following measurements are attained after light pressing : round bust, 36 inches , length from shoulder to edge of waist-band, 17½ inches : underarm seam of sleeve, 4 inches.

TO WORK : Begin with the sleeves, and using the No. 12 needles and the orange wool, cast on 96 sts. Work 15 rows of single rib (k. 1 and p. 1 alternately).

Now change to No. 10 needles and white wool, and begin the coloured bands.

1ST AND 2ND ROWS : K. plain.
3RD ROW : Purl.
4TH ROW : K. plain.
5TH ROW : Purl.
6TH ROW : K. plain.
7TH ROW : Change to chocolate and k. plain.

Work 4 rows more in s.s. in this colour, then 5 rows in orange. These 16 rows form the pattern, 10 of them being in s.s. and 6 rows are worked in white so that the p. side is on the right side of the work.

Change to white and repeat from the 1st row to the 10th row once

To shape the top of the sleeve, continue in the same pattern and order of colour, taking 2 sts tog. at the beginning and end of every row until the sts. are reduced to 32. There should now be 4 stripes each of white and chocolate and 3 of orange Cast off on the wrong side after the 5th row of the last chocolate band.

THE BACK : Cast on 120 sts. using No. 12 needles and orange wool. Work 35 rows in single rib.

Change to No. 10 needles and white wool and work in pattern as directed for the sleeve until 2 stripes of orange are completed. In the next, and every 8th row, increase (by knitting 2 into the same st.) at both ends of the row, until there are 130 st. Continue without increase until 6 chocolate stripes can be counted when the armhole will be reached.

To shape the armhole cast off 4 sts. at the beginning of each of the next 4 rows.

NEXT ROW : In orange, p. without dec.

Continue in pattern. but on the next and every 5th row, take 2 tog. at both ends of needle, until the sts. are reduced to 100. Complete the orange band, and in the last row of it, divide the sts. for the shoulders thus : p. 44, cast off 12 in centre, p. 44.

FIRST SHOULDER.—1ST ROW : K. in white.
2ND ROW : K., casting off 4 at the beginning of the row (neck end).
3RD ROW . P. 40.
4TH ROW : Cast off 4, k. to the end where take the last 2 tog.
5TH ROW : P. 35.
6TH ROW : Take 2 tog. and k. to end.
7TH ROW : Change to chocolate and k. 34.
8TH ROW : P.
9TH ROW : K., dec. at both ends.

Continue in pattern, decreasing at both ends of every 5th row until the sts are reduced to 27. Do one more dec. at the neck end of the work, then complete the 10th chocolate band on 26 st. Cast off.

For the second shoulder join the wool to the neck end and work to match the first shoulder, bearing in mind that the 1st row is already worked, so the first 4 sts. can be cast off at the beginning of the first row on the wrong side of the work.

THE FRONT : This is worked in the same way as the back. but with a lower neck-line. Work only 6 complete patterns, and the 7th as far as the first 4 orange rows. In the last row p. 47, cast off 14, p. 47.

FOR LEFT SHOULDER.—1ST ROW : K. 47 in white.
2ND ROW : Cast off 4 at the neck end, k. to end.
3RD ROW : P. 43.
4TH ROW : Cast off 4. K. to end.

5TH ROW : Take 2 tog. and p. to end.
6TH ROW : Take 2 tog. and k. to end.
7TH ROW : Change to chocolate wool and k. 37.
8TH ROW : P. 2 tog , and p. to end.
9TH ROW : K. 36.
10TH ROW : P., decreasing at both ends.
11TH ROW : Change to orange wool and k.
12TH ROW : P., decreasing at the beginning of the row.
13TH ROW : K. 33.
14TH ROW : P. 33.
15TH ROW : K., decreasing at the end.

Now continue in pattern, decreasing at both ends of every 5th row until the sts. are reduced to 27. Decrease once more at the neck end of the work and continue on 26 sts. until there are 10 complete chocolate bands from the beginning.

Change to orange wool, and on every other row cast off 6 sts. at the armhole end of the work, until 14 sts. remain, then cast off.

THE SECOND SHOULDER : Join the wool at the neck end of the opposite shoulder sts., and cast off 4 at the beginning of the 1st row, then work to match the first shoulder.

THE NECK BAND : With the No. 12 needles pick up 108 st. round the front neck opening, and k. 15 rounds of single rib. Cast off. Pick up 88 sts. round the back neck and work to match the front.

TO MAKE UP THE JUMPER : First press all pieces on the wrong side, putting a damp cloth over the work and using a hot iron. Press the ribbing very lightly. Now sew up the shoulder seams including the neck band. Sew the sleeves into the armhole and press these seams while the work is open. Sew up the side seams and press.

THE CAP

THE head measurement of this cap is 20 inches, but it will stretch further. Begin at the edge of the brim and with No. 10 needles and orange wool, cast on 110 sts.

Work 5 rows in s.s., then change to chocolate wool and work 5 rows more in s.s. Change to white wool and work the stripe of 6 rows as on the jumper, also one chocolate stripe more.

Change to orange wool and work 32 rows of single rib, with the wrong side of the coloured bands facing the worker.

Here begin to shape the top of the cap.

1ST DECREASE ROW : *K 9, k. 2 tog., repeat from * all along.
2ND ROW : Purl.

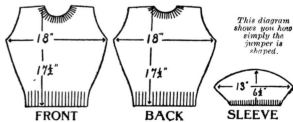

FRONT   **BACK**   **SLEEVE**

This diagram shows you how simply the jumper is shaped.

3RD ROW : *K 7, k. 2 tog., repeat from * all along.
4TH ROW : Purl.
5TH ROW : *K. 6, k. 2 tog., repeat from * all along.

Change to chocolate wool and work 5 rows of s.s. without dec.

With orange wool take 2 sts. tog. all round.

NEXT ROW : No decrease.

Repeat the last 2 rows once, then with the No. 12 needles, k. one row. Cut the wool, leaving about half a yard, which thread into a darning needle, and pass it twice through the sts., then slip them off the needles, draw up and secure for centre of cap. Join the seam up neatly using self-coloured wool on each part.

Turn the hat so that the wrong side of the turned-up brim is facing the worker, and with the No. 1 steel crochet hook work d.c. into the knitted sts., putting 1 in each st., but miss a st. here and there to prevent the edge from fluting. Work 3 rounds more (not rows) taking up the back thread of the st. only. Fasten off.

Press the cap on the wrong side, touching the ribbing lightly, but press the centre top well, putting it over some round object, or the corner of the table to do so. Turn up the brim to the right side and press this in position.

SUMMER STITCHERY

An easy piece of knitting for the garden or beach.

ABBREVIATIONS

st., stitch ;
k., knit ;
p., purl ;
in., inch.

A SLEEVELESS PULLOVER IN CABLE-STITCH

MATERIALS

Ten ozs. of Baldwin & Walker's Chubby wool in white, a set of long No. 5 knitting needles, a pair No. 4 knitting needles.

MEASUREMENTS

Length from the top of the shoulder—22½ ins.

Width all round, below sleeves—38 ins.

Round armhole—16 ins. stretching to 22 ins.

TENSION

7 sts. to 2 ins. in width without opening the pattern.

T HE *Back.*—Begin at the lower edge by casting on 66 sts., using the No. 5 needles.

Work in k. 1, p. 1 rib for a depth of 3½ ins., working into the backs of the sts. on the first row.

Change to No. 4 needles and the following pattern :

1st row : P. 1, * k. 4, p. 2, and repeat from * all across, ending k. 4, p. 1.

2nd row : K. 1, * p. 4, k. 2, and repeat from * all across, ending p. 4, k. 1.

3rd row : As for the 1st row.

4th row : As for the 2nd row.

5th row : As for the 1st row.

6th row : As for the 2nd row.

7th row : P. 1, * pass the next 2 sts. to a spare needle, k. the next 2 sts., pass the sts. on the spare needle back again to the one holding the sts. in working, and k. these, p. the next 2 sts., and repeat from * all across, purling the last st.

The last 6 rows from row 2 to 7 inclusive form the pattern. Continue quite straight till the 6th pattern from the beginning is completed. Shape the armhole by casting off 3 sts. at the beginning of each of the next 4 rows, then continue in the pattern over the remaining 54 sts. till a depth of 11 patterns from the beginning has been worked, with the exception of the last row of the 11th pattern. On the next row cast off, working the cable pattern as usual.

The Front.—Work this in exactly the same way as for the back till the position for the armholes is reached. On the next row cast off 3 sts. and work over the next 29 sts. Pass the remaining sts. to a safety-pin. Continue over the sts. on the needle, decreasing the edge sts. at the beginning of the next row.

On the following row cast off 3 sts. and complete the row. Now continue to decrease the edge sts. at the neck edge on every 4th row, till there are 9 decreases in all. The correct length for the front will now have been worked. Cast off on the last row of the pattern. Join the wool to the front edge of the opposite side and complete this side to match the first.

Sew the shoulders of the back and front together.

Using No. 5 needles, pick up and knit through every cast-off st. and the edge of every row along the armhole edge—this to be done holding the right side of the work towards you. Work one row of ribbing all across.

On the next row work as far as the shoulder seam, work 3 sts. together and complete the row. Work the next row straight. Repeat the last 2 rows once more. Cast off.

Complete the second armhole to match.

The Neck. — Holding the right side of the work towards you, pick up and knit through every cast-off st. and the edge of every row round the neck. The set of needles will be required for this.

Work one round in the ribbing, increasing across the back of the neck in every 3rd st. Work 4 rounds more in the ribbing, decreasing at each side of the V at the front of the neck on every row.

Cast off, decreasing at the same time.

Press out the work—without opening the pattern—on the wrong side with a hot iron over a damp cloth.

Sew up the side and sleeve seams and press these.

YOU WILL LOOK WELL-DRESSED

In This Interesting Jumper with Its High Square Neck-line and Its Buckled Strap

The belt-buckle matches the one on the high neck-line.

THIS charming jumper is knitted on tailored lines and has diagonal stripes on the lower part of the back and front all round. The shaping at the waist is effected by a change of needles, so the beginner need not have any qualms about keeping the pattern correct.

Materials

Six ounces of " Greenock " 3-ply Super Fingering No. 395 light green (obtainable only at branches of the Scotch Wool and Hosiery Stores), a pair of knitting needles No. 8 and No. 11, and a spare needle. Two slides to match the wool.

Tension and Measurements

Worked at a tension of 7 sts. to the inch in width on the s.s. with No. 8 needles, the following measurements are attained after pressing : Round bust, 39 inches ; length from shoulder fold to lower edge, 21½ inches ; side seams, 14¼ inches ; sleeve seam, 18½ inches.

Abbreviations

K., knit ; p., purl ; tog., together ; inc., increase ; (by working into the back and front of the same st.) ; st., stitch ; m.s., moss-st. (k. 1 and p. 1 alternately and on successive rows a k. must come over a p., and vice versa) ; s.s., stocking-stitch (k. on the right side and p. back). Directions in brackets are worked the number of times stated immediately after the brackets.

To Work the Back

Begin at the lower edge and with No. 8 needles cast on 112 sts.

Work the m.s. border as follows :

1st row : With right side facing, * k. 1, p. 1 ; repeat from * to end of row.

2nd row : * P. 1, k. 1 ; repeat from * to end.

Repeat these 2 rows 3 times more, than begin the pattern as follows :

1st row : With right side facing, * k. 7, m.s. 7, (note that the m.s. 7 on right side rows begins and ends with p. 1) ; repeat from * to end.

2nd row : P. 1, * m.s. 7, p. 7 ; repeat from *, ending the last repeat with p. 6 (note that the m.s. 7 on the wrong side rows begins and ends with k. 1).

3rd row : K. 5, * m.s. 7, k. 7 ; repeat from *, ending with k. 2.

4th row : P. 3, * m.s. 7, p. 7 ; repeat from *, ending with k. 4.

5th row : K. 3, * m.s. 7, k. 7 ; repeat from *, ending with k. 4.

6th row : P. 5, * m.s. 7, p. 7 ; repeat from *, ending with p. 2.

7th row : K. 1, * m.s. 7, k. 7 ; repeat from *, ending with k. 6.

8th row : * P. 7, m.s. 7 ; repeat from * to end.

9th row : K. 1, m.s. 5, * k. 7, m.s. 7 ; repeat from *, ending with k. 7, p. 1.

10th row : P. 1, k. 1, * p. 7, m.s. 7 ; repeat from *, ending with m.s. 5.

11th row : (K. 1, p. 1) twice, * k. 7, m.s. 7 ; repeat from *, ending with m.s. 3.

(*Continued on page 23*)

THE SQUARE-NECKED JUMPER
Continued

12th row : (P. 1, k. 1) twice, * p. 7, m.s. 7 ; repeat from *, ending with k. 1, p. 1, k. 1.

13th row : K. 1, p. 1, * k. 7, m.s. 7 ; repeat from *, ending with m.s. 5.

14th row : (P. 1, k. 1) 3 times, * p. 7, m.s. 7 ; repeat from *, ending with k. 1.

Work these 14 rows once more.

Change to No. 11 needles and work the pattern of 14 rows again. With No. 8 needles work 28 rows more (2 patterns).

Now work in S.S., increasing 1 st. at each end of the 5th, 11th, 17th, 23rd, and 28th row. There are now 122 sts. on which continue until there are 52 rows of s.s. altogether, when the armholes will be reached.

To Shape the Armholes: Take 2 sts. together at each end of the next 7 rows, then 2 sts. tog. at each end of every alternate row for 7 dec. rows more, which leaves 94 sts.

S.s. 19 rows, beginning and ending, with a p. row.

Work 10 rows more in s.s., taking 2 sts. tog. at each end of every row, which leaves 74 sts.

Next row · K. 2 tog., k. 8, p. 1, (k. 1, p. 1) 12 times, k. 2 tog., p. 1, (k. 1, p. 1) 13 times, k. 8, k. 2 tog. (71 sts.).

Work 9 rows more, keeping the centre 53 sts. in m.s. and the sts. at each side of these in s.s., but take 2 sts. tog. at each end of every row. 53 sts. will remain on which work 2 rows in m.s., casting off 5 sts. at the beginning of each. Cast off the remaining sts.

THE FRONT : With No. 8 needles cast on 126 sts. and work exactly as for the back except that there are 14 sts. more all the time, and there will be 136 sts. at the armhole.

To Shape the Armholes : Take 2 sts. tog. at each end of the next 21 rows. There are 94 sts. left on which work 17 rows in s.s.

THE LEFT SHOULDER : *1st row :* K. 20, m.s. 11. (Pass the remaining 63 sts. on a spare needle for the right front and neck.)

2nd row : M.s. 11, p. 20.

Continue with the sts. in this order and take 2 tog. at the armhole end of the next 20 rows, which leaves only 11 sts.

Work 14 rows in m.s. and cast off.

THE RIGHT SHOULDER : First cast on 30 sts. for the tab at the left side of the neck and work one row of p. 1 and k. 1 alternately on these sts. On the same needle work the 63 spare needle sts. as follows : With the right side facing m.s. 43 for the yoke, k. 20.

Next row : P. 20, m.s. 73.

** Work 4 rows with the sts. in the same order, taking 2 tog. at the arm end of every row.

On the next row, beginning at the tab end, m.s. 30, turn and m.s. 30 back to the tab end. Repeat from ** once more.

Work 2 rows more on all the sts., taking 2 sts. tog. at the arm end of each row. (83 sts.)

Next row : From the tab end cast off 62 sts., m.s. 11 (including the one on the needle after casting off), k. 8, k. 2 tog.

Work 9 rows more, taking 2 sts. tog. at the arm end of each row, and keep 11 sts. in m.s. at the neck end. There

are now 11 sts. left on which m.s. 15 rows, and cast off.

THE SLEEVES : Begin at the top and cast on 8 sts. with No. 8 needles. K. one row and p. one row.

1st inc. row : Inc. in the first st., k. until 2 sts. remain, inc. in the next st., k. 1.

2nd row : All purl.

Repeat these 2 rows until there are 42 sts. on the needle, then p. one row. Work s.s., increasing in the first and last st. on every row until there are 84 sts. on the needle.

Work 5 rows in s.s.

Continue in s.s. taking 2 sts. tog. at each end of the next row, and every following 8th row, until the 13th dec. row is worked with 58 sts.

P. one row.

Now work the pattern as follows :

1st row : K. 2, * m.s. 7, k. 7 ; repeat from * to end.

2nd row : K. 1, * p. 7, m.s. 7 ; repeat from *, ending with p. 1.

3rd row : * M.s. 7, k. 7 ; repeat from *, ending with m.s. 2.

4th row : M.s. 3, * p. 7, m.s. 7 ; repeat from *, ending with m.s. 6.

5th row : M.s. 5, * k. 7, m.s. 7 ; repeat from *, ending with m.s. 4.

6th row : M.s. 5, * p. 7, m.s. 7 ; repeat from *, ending with m.s. 4.

Now continue in pattern, keeping the stripe in the diagonal direction as set in the above 6 rows, but work 2 sts. tog. at each end of the next row and every following 8th row, until there are 46 sts. left.

Work 8 rows straight, then m.s. 8 rows and cast off.

(Beginners who cannot decrease and keep the pattern correct, can finish the sleeve in s.s. with a m.s. border as directed, or a deeper cuff.)

THE BELT : With No. 8 needles cast on 11 sts. and work m.s. for the length required and cast off. Sew one end of the belt to the centre bar of the slide with over-cast stitches.

TO MAKE UP : First sew the cast-off edges of the front neck-bands to the matching parts of the back yoke. Sew the sleeves in place. Now press all with a hot iron and a damp cloth over the wrong side of the work. Join the sleeve and side seams and press these Sew the centre bar of the slide to the left side of the yoke on the m.s., and slip the knitted tab end through ; tack in place.

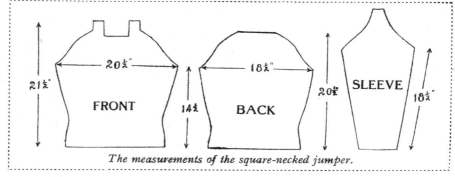

The measurements of the square-necked jumper.

The new Triumph Six Flow Free Saloon

Scaioni Photographs

Her PINAFORE FROCK

And the Trim Little Blouse
that Belongs to It

19th row.—K. 2 tog., k. 30, k. 2 tog., k. 30, k. 2 tog., k. 30, k. 2 tog. (94).

25th row.—K. 2 tog., k. 28, k. 2 tog., k. 30, k. 2 tog., k. 28, k. 2 tog. (90).

31st row.—K. 2 tog., k. 26, k. 2 tog., k. 30, k. 2 tog., k. 26, k. 2 tog. (86).

37th row.—K. 2 tog., k. 24, k. 2 tog., k. 30, k. 2 tog., k. 24, k. 2 tog. (82). Work 5 rows st.-st.

Change to No. 12 needles and work 1 in. k. 1, p. 1 rib. Change to No. 10 needles and st.-st. for 24 rows, inc. 1 st. at both

THE model, to fit a child of 4 to 6, is knitted in shrimp pink and white.

MATERIALS.—6 oz. of Sirdar 4-ply "Majestic" Knitting Wool in shrimp pink; and 4 oz. in white; 1 pair each of Nos. 10 and 12 Stratnoid knitting needles; 12 buttons, 3 press studs.

Measurements.—Length from shoulder, 18 in.; width all round under the arms, 26 in. *Blouse:* Length from back neck, 10 in.; width all round under the arms, 24 in.; length of sleeve seam, 10½ in.

Tension.—7 stitches to 1 in. in width and 10 rows to 1 in. in depth.

Abbreviations.—K., knit; p., purl; sts., stitches; dec., decrease; inc., increase; tog., together; sl., slip; p.s.s.o., pass slipped stitch over; d.c., double crochet; st.-st., stocking-stitch.

The Back

BEGIN at the lower edge with No. 10 needles and pink wool. Cast on 130 sts., but do not work into the back of the first row. Continue in st.-st. for 1½ in., finishing after a p. row. With a No. 12

needle pick up every cast-on loop, then work the next row together with these sts., thus forming a hem.

Continue in st.-st., but dec. 1 st. at both ends of the 7th row and then on every 6th row following until 110 sts. remain, finishing after 5 rows st.-st. Now shape front thus:

1st row.—K. 2 tog., k. 36, k. 2 tog., k. 30, k. 2 tog., k. 36, k. 2 tog., (106). Always work 5 rows st.-st. between each dec.

7th row.—K. 2 tog., k. 34, k. 2 tog., k. 30, k. 2 tog., k. 34, k. 2 tog., (102).

13th row.—K. 2 tog., k. 32, k. 2 tog., k. 30, k. 2 tog., k. 32, k. 2 tog. (98).

ends of the 5th, 13th and 21st rows (88).

Now shape armholes by casting off 4 sts. at beginning of the next 2 rows, then dec. 1 st. at both ends of the next 4 rows, then 1 st. at both ends of the next 2 k. rows. (10 sts. taken off each side and 68 sts. remain.) Now shape neck:

1st row.—K. 30, cast off 8, k. 29.

(*Continued on page 25*)

Her Pinafore Frock
Continued

2nd row.—P. 30, then slip remaining 30 sts. on to a st. holder for the present. Cast off 3 sts. at the beginning of every k. row until 12 sts. remain, then continue without dec. for 4½ ins. Cast off.

Rejoin wool at neck, work other side to match, casting off 3 sts. at beginning of p. rows.

The Front

WORK this in exactly the same way as the back until the waist ribbing has been worked, then shape thus :

1st row.—On No. 10 needles, k. 38, and leave remaining 44 on a st. holder for the present. *Next row.*—Cast on 10 sts., p. to end. Continue working this side in st.st., inc. 1 st. at beginning of 5th, 13th and 21st rows, then shape armholes as on back, finishing after a k. row.

Cast off 10 sts. at the beginning of next p. row, then 3 sts. at beginning of every p. row until 12 sts. remain. Continue without dec. for 5 ins., then dec. 1 st. at both ends of every row until all sts. are dec.

Rejoin wool at neck. Work other side to match, omitting the 10 cast-on sts., and casting off 10 sts. at the beginning of a k. row and the 3 sts. at the beginning of every following k. row.

Press the work on both sides with a warm iron and damp cloth. Join sides, then work 2 rows of d.c. round neck and armholes. Press, then sew shaped end of strap to back and sew one button on each shoulder. Sew three buttons down front opening and fasten with press-studs.

The Blouse

BEGIN at the lower edge of the back· Cast on 90 sts. on No. 12 needles, with white wool, and work 6 rows k. 1, p. 1 rib. *Next row*—K. 1, * w. fd., k. 2 tog. Rep. from *, finishing p. 1. Work 7 more rows k. 1, p. 1 rib. Change to No. 10 needles and st.st. for 4 ins., finishing after a p. row.

The Armholes.—Cast off 4 sts. at beginning of next 2 rows, then dec. 1 st. at both ends of next 4 rows, then 1 st. at both ends of next 2 k. rows. (70 sts. left). Continue without dec. for 3 ins., then shape shoulders.

1st row.—K. 26, cast off 18, k. 25. *2nd row.*—P. 24, p. 2 tog., leave remaining sts. on a holder for the present. *3rd row.*—K. 2 tog., k. 19, turn, p. 18, p. 2 tog. *5th row.*—K. 2 tog., k. 13, turn, p. 12, p. 2 tog. *7th row.*—K. 2 tog., k. 7, turn, p. 8. *9th row.*—K. 4, turn, p. 4. Cast off all shoulder sts.

Rejoin wool to other set of sts., and work to match by reversing all decs. and leaving sts. at ends of p. rows.

The Front

WORK in same way as back until armholes have been worked, then work opening. *Next row.*—K. 35, and leave remaining 35 sts. on a st. holder. Work 3 ins. st.st., finishing after a k. row, then shape neck.

1st row.—Cast off 4, p. to end. *2nd row.*—K. 29, k. 2 tog. *3rd row.*—P. 2 tog., p. 28. *4th row.*—K. 27, k. 2 tog. *5th row.*—P. 2 tog., p. 26. *6th row.*—K. 25, k. 2 tog. *7th row.*—P. 2 tog., p. 24. *8th row.*—K. 23, k. 2 tog. *9th row.*—P. 2 tog., p. 22. *10th row.*—K. 21, k. 2 tog. *11th row.*—P. 2 tog., p. 20. **12th row.—K. 19, k. 2 tog. Now shape shoulder thus : P. until 4 sts. remain, turn and work back to neck. P. until 8 sts. remain, turn and work to neck. Continue in this way leaving 4 sts. unworked at the end of every p. row until 4 sts. remain. Cast off. Work other side of neck to match, leaving sts. at end of k. rows.**

The Sleeves.

—Begin at the cuff edge with No. 12 needles. Cast on 46 sts. and work 2½ ins. k. 1, p. 1 rib. Change to No. 10 needles and st.st., inc. 1 st. at both ends of 7th, then every 8th row following until there are 66 sts., finishing after 7 rows st.st. Shape top by dec. 1 st. at both ends of every row until 20 remain. Cast off.

Press work on both sides with a warm iron over damp cloth. Join shoulders and press seams, sew sleeves into armholes and press, then join up side and sleeve seams and press.

With No. 10 needles pick up 74 sts., round neck and work 2 ins. k. 1, p. 1 rib, then 4 rows in pink. Cast off in rib.

For front piece, pick up with No. 10 needles 80 sts. down front, folding the work from the centre opening and working into each stitch. Work in k. 1, p. 1 rib for 4 rows, then on 5th and 6th rows work buttonhole thus : K. 1, p. 1, k. 1, * cast off 2 sts., rib 10. Rep. from * finishing cast off 2, rib 3. Cast on 7 sets of 2 sts. in next row to replace those cast off, then finishing with 4 rows, k. 1, p. 1 rib and cast off in rib.

Give work a final press and insert elastic at waist and sew buttons on front.

A Boy's School Jersey

Designed by Margaret Raven

for shoulders and neck. Knit 24 stitches (slip on to a stitch-holder), cast off 22, knit 24. Work on the last 24 stitches. Purl back, knit to the end of the row. Purl back, knit 12. Purl back. Cast off. Work the other shoulder similarly.

Front

Work as directed for the back until the armhole decreases have been worked, then divide for the front opening. Knit 35 (slip on to the stitch-holder), work on the last 35 stitches as directed for the back until the neck and shoulders have been reached, then cast off 11 stitches for the neck. Work on 24 stitches for the shoulder as for the back. Work the other half similarly.

THIS jersey is very practical for school wear and has a " Zipp " fastener down the front.

MATERIALS REQUIRED : 12 ounces of Sirdar " Majestic " Knitting Wool ; ½ ounce of contrasting shade for collar ; " Zipp " fastener, 5 inches long ; 1 pair of Stratnoid needles No. 11, and 1 pair No. 12 ; 1 Stratnoid crochet hook, No. 15.

MEASUREMENTS : Length from shoulder to lower edge, 20 inches ; width all round under arms, 28 inches ; sleeve seam (including cuff), 18 inches.

TENSION : 6 stitches to 1 inch in width ; 9 rows to 1 inch in depth.

METHOD : The jersey is worked in the following pattern :—
1st row.—1 plain, 1 purl, to the end of the row.
2nd row.—Purl.
3rd row.—1 purl, 1 plain, to the end of the row.
4th row.—Purl.

Back

With No. 12 needles cast on 84 stitches and rib in 2 plain, 2 purl for 1½ inches. Change to No. 11 needles and work in pattern for 12 inches. Here decrease for armholes.

Armholes

Cast off 3 stitches at the beginning of the next 2 rows, then knit 2 together at the beginning and end of the next 4 rows (70 stitches left). Knit without decreasing for 4 inches, then divide

Sleeves. (Both alike)

With No. 12 needles cast on 48 stitches and rib for 2½ inches. Change to No. 11 needles and work in pattern, increasing 1 stitch on every eighth stitch to the end of the row (54 stitches). Increase 1 stitch at each end on every eighth row, until there are 76 stitches, then knit without increasing until the sleeve measures 18 inches (cuff included). Cast off 2 stitches at the beginning of each row until there are 20 stitches left. Cast off.

Collar

Join the shoulders together. Holding the right side of the work towards you, pick up the stitches all the way round (62 approximately) and knit in stocking-stitch except for the first and last 8 stitches, which are knitted in pattern. Increase 1 stitch at each end inside the border on every plain row. Knit 14 rows, then join on contrasting colour. Knit 14 rows, then change to main colour and work 2 rows in stocking-stitch. Work in pattern right across for 14 rows (without increasing). Cast off loosely.

To Make Up

Work a row of double crochet down the side of the collar and front opening. Stitch in the sleeves, then open the garment out flat and press on the wrong side with a warm iron and a damp cloth. Sew up the under-arm and sleeve-seams and press them. Stitch the " Zipp " fastener in position. Work 2 strips in pattern about 5½ inches long with 8 stitches. Sew the strips on the wrong side of the jersey, where the " Zipp " fastener was stitched. Press.

A Young Girl's Jumper

The model is in light green, expressing youth and springtime, but it is charming in any colour. Designed to fit 30 to 32-inch bust

So Delightfully Simple is this Design that your Schoolgirl Daughter may like to Knit it for Herself

The Back

Work exactly as for front, including armhole shaping. Then knit four more patts. without decreasing.

Next row.—K. 3, p. 4, k. 10, p. 4, turn, and continue in the patt. on these 21 sts. until 2 more patts. have been worked. Cast off.

Pass the next 70 sts. on to a st.-holder for the present. Join in wool and work on the remaining 21 sts. for the same depth as on the opposite side. Cast off.

The Sleeves

Cast on 60 sts., using No. 12 needles. K. 1, p. 1, rib for 4 in., change to No. 10 needles.

Row 1.—* p. 4 ; k. 2 tog., and wl. fwd. 4 times, k. 2 tog., wl. *over* needle * rep. from * to * ending p. 4.
Row 2.—* k. 4, p. 10, * rep. from * to * ending k. 4.
Row 3.—* p. 4, k. 10, * rep. from * to * ending p. 4.
Row 4.—As 2nd row.

Now continue in patt., inc. 1 st. at both ends of needle on next row and on every following 8th row (working the inc. sts. into the patt. as you go) until there are 94 sts. on needle. Work a few more rows until work measures 18½ in. from the beginning, then shape top by casting off 2 sts. at beginning of every row until 24 sts. remain. Cast off.

The Neck Border

First, sew up shoulder seams and press them with damp cloth. Now take the 5 No. 12 steel needles and work neck as follows :—Slip the sts. of the back neck on to one needle, then slip the sts. of the front neck on to another. Take another needle and knit up and draw through 45 sts. down one side of neck ; with a fourth needle knit up 45 sts. on the other side of neck, making 230 sts. altogether. Now knit in a k. 1, p. 1 rib for 1 in., knitting 2 sts. tog. at each corner on alternate rows. Cast off still working in the rib.

Making Up

Press all pieces, except the ribbing, on the wrong side under a damp cloth with a hot iron. Sew tops of sleeves into armholes and press. Then sew up under-arm and side seams. *Press all seams.*

MATERIALS. — 9 ozs. Patons' 4-ply Super Scotch Fingering ; 1 pair each of No. 10 and No. 12 knitting needles ; and 5 No. 12 steel sock needles.

Measurements.—Length from shoulder, 19 in. ; width all round under the arms, 30 in., stretches to 32 in. Length of sleeve seam, with cuff turned down, 19 in.

Tension.—7 stitches in width ; 10 rows to 1 in. in depth.

Abbreviations.—K., knit ; p., purl ; st., stitches ; tog., together ; dec., decrease ; inc., increase ; rep., repeat ; wl. fwd., wool forward ; patt., pattern.

The Front

Begin at the lower edge, cast on 112 sts., using No. 12 needles, and work in k. 1, p. 1 rib for 3 in. Change to No. 10 needles and work in pattern as follows :—

Row 1.—P. 2, * k. 2 tog., wl. fwd., 4 times, k. 2 tog., wl. *over* needle ; p. 4, * rep. from * to * ending with p. 2.
Row 2.—K. 2, * p. 10, k. 4 * rep. from * to * ending with k. 2. *Row 3.*—P. 2, * k. 10, p. 4 * rep. from * to * ending with p. 2.

Rep. last two rows 3 times ; then row 2 once. These 10 rows complete one pattern. Work 9 more patts. (10 in all), then rep. 1st and 2nd rows once more, then shape for armholes as follows :—

Row 1.—Cast off 3, k. 8, p. 4, * k. 10, p. 4, * rep. from * to * ending with p. 2.
Row 2.—Cast off 3, p. 8, k. 4, * p. 10, k. 4, * rep. from * to * ending with p. 9.
Row 3.—Cast off 2, k. 6, p. 4, * k 10, p. 4, * rep. from * to * ending with k. 9.
Row 4.—Cast off 2, p. 6, k. 4, * p. 10, k. 4, * rep. from * to * ending with p. 7.
Row 5.—Cast off 2, k. 4, p. 4, * k 10, p. 4, * rep. from * to * ending with k. 7.
Row 6.—Cast off 2, p. 4, k. 4, * p. 10, k. 4, * rep. from * to * ending with p. 5.
Row 7.—Cast off 2, k. 2, p. 4, * k. 10, p. 4, * rep. from * to * ending with k. 5.
Row 8.—Cast off 2, p. 2, k. 4, * p. 10, k. 4, * rep. from * to * ending with p. 3.

Next Row.—K. 3, p. 4, k. 10, p. 4, turn, and continue in the patt. on these 21 sts. until 5 more patts. have been worked. Cast off.

Pass the next 70 sts. on to a st.-holder for the present. Join in wool to the neck edge of the remaining 21 sts., and work up this side for the same depth as on the opposite side. Cast off.

A Quickly-made PULL-OVER

The Man of the Family Will be Sure to Welcome a Gift Like This

ISN'T it possible that a pull-over like the one for which we are giving knitting instructions this week will solve your problem of what to give husband, father or brother for Christmas ?

Nothing could be simpler than the two-row pattern in which it is worked. And nothing could be cosier than such a garment for wear during the cold days of winter.

MATERIALS

To make the pullover, you will require 8 ozs. Patons and Baldwins 4-ply Crocus Non-Shrink knitting wool. One pair No. 10 Beehive knitting needles and a set of No. 12.

MEASUREMENTS.—Length from the top of the shoulder, 22½ ins. Width all round, 37 ins.—stretching. Round armhole, 19 ins.

TENSION.—7 sts. to 1 in. in width. 8 rows to 1 in. in depth.

THE BACK

Begin at the lower edge by casting on 128 sts., using a pair of the No. 12 needles.

Work in k.1, p.1 rib for a depth of 3 ins., working into the backs of the stitches on the first row.

Change to No. 10 needles and work in the following pattern :—1st row : p.1 * k.2, p.2 and repeat from * all across ending p.1. 2nd row : Purl all across. Repeat these two rows for the pattern. Continue quite straight till the work measures a depth of 13½ ins. from the beginning.

Shape the armholes by casting off 4 sts. at the beginning of each of the next 6 rows, then by decreasing the edge sts. at both ends of the needle on alternate rows till there are seven decreases at each edge. You will then find that 90 sts. remain on the needle.

Work quite straight for a depth of 6 ins. Then start to shape the neck and shoulders.

1st row : Work to within 6 sts. of the end, turn. 2nd row : Work to within 6 sts. of the opposite end, turn. 3rd row : Work to within 13 sts. of the end, turn. 4th row : Work to within 13 sts. of the opposite end, turn. 5th row : Work over 24 sts., cast off 16 sts., then work to within 20 sts. of the end, turn. 6th row : Work back to neck. 7th row : Cast off 10 sts. and work across the remainder. 8th row : Cast off. 9th row : Join the wool to neck edge of the opposite side and work to within 20 sts. of the end, turn. 10th row : Work back to neck.

11th row : Cast off 10 sts. and work across the remainder. 12th row : Cast off.

THE FRONT

Work this exactly the same way as for the back to within one inch of the armholes.

On the next row work over 64 sts., and pass the remaining stitches to a Beehive Stitch Holder.

Continue over the stitches on the needle, and work back to the side edge. Work back again to the neck.

On the next row decrease and work back to the side edge. Then work three rows straight.

Now continue with the neck shaping, decreasing on the next and every following 4th row till there are 18 decreases in all at this edge, but at the same time, when the side edge is the same depth as that of the back of the armhole, shape this by casting off 4 sts. at the beginning of each of the next three rows, commencing at this edge. Then decrease the edge sts. on the same edge on alternate rows, till there are 7 decreases in all.

Continue with this edge straight till the front armhole edge is 6 rows longer than that of the back, then shape the shoulder.

1st row : Working from the neck edge work to within 6 sts. of the end, turn. 2nd row : Work back to neck. 3rd row : Work to within 13 sts. of the end, turn. 4th row : Work back to neck. 5th row : Work to within 20 sts. of the end, turn. 6th row : Work back to neck. 7th row : Work across all stitches. 8th row : Cast off. Join the wool to the front edge of the opposite side and complete this side to match the first.

NECK RIBBING

Sew the shoulders of the back and front together.

Using the set of No. 12 needles, and holding the right side of the work towards you, join the wool to a shoulder seam, then pick up and knit through every stitch and the edge of every row across the back of the neck, making 42 sts. here. Now continue along the sides of the neck, making 90 sts. on each side.

Work all round in k.1, p.1 rib.

Continue in the ribbing, decreasing on each side of the lower V of the front, on every row till the ribbing is one inch in depth. Cast off.

AND ARMHOLES

Holding the right side of the work towards you, pick up and knit through every stitch and the edge of every row on the armhole shaping, then along the straight edge miss the edge every third row till the shaping of the opposite side of the armhole is reached.

Here again pick up and knit through every stitch and the edge of every row. On the original there were 128 stitches on the needle.

Work nine rows in k.1, p.1 rib. Cast off.

Complete the second armhole in the same way.

Press out the work on the wrong side with a hot iron over a damp cloth. Press again lightly on the right side.

Sew up the side and sleeve seams, and press these on the wrong side.

There are many ways of keeping warm

A Knitted Frock for a Three-Year-Old

MATERIALS REQUIRED : 4 ounces of Sirdar Super Shetland 3-ply wool ; 1 ball of rabbit wool ; 1 pair of Stratnoid No. 12 needles ; 1 pair of Stratnoid No. 14 needles.

TENSION : 7½ stitches to the inch, in stocking-stitch.

MEASUREMENTS : Length, 19 inches ; chest measurement, 24 inches.

Cast on 140 stitches. Knit first row into back of stitches.

Pattern as follows :—

1st row.—Knit 1. Knit 2 together all along. Knit 1.

2nd row.—Knit 1. Knit 1, make 1, by picking up a thread between the 2 stitches, all along. Knit 1.

3rd row.—Knit.

4th row.—Purl.

These 4 rows form the pattern.

Work 10 patterns (40 rows). Then join rabbit wool.

Work first 2 rows of pattern in rabbit wool, then finish pattern in 3-ply wool, and continue for 6 more patterns.

Then 2 more rows of pattern in rabbit wool.

Now knit in stocking-stitch, till work measures 12 inches, finishing with a purl row.

Knit 2 together twenty-five times, knit 40, knit 2 together twenty-five times. (90 stitches on needle now.)

Purl next row.

Row of holes : Knit 1. Knit 2 together, wool forward, all along. Knit 1.

Purl next row.

Knit 8 rows stocking-stitch.

Now knit 55, knit 2 together ten times, knit 15.

Purl 15, next 20 as pattern, purl 55.

Knit.

Purl.

Knit 51, knit 2 together ten times, knit 19.

Purl 19, next 20 as pattern, purl 51.

Knit 2 rows stocking-stitch.

Knit 47, knit 2 together ten times, knit 23.

Purl 23, 20 as pattern, purl 47.

Knit 2 rows stocking-stitch.

When bodice measures 3 inches, cast off 5 stitches at each end.

Knit 8 rows stocking-stitch.

Knit 18, knit 2 together ten times, knit 42.

Purl 42, 20 as pattern, purl 18.

Knit 2 rows stocking-stitch.

Knit 14, knit 2 together ten times, knit 46.

Purl 46, 20 as pattern, purl 14.

Knit 2 rows stocking-stitch.

Knit 10, knit 2 together ten times, knit 50.

Purl 50, 20 as pattern, purl 10.

Knit 2 rows stocking-stitch.

Shape for Neck

Knit 30, cast off 20, knit 30.

Purl 30.

Knit 1, knit 2 together, and knit to the end of the row.

Purl.

Repeat till there are 24 stitches, then work 4 rows stocking-stitch. Cast off. Then work the other side of neck to correspond. The back and front are alike, except left shoulder of back, where 12 stitches are left at neck edge. Knit 4 rows plain.

Pick up 50 stitches round the neck of each half, and knit 4 rows of pattern. Join rabbit wool for 2 rows, then finish the other 6 rows of pattern with wool. Cast off.

Either press studs or buttons and loops may be sewn to shoulder.

Sleeves

Cast on 50 stitches on No. 14 needles. Knit 1 and purl 1 for 5 rows.

Next row make 1 every other stitch (76 stitches now).

Change to No. 12 needles. Work 12 rows stocking - stitch and 4 rows pattern.

Next 2 rows pattern with rabbit wool.

Finish pattern in 3-ply wool, then work 4 more rows pattern. Cast off 2 stitches at the beginning of every row, until there are 48 stitches. Cast off.

Press carefully with a warm iron, sew up sides and shoulder, ease in the sleeves. A ribbon or a cord may be threaded through the holes if wished. The original has a chain of rabbit wool, with two crocheted discs to finish.

Designed by

Florence Edwards

"NEXT TO NOTHINGS"

As brief as your briefest summer set,
but cosy enough for the coldest day!

A Dainty Set of Vest and Panties

"FINELLA'S" own design for your winter woollies. They are very simple to knit and delightful to wear; in fact, they will be favourites all round!

MATERIALS

Six ozs. Greenock 2-ply super fingering (which can be obtained from the branches of the Scotch Wool and Hosiery Stores), a pair each of Nos. 11 and 14 knitting needles, 2½ yards of narrow ribbon to match wool.

MEASUREMENTS

Length of vest, 23 inches; all round bust, 31 inches (to fit a 33 to 34-inch bust); length of panties, 14 inches; width round widest part, 36 inches (to fit 36 to 38 hips).

TENSION

On No. 11 needles over st.st. 8 sts. to 1 inch in width; 19 rows to 2 inches in depth.

NOTE.—Always work into the backs of sts. on the first row of every part of garment to give a firm edge.

The Vest Back.—With No. 11 needles cast on 127 sts. and work in the following pattern:

1st row: Sl. 1, * m. 1, k. 1, (p. 3, k. 1) 4 times, m. 1, k. 1. Repeat from * to end of row.

2nd row: P. 3, * (k. 3, p. 1) 3 times, k. 3, p. 5. Repeat from * to end of row, ending p. 3 instead of p. 5.

3rd row: Sl. 1, k. 1, * m. 1, k. 1, (p. 3, k. 1) 4 times, m. 1, k. 3. Repeat from * to end of row, ending k. 2.

4th row: P. 4, * (k. 3, p. 1) 3 times, k. 3, p. 7. Repeat from * to end of row, ending p. 4.

5th row: Sl. 1, k. 2, * m. 1, k. 1, (p. 3, k. 1) 4 times, m. 1, k. 5 Repeat from * to end of row, ending k. 3.

6th row: P. 5, * (k. 3, p. 1) 3 times, k. 3, p. 9. Repeat from * to end of row, ending p. 5.

7th row: Sl. 1, k. 3, * m. 1, k. 1, (p. 2 tog., p. 1, k. 1) 4 times, m. 1, k. 7 Repeat from * to end of row, ending k. 4.

8th row: P. 6, * (k. 2, p. 1) 3 times, k. 2, p. 11. Repeat from * to end of row, ending p. 6.

9th row: Sl. 1, k. 4, * m. 1, k. 1, (p. 2 tog., k. 1) 4 times, m. 1, k. 9 Repeat from * to end of row, ending k. 5.

10th row: P. 7, * (k. 1, p. 1) 3 times, k. 1, p. 13. Repeat from * to end of row, ending p. 7.

11th row: Sl. 1, k. 5, * m. 1, (k. 2 tog., k. 1) 3 times, m. 1, k. 11. Repeat from * to end of row, ending k. 6.

12th row: (P. 17, p. 2 tog.) 6 times, p. 18, p. 2 tog.

Now change to st.st. and continue until work measures 9 ins. from the beginning. Then change to No. 14 needles and k. 2, p. 2 ribbing, and work 1¼ ins.

Change back to No. 11 needles and st.st. and work for 12 ins. As this is lower edge of vest it may be made any length desired. Cast off loosely.

The Front of Vest.—Using No. 11 needles cast on 127 sts. and work the first 12 rows exactly as for back of vest.

13th row: K. 19, * m. 1, k. 1, (p. 3, k. 1) 4 times, m. 1, k. 1. Repeat from * 4 times more, k. 18.

This reduces the number of patterns across front of vest from 7 to 5, the extra sts. at either side being kept in st.st. and 1 more st. being worked in st.st. on every odd numbered row (i.e. 15th row will start k. 20; 17th row k. 21, etc.). Continue thus for 10 more rows and complete one pattern, then:

24th row: P. 35, p. 2 tog (p. 17, p. 2 tog.), 3 times, p. 18, p. 2 tog., p. 18.

25th row: K. 37, * m. 1, k. 1, (p. 3, k. 1) 4 times, m. 1, k. 1. Repeat from * twice more, k. 36.

The number of patterns is now reduced to 3, with an increased number of sts. in st.st. at each side. Work as before, keeping to these sts. for 10 rows.

36th row: P. 53, p. 2 tog., p. 17, p. 2 tog., p. 18, p. 2 tog., p. 36.

37th row: K. 55, m. 1, k. 1, (p. 3, k. 1) 4 times, m. 1, k. 54.

There is now only one pattern in centre, the remainder of sts. all being in st.st. Continue for 10 more rows.

48th row: P. 2 tog., p. to within last 2 sts., p. 2 tog.

Now change to st.st. and continue until work measures 9 ins. Then finish front of vest exactly to match back.

Right Leg of Panties.—Cast on 145 sts. on No. 11 needles and work in pattern exactly as for the back of vest for the first 11 rows.

12th row: (P. 17, p. 2 tog.) 7 times, p. 18, p. 2 tog.

Repeat these 12 rows once more.

25th row: K. 19, * m. 1, k. 1, (p. 3, k. 1) 4 times, m. 1, k. 1 Repeat from * 5 times more, k. 18.

This gives six patterns instead of eight with st.st. at either end. Continue the next ten rows of pattern as before, but keeping these end sts. in st.st. as for vest and working 1 more st. in st.st. on each row (i.e. 27th row will start k. 20; 29th row k. 21, etc.).

36th row: P. 35, p. 2 tog., (p. 17, p. 2 tog.) 4 times, p. 18, p. 2 tog., p. 18.

37th row: K. 37, work 4 complete patterns as before, ending k. 36. There are now only 4 patterns, the sts. in st.st. having been increased Work next 10 rows of pattern accordingly, then:

48th row: P. 53, p. 2 tog., p. 17, p. 2 tog., p. 17, p. 2 tog., p. 18, p. 2 tog., p. 36.

49th row: K. 55. Work 2 patterns as before, ending k. 54.

Continue for next 10 rows of pattern as before, keeping the increased number of sts. at each end in st.st.

60th row: P. 2 tog., p. to within last 2 sts., p. 2 tog.

Now change to st.st. and work 64 rows. Now work thus:

1st row: K. all sts.

2nd row: P. 56, turn and work back.

4th row: P. 50, turn and work back.

6th row: P. 44, turn and work back.

Work another 5 p. rows, working 6 sts. less on each row, then k. remaining sts., turn and p. right across all sts. Change to No. 14 needles and k. 2, p. 2 rib and work for 1½ ins. On next row k. 2 tog., m. 1 to end of row. P. all sts. on next row. Cast off.

Left Leg of Panties.—This is made in exactly the same way as the right leg, but all shapings should be reversed, so that they come on the opposite side.

The Gusset.—On No. 11 needles cast on 2 sts. and working in st.st., inc. 1 st. at beginning and end of every p. row until there are 40 sts. on the needle.

Now dec. 1 st. at beginning and end of next 2 rows, then work 1 row without dec. Continue thus, always working the 3rd row without dec. until 1 st. remains. Cast off.

TO MAKE UP

Press work lightly on wrong side with a warm iron over a damp cloth. Sew up side seams of vest and sew on ribbon to form shoulder straps.

Sew in gusset with longer side at the back, placing point 7 ins. from lower edge of legs. Sew up leg seams and front and back seams, thread remainder of ribbon through holes in ribbing.

KEEPING THEM LOVELY

ONE of the secrets of keeping your woolly garments soft and beautiful to the end of their days is in careful washing.

To begin with, always wash woollies quite separately. Have plenty of water to which some good soapflakes (which are guaranteed not to contain soda) have been added, then add cold water until the temperature is just about lukewarm.

When a good lather is obtained, squeeze the garment in the water until all dirt is removed. Do not, on any account, twist or rub the garment, but if it is very grubby, use several waters.

When quite clean, rinse in clean, lukewarm water, squeeze again, then wrap in a dry towel. Bang with the hand several times in order to remove as much moisture as possible, then dry by laying out flat on another dry towel, or hang over a drying rail, keeping the shape as near correct as possible. Do not dry in the heat and never allow the garments to lie about in a damp state. The best place to dry them is where a current of air can play underneath.

The skirt is so trim, and the jacket is snug !

The ROUGH TWEED Effect

The Whole Suit Is Made In Stocking Stitch, And The Revers of Single Rib

HERE is such a fascinating suit of coat, skirt and cape knitted in a wool which forms its own pattern; stocking-stitch is therefore employed, and the purl side forms the right side of the suit. The revers and belt are knitted in a wool crêpe.

MATERIALS

MUNROSPUN Heatherglen in black and white mixture, as follows: 19 ounces for the skirt, 16 ounces for the coat, and 6 ounces for the cape; 4 ounces of 3-ply Munrospun Crêpe in black; a pair each of No. 11 and No. 9 Aero knitting needles; a black buckle for coat belt; and 1 yard of petersham.

TENSION AND MEASUREMENTS

WORKED at a tension of 6 stitches to the inch in width with the No. 9 needles, the following measurements are attained after pressing:

THE SKIRT: Round waist, 28 inches; round hips, 40 inches (measured 9 inches down from the top of the waist); length, 32 inches.

THE COAT: Across the back at the under-arms, 20 inches; across each front at the underarms without the revers, $10\frac{1}{2}$ inches; front length from shoulder seam to lower edge, 22 inches; back length, 20 inches; side seam, 15 inches; sleeve seam, 19 inches.

THE CAPE: Round the lower edge, 42 inches; neck edge, 17 inches; length at centre back, 16 inches.

ABBREVIATIONS

K. knit plain; p., purl; sl., slip; st., stitch; tog., together; s.s., stocking-st. (k. on the right side and p. back); inc., increase (by knitting in the front and back of the same st.); single rib is k. 1 and p. 1 alternately.

THE SKIRT

THIS is worked in two pieces, beginning at the waist, so that any length can be knitted downwards according to requirements. It is advisable to work it a few inches shorter than the desired length to allow for dropping in wear.

THE FRONT: Using No. 9 needles throughout the skirt, cast on 90 sts. and work in s.s., increasing 1 st. at both ends of every plain row until there are 158 sts. Continue on these sts., increasing 1 st. at the beginning and end of every 12th row every 2 inches of knitting until there are 184 sts. Work without further shaping on these sts. until the skirt is 31 inches or length required.

K. 8 rows in garter-st. and cast off.

THE BACK: Cast on 58 sts. and work as on the front until there are 76 sts.

Continue as on the front, increasing at both ends of every 12th row until there are 102 sts.,

Is The Simplest Knitting

The Finished Knitting Looks Just Like One Of The New Knobbly Tweeds

after which work straight down until there are as many rows as on the front, finishing with the garter-st. border.

THE COAT

BEGIN at the lower edge of the back by casting on 116 sts. with No. 9 needles and k. plain, taking 2 tog. at both ends of every 4th row, until 8 rows have been worked. Now proceed in s.s., beginning with a purl row and still decreasing on every 4th row until the sts. are reduced to 100 (8 decrease rows altogether from the beginning).

Work 16 rows plain, then begin the slope of the side seam. Inc. 1 st. at both ends of every 8th row until there are 110 sts., after which inc. 1 st. at both ends of every 4th row, until there are 116 sts., when the armhole will be reached.

To Shape the Armholes: Take 2 tog at both ends of every row, until the sts. are reduced to 84. On these sts. work 36 rows without further alteration up to the shoulder-line.

To Slope the Shoulders: Cast off 7 sts. at the beginning of each of the next 8 rows, then cast off the remaining 28 sts.

The Left Front: Cast on 44 sts. with No. 9 needles, and k. 8 rows, shaping as follows: Work 3 rows without alteration. On the 4th row inc. in each of the first 2 sts. and k. 2 tog. at the end of the row (side seam). Work 3 rows plain.

8TH ROW: As 4th row.

Now change to s.s., beginning with a purl row, and work the 12th, 16th, 20th, and 24th row as 4th row (50 sts.).

Work on these sts. until there are 5 inches from the beginning. Now, with the right side of work facing (purl side), inc. 1 st. at the beginning of the next row and every 8th row, until there are 56 sts., after which inc. 1 st. at the beginning of every 4th row until there are 60 sts. On these sts. work until the side seam measures exactly the same as the back up to the armhole.

To Shape the Armhole: With the purl side of the work facing, p. 2 tog., p. until 2 remain, p. 2 tog. for front neck decrease.

NEXT ROW: K. plain, ending with k. 2 tog. for the armhole decrease.

NEXT ROW: P. 2 tog., p. to the end of the row (no decrease at front end).

NEXT ROW: Plain knitting, ending with k. 2 tog.

Repeat these 4 rows 3 times more, when there will be 40 sts. left. This finishes the armhole decreases, but continue to p. 2 tog. at the end of every alternate *purl* row, until 29 sts. remain. Work one row more back to arm end.

To Slope the Shoulder: Cast off 7 sts. at the beginning of the next row and every alternate row (arm end) until 1 st. remains, draw wool through and fasten off.

Continued overleaf

To give a touch of chic, add the little cape across the shoulders.

THE RIGHT FRONT: Work this from the same directions as the left front, but remember to reverse the shaping right from the beginning by decreasing 1 st. at the beginning of the 4th row and increasing in the last 2 sts. This also applies to the armhole and front neck shaping, but as it is all in stocking-st. this is very easy. Cast off the shoulder stitches with the plain side facing.

THE REVERS: Cast on 2 sts. with the No. 11 needles and black crêpe wool. Work in single rib, always working the k. st. into the back of the sts., and increasing 1 st. at the beginning of every alternate row, until there are 60 sts.

Cast off 36 sts. beginning at the straight edge (1 st. now on the right-hand needle) and work across the remaining 23 sts.

NEXT ROW: Work to the end of the row and there cast on 26 sts. (50 sts. now on).

Work on these 50 sts. for 16 inches.

Now, beginning at the outside edge of the collar, cast off the 26 sts. that were cast on at the beginning of the straight piece, and work to the end of the row.

NEXT ROW: Work to the end of the remaining 24 sts., then cast on 36 sts., making 60 altogether.

Now k. 2 tog. on the inside edge (that is the opposite side to the casting on) on every other row until 2 remain, then cast off.

THE BELT

CAST on 24 sts. with No. 11 needles and work single rib as on the revers until the strip measures 31 inches or the length required.

Now k. 2 tog. at the beginning of every row until all are worked off.

THE SLEEVES

CAST on 54 sts. and k. 8 rows plain. Proceed in s.s., increasing 1 st. at both ends of every 8th row until there are 80 sts. and the work measures 19 inches.

Now k. 2 tog. at both ends of every row until 24 sts. remain. Cast off.

THE CAPE

CAST on 242 sts. with No. 9 needles and k. 8 rows plain. Proceed in s.s. but now work the first and last 8 sts. plain on the purl rows also.

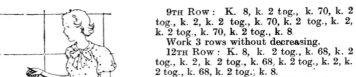

9TH ROW: K. 8, k. 2 tog., k. 70, k. 2 tog., k. 2, k. 2 tog., k. 70, k. 2 tog., k. 2, k. 2 tog., k. 70, k. 2 tog., k. 8.

Work 3 rows without decreasing.

12TH ROW: K. 8, k. 2 tog., k. 68, k. 2 tog., k. 2, k. 2 tog., k. 68, k. 2 tog., k. 2, k. 2 tog., k. 68, k. 2 tog., k. 8.

Repeat the last 4 rows (that is, 3 rows in s.s. without decreasing), then a repetition of the 12th row, until 98 sts. remain, but note that on every decrease row there are 2 sts. less to knit plain between the 2 decreases.

Now work without decreasing until the cape measures 16 inches at the centre back. Cast off.

TO MAKE UP THE SUIT

FIRST press all pieces on the wrong side (plain knitting), putting a damp cloth over the knitting.

Join up the side seams of the skirt, leaving 7 inches open on the left hip, where the fastening goes towards the back. Face the front of the opening with black silk. Make a flap of the same material about 1 inch wide on the back of the opening. Attach petersham at the top.

To make up the coat sew up the shoulder seams and set sleeves to armholes, press these seams while the work is open, then sew up the sleeve and side seams in one continuous line. Sew on the revers, beginning at the centre back of the neck and marking the centre of the collar with a pin. Sew down each side to the end of the rever, but leave a 1-inch slit just opposite the break in the revers. Press seams and revers flat. Sew one press-stud at the bottom of the revers where the coat just meets. Sew buckle to belt.

Work two ties for the cape as follows: Cast on enough stitches to make about 9 inches, and k. 6 rows in garter stitch. Cast off loosely. Sew these to the top corners of the cape.

NOTE.—If you should have any difficulty in obtaining the wool specified locally, it may be obtained, price 7½d. per ounce, from any of the undermentioned firms:—

Messrs. Bourne and Hollingsworth, Ltd., Oxford Street, London, W.1; Messrs. Marshall and Snellgrove, Ltd., Oxford Street, London, W.1; and Messrs. Liberty's, Regent Street, London, W.1.

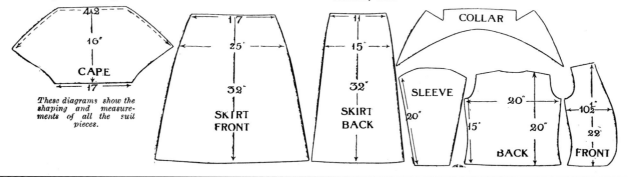

These diagrams show the shaping and measurements of all the suit pieces.

CAPE 4½ 16" 17

SKIRT FRONT 17 25 32

SKIRT BACK 14 15 32

COLLAR SLEEVE 20 20 15 BACK 20 FRONT 10½ 22

Film News

WHEN you see "Sixty Glorious Years" you will see Anna Neagle driving in the real State Coach drawn by the famous Windsor Greys. The King was so interested in the making of this film, that he gave permission for the coach to be used and also for some shots to be made inside Buckingham Palace. The filming took just over two hours, and was the first time a "talkie" had been made there.

Hedy Lamarr is hailed in New York as the most glamorous foreign beauty since Marlene. With Charles Boyer she will appear in "Algiers," which is the English version of a French film called "Pèpè le Moko." It has enormous success in London, and for that reason is to be re-issued in English for general release.

WIDE LAPELS *Are Chic and* VERY NEW

A Woolly That is Knitted in a Most Attractive Pattern

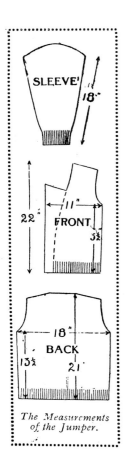

The Measurements of the Jumper.

The alternating pattern is very intriguing.

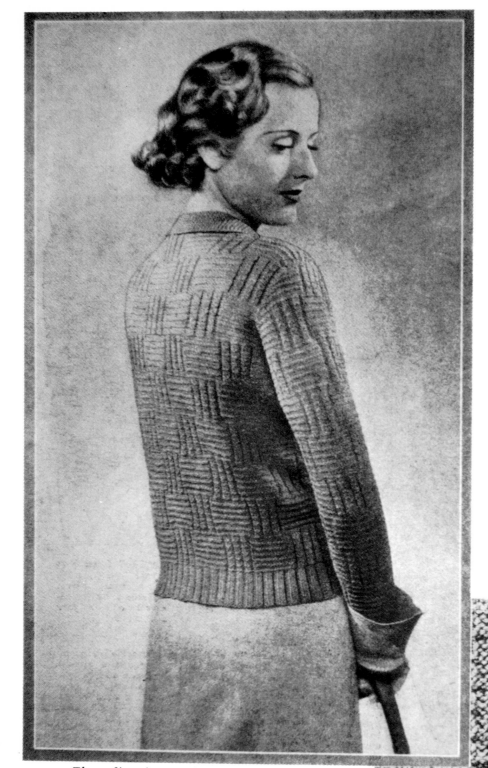

The cardigan is a cosy length for winter days.

DESIGNED
for a
LADY
Who Likes
TO BE
WARM

A Stylish New Cardigan that You Will Want to Wear and Wear

TENSION AND MEASUREMENTS:
Worked at a tension of 7 sts. to the inch in width on No. 8 needles the following measurements are attained after light pressing : Across the back at the under-arms, 18 inches ; across each front at the same point, 11 inches ; front length from shoulder seam to edge, 22 inches ; back length, 21 inches ; side seam, 13½ inches ; sleeve seam, 18 inches.

A " close-up " of the stitch.

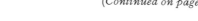

MATERIALS :
Ten ounces of " Ramada " 4-ply Superfine Pure Wool Knittings ; a pair each of Aero knitting needles, No. 8 and No. 10 ; two buttons.

ABBREVIATIONS : *K., knit ; p., purl ; tog., together ; inc., increase (by working into the back and front of the same stitch) ; st., stitch ; rib is k. 2 and p. 2 alternately. Directions in brackets are worked the number of times stated immediately after the brackets.*

(Continued on page 37)

BEGIN at the back and using No. 10 needles, cast on 126 sts. and work in rib as follows :

1st row (right side facing) : P. 2, * k. 2, p. 2 ; repeat from * to end.

2nd row : K. 2, * p. 2, k. 2 ; repeat from * to end.

Repeat these 2 rows until 19 rows have been worked, then k. 1 row with the wrong side facing. Change to No. 8 needles and work in pattern as follows :

1st row (right side facing) : P. 2, (k. 2, p. 2) 3 times, * k. 14, p. 2, (k. 2, p. 2) 3 times ; repeat from * to end.

2nd row : K. 2, (p. 2, k. 2) 3 times, * p. 14, k. 2, (p. 2, k. 2) 3 times ; repeat from * to end.

3rd row : All p.

4th row : As 2nd row.

5th row : As 1st row.

6th row : All k.

Repeat these 6 rows twice more, which makes 18 rows in pattern.

19th row : K. 14, * p. 2, (k. 2, p. 2) 3 times, k. 14 ; repeat from * to end.

20th row : P. 14, * k. 2, (p. 2, k. 2) 3 times ; p. 14 ; repeat from * to end.

21st row : All p.

22nd row : As 20th row.

23rd row : As 19th row.

24th row : All k.

Repeat the 19th to 24th rows twice more (36 rows in pattern).

Repeat these 36 pattern rows once more, then 24 rows of next pattern to armholes.

To SHAPE THE ARMHOLES : Continue in pattern, casting off 2 sts. at the beginning of each of the next 10 rows, then work 2 sts. tog. at the beginning of each of the following 8 rows (98 sts.).

Work 38 rows straight in pattern to shoulder.

To SLOPE THE SHOULDERS : Cast off 7 sts. at the beginning of each of the next 8 rows. Cast off the remaining sts.

THE LEFT FRONT : With No. 10 needles cast on 56 sts. for the lower edge. Work 19 rows in rib, beginning every row with k. 2.

Next row (wrong side facing) : All k. Change to No. 8 needles and work in pattern as follows :

1st row (right side facing) : * k. 14, p. 2, (k. 2, p. 2) 3 times ; repeat from * to end.

2nd row : * k. 2, (p. 2, k. 2) 3 times, p. 14 ; repeat from * to end.

3rd row : All p.

4th row : As 2nd row.

5th row : As 1st row.

6th row : All k.

Repeat these 6 rows twice more (18 rows).

19th row : * p. 2, (k. 2, p. 2) 3 times, k. 14 ; repeat from * to end.

20th row : * p. 14, k. 2, (p. 2, k. 2) 3 times ; repeat from * to end.

21st row : All p.

22nd row : As 20th row.

23rd row : As 19th row.

24th row : All k.

Repeat the 19th to 24th row twice more, . which completes 36 rows in pattern.

Work the first 18 rows (3 sets of squares), then continue in pattern, beginning with the 19th row and take 2 sts. tog. at the end of next and every following 8th row (front end) until the 6th decrease row has been worked, then 1 row more to armhole.

** To SHAPE THE ARMHOLE : Continue in pattern, still decreasing at the front end as before, and cast off 2 sts. at the beginning of next and every following alternate row (armhole end) 5 times, then work 2 sts. tog. at the beginning of alternate rows (armhole end) for 4 times.

Continue straight at armhole end, but still work the front decreases as before until 30 sts. remain.

Work 19 rows straight on these sts. (20 rows on right front) to shoulder.

To SLOPE THE SHOULDERS : Continue in pattern, casting off 6 sts. at the beginning of next and every following alternate row (armhole end) until all are worked off.

THE RIGHT FRONT : With No. 10 needles cast on 56 sts. for the lower edge and work 19 rows in rib (beginning every row with p. 2).

Next row (wrong side facing) : All k. Change to No. 8 needles and work in pattern as follows :

1st row (right side facing) : * p. 2, (k. 2, p. 2) 3 times, k. 14 ; repeat from * to end.

2nd row : * p. 14, k. 2, (p. 2, k. 2) 3 times ; repeat from * to end.

3rd row : All p.

4th row : As 2nd row.

5th row : As 1st row.

6th row : All k.

Repeat these 6 rows twice more (18 rows).

19th row : * K. 14, p. 2, (k. 2, p. 2) 3 times ; repeat from * to end.

20th row : * K. 2, (p. 2, k. 2) 3 times, p. 14 ; repeat from * to end.

21st row : All p.

22nd row : As 20th row.

23rd row : As 19th row.

24th row : All k.

Repeat the 19th to 24th rows twice more, which completes 36 rows in pattern. Work from the 1st to the 18th row inclusive, then continue in pattern, taking 2 sts. tog. at the beginning of next and every following 8th row (front end) for 6 decreases, and then 2 rows more. (7 rows of 6th set of squares.) To shape the armhole continue from left front instructions from ** to end.

THE SLEEVES : With No. 8 needles cast on 26 sts. and k. 1 row.

Now work in increase pattern as follows :

1st row (right side facing) : Inc., k. 5, p: 2 (k. 2, p. 2) 3 times, k. 5, inc.

2nd row : Inc., p. 6, k. 2 (p. 2, k. 2) 3 times, p. 6, inc.

3rd row : Inc., p. until 1 remains, inc.

4th row : Inc., p. 8, k. 2, (p. 2, k. 2) 3 times, p. 8, inc.

5th row : Inc., k. 9, p. 2, (k. 2, p. 2,) 3 times, k. 9, inc.

6th row : Inc., k. until 1 remains, inc.

7th row : Inc., k. 11, rib 14, k. 11, inc.

8th row : Inc., p. 12, rib 14, p. 12, inc.

9th row : Inc., p. until 1 remains, inc.

10th row : Inc., p. 14, rib 14, p. 14, inc.

11th row : Inc., p. 1, k. 14, rib 14, k. 14, p. 1, inc.

12th row : Inc., k. until 1 remains, inc.

13th row : Inc., k. 3, rib 14, k. 14, rib 14, k. 3, inc.

14th row : Inc., p. 4, rib 14, p. 14, rib 14, p. 4, inc.

15th row : Inc., p. until 1 remains, inc.

16th row : Inc., p. 6, rib 14, p. 14, rib 14, p. 6, inc.

17th row : Inc., k. 7, rib 14, k. 14, rib 14, k. 7, inc.

18th row : Inc., k. until 1 remains, inc.

19th row : Inc., k. 9, rib 14, k. 14, rib 14, k. 9, inc.

20th row : Inc., p. 10, rib 14, p. 14, rib 14, p. 10, inc.

21st row : Inc., p. until 1 remains, inc.

22nd row : Inc., p. 12, rib 14, p. 14, rib 14, p. 12, inc.

23rd row : Inc., k. 13, rib 14, k. 14, rib 14, k. 13, inc.

24th row : Inc., k. until 1 remains, inc.

25th row : Inc., p. 1, k. 14, (rib 14, k. 14) twice, p. 1, inc.

26th row : Inc., k. 2, p. 14, (rib 14, p. 14) twice, k. 2, inc.

27th row : Inc., p. until 1 remains, inc.

28th row : Inc., p. 2, k. 2, p. 14, (rib 14, p. 14) twice, k. 2, p. 2, inc.

29th row : Inc., p. 1, k. 2, p. 2, k. 14, (rib 14, k. 14) twice, p. 2, k. 2, p. 1, inc.

There are now 84 sts. on needles on which work 1 row in plain knitting which completes the pattern square.

31st row : K. 7, rib 14, * k. 14, rib 14 ; repeat from * until 7 remain, k. 7.

32nd row : P. 7, rib 14, * p. 14, rib 14, repeat from * until 7 remain, p. 7.

33rd row : All p.

34th row : As 32nd row.

Continue in pattern taking 2 sts. tog. at each end of next and every following 8th row until 52 sts. remain. Work 1 row in plain knitting.

Change to No. 10 needles and work 30 rows in rib. Cast off.

Work a second sleeve in the same manner.

THE RIGHT FRONT REVER : With No. 10 needles cast on 16 sts. and k. 25 rows.

1st buttonhole row : K. 3, cast off 5, k. 8.

2nd buttonhole row : K. 8, cast on 5 over those cast off, k. 3.

K. 36 rows and then repeat the 2 buttonhole rows.

K. 15 rows (on the left front rever begin with 16 sts. and k. 80 rows to this point, both fronts are then worked alike from here.)

Continue all in plain knitting, inc. in the last st. on next and every following 6th row (the same edge as narrow end of buttonhole band) until there are 31 sts. on row, then k. 5 rows.

Now build up as follows at the straight edge : K. 29, turn, k. 29 ; k. 28, turn, k. 28 ; k. 26, turn, k. 26 ; k. 25, turn, k. 25 ; k. 23, turn, k. 23 ; k. 22, turn, k. 22 ; k. 20, turn, k. 20 ; k. 19, turn, k. 19 ; k. 17, turn, k. 17 ; k. 16, turn, k. 16 ; k. 14, turn, k. 14 ; k. 13, turn, k. 13 ; k. 11, turn, k. 11 ; k. 10, turn, k. 10 ; k. 8, turn, k. 8 ; k. 7, turn, k. 7 ; k. 5, turn, k. 5 ; k. 4, turn, k. 4 ; k. 2, turn, k. 2.

Now k. 2 rows on all the sts. and then build up in the reverse way, that is, begin with k. 2 and end with k. 29.

Continue in plain knitting on all the sts. taking 2 sts. tog. at the end of the next and every following alternate row (same end as increases) until 24 remain. Now take 2 sts. tog. at the end of every 4th row until 18 remain. K. 30 rows and cast off. Work the left rever in same manner.

To MAKE UP THE CARDIGAN : Join the shoulder seams, taking 1 st. from each side at a time, then sew the centre-back seam of the collar. Join the collar and revers to neck and front edges, and press all seams. Set the sleeves into armholes and join the sleeve and side seams in one continuous line and press. Stitch buttons to left front matching the buttonhole.

A PAIR OF JUMPERS FOR THE

This easy-fitting jumper is ideal for putting on first thing in the morning when there is work to be done round the house. A simple plain-and-purl diamond pattern and panels of moss-stitch give interesting detail in the front, and the collar can be made larger, or to close up round the throat in polo style, if desired

FOR

MORNING

Materials Required : 9 oz. Rosedale 3-ply fingering wool. A pair each of No. 10 and No. 13 knitting needles. 3 buttons. **Measurements (after pressing) :** Length from lower edge to top of shoulder, 19½ in. ; length of sleeve, along seam, 20 in. ; width all round, under arms, 37 in. **Abbreviations :** Sts., stitches ; k., knit ; p., purl ; tog., together ; rep., repeat ; rem., remain (s), (der), (ing) ; inc., increase (ing) ; dec., decrease (ing) ; Moss-st., k. 1, p. 1 alternately, working next row so that the k. st. comes over a p. st., and the p. st. over the k. st. in previous row.

The Back : With the No. 13 needles cast on 100 sts., and work in single rib (k. 1, p. 1 alternately) for 3 in., then—Next row : Inc. to 120 sts. by knitting into the front and the back of every 5th st.

Now change over to No. 10 needles, and commence in pattern, as follows—**Row 1 :** * k. 5, p. 5, rep. from * to end. **Row 2 :** K. 6, * p. 5, k. 5, rep. from *, ending row by p. 4. **Row 3 :** K. 3, * p. 5, k. 5, rep. from *, ending row by k. 2 (instead of k. 5). **Row 4 :** P. 3, * k. 5, p. 5, rep. from *, ending row by p. 2 (instead of p. 5). **Row 5 :** K. 1, * p. 5, k. 5, rep. from *, ending row

by k. 4 (instead of k. 5). **Row 6 :** * P. 5, k. 5, rep. from * to end.

These 6 rows comprise the pattern. Work 20 more patterns. **Shape the arm-holes,** as follows : Cast off 5 sts. at the beginning of each of the next 2 rows, then k. 2 tog. at both ends of the next 5 rows, until 100 sts. rem.

Continue to work without further dec. until 28 patterns from the beginning have been completed, then work for 20 rows in moss-st. Then cast off 26 sts. (one st. now on the needle), work 47 sts., cast off 26.

On the rem. 48 sts. work for 32 rows in single rib (more rows if a deeper collar is desired). Cast off.

The Front : Work as for the back, until the first pattern has been completed, then : **2nd Pattern, Row 1 :** * K. 5, p. 5, rep. from * 3 times more, then k. 5 (45 sts. in all), now work the next 30 sts. in moss-st., then * p. 5, k. 5, rep. from *, ending row by p. 5. **Row 2 :** K. 6, * p. 5, k. 5, rep. from * twice more, then p. 5, k. 4, work the next 30 sts. in moss-st., then k. 1, * p. 5, k. 5, rep. from *, ending row by p. 4. **Row 3 :** K. 3, * p. 5, k. 5, rep. from * 3 times more, p. 2, work the next 30 sts. in

moss-st., p. 3, * k. 5, p. 5, rep. from *, ending row by k. 2. **Row 4 :** P. 3, * k. 5, p. 5, rep. from * 3 times more, k. 2, work 30 sts. in moss-st., k. 3, * p. 5, k. 5, rep. from *, ending row by p. 2. **Row 5 :** K. 1, * p. 5, k. 5, rep. from * 3 times more, p. 4, work 30 sts. in moss-st., k. 6, * p. 5, k. 5, rep. from *, ending row by k. 4 (instead of k. 5). **Row 6 :** * P. 5, k. 5, rep. from * 4 times, p. 5, work 30 sts. in moss-st., * k. 5, p. 5, rep. from *, ending row by k. 5.

Rep. the last 6 rows 18 times more, then shape for arm-holes as for the back, and continue to work without further dec. until 28 patterns from the beginning have been completed. Now work for 6 rows in moss-st., then shape neck-opening, thus : **Row 7 :** Work moss-st. for 42 sts., turn the work, and work the return row. Repeat this 8 more times, working 2 sts. less each time, until with row 23 only 26 sts. are worked.

Work for 10 more rows in moss-st. on these 26 sts. Cast off. Now pick up 8 sts. along the inside straight edge of neck, and work the entire row in moss-st. (82 sts.). Then work the right side exactly as the left side. (This leaves 64 sts. on the needle.) Now work for 12 rows in single rib on these sts.

If a round collar without any opening at the front is desired, continue to work straight, but if the design illustrated is preferred, then : **Next Row :** Rib 34 sts., turn the piece, and leave the rem. 34 sts. on a spare needle for the present. Work in rib for 20 rows on these sts. (more if longer collar desired). Cast off. Now pick up the sts. from spare needle, and work the opposite side in the same manner.

The Sleeve (two alike) : With No. 13 needles cast on 50 sts., and work for 30 rows in single rib, then change over to No. 10 needles, and commence in pattern, as for the back, inc. 1 st. at each end of every following 10th row, until there are 78 sts. Continue to work without further inc. to the length required, then k. 2 tog. at each end of every row, until 8 sts. rem. Cast off.

Make up and Finish : Seam up the shoulders, and neatly sew the tops of sleeves into the arm-holes. Carefully press the work open under a damp cloth with a hot iron. Sew up sleeve and side seams in one operation. Sew on buttons and press seams.

KNITTED SUITABLE AUTUMN

When something pretty and feminine is required, this delightful angora jumper is very attractive. The pattern is a simple fern design, easy to knit, and a band of stocking-stitch at the neck edge rolls back to give a becoming line, finished by a pearl buckle. The sleeves are knitted out from the shoulders to avoid an ugly join

Materials : 10 balls Paton and Baldwin's " Beehive " fine-spun angora. 1 mother-of-pearl buckle. 2 No. 9 knitting needles. 1 crochet hook. 2 No. 11 knitting needles. **Measurements :** Length from shoulder, 19 inches. To fit 33- or 34-inch bust. **Abbreviations :** k., knit ; p., purl ; tog., together ; rep., repeat ; w.fd., wool forward over needle ; s. 1, slip one ; p.s.s.o., pass slipped stitch over ; patt., pattern.

Front.—With No. 9 needles cast on 87 sts. and knit off from back of loop. Change to No. 11. K. 1, p. 1 for 5 inches.

1st Row after rib : Rib 5, k. 6, * k. 2 tog., k. 5. Repeat from * to within 13 sts. of end, then k. 2 tog., k. 6, rib. 5 = 76.

2nd Row : Rib 5, p. 66, rib 5.

The next row begins pattern, divisible by 14 with 2 over. At each side before the pattern begins there are 9 stitches which are worked as a rib of k. 1, p. 1, k. 1, p. 1, k. 1, and then 4 sts. in stocking-st. (reversed at the end of the row to bring the 4 stocking-sts. next to the pattern). These nine should be knitted at the beginning and end of all the following rows, though they are not referred to again until under-arms are reached.

1st Patt. Row (58 sts. for pattern, with 9 each end, making 76 in all) : Change to No. 9 needles. P. 2, * k. 2, w.fd., k. 1, w.fd., k. 1, k. 1, s. 1, k. 1, p.s.s.o., k. 3, k. 2 tog., k. 1, p. 2. Repeat from * for 58 sts.

2nd and every alternate Row : K. 2, p. 12, ending k. 2. **3rd Patt. Row :** P. 2, * k. 2, w.fd., k. 3, w.fd., k. 1, s. 1, k. 1, p.s.s.o., k. 1, k. 2 tog., k. 1, p. 2. Rep. from *. **5th Patt. Row :** P. 2, * k. 2, w.fd., k. 5, w.fd., k. 1, s. 1, k. 2 tog., p.s.s.o., k. 1, p. 2. Rep. from *. **7th Patt. Row :** P. 2, * s. 1, k. 1, p.s.s.o., k. 3, k. 2 tog., k. 1, w.fd., k. 1, w.fd., k. 3, p. 2. Rep. from *. **9th Patt. Row :** P. 2, * s. 1, k. 1, p.s.s.o., k. 1, k. 2 tog., k. 1, w.fd., k. 3, w.fd., k. 1, p. 2. Rep. from *. **11th Patt. Row :** P. 2, * s. 1, k. 2 tog., p.s.s.o., k. 1, w.fd., k. 5, w.fd., k. 3, p. 2. Rep. from *.

Continue repetition of pattern until there are 3 complete ones.

Then continue patt. on first 16, k. 26, patt. on last 16 = 58. **2nd Row :** K. 2, p. 12, k. 2, p. 26, k. 2, p. 12, k. 2. Continue in this order until a 4th Patt. is completed.

Work on Right Side, cast off for under-arms. Cast off 4. Continue with 1st row of 5th patt., knitting 26 sts. in centre as

before. **2nd Row :** Cast off 4. Continue to end of row. Complete the under-arm shaping as follows: At beginning of 3rd, 5th, 7th, 9th and 11th rows, k. 1, k. 2 tog. At end of 3rd, 5th, 7th, 9th and 11th rows, s. 1, k. 1, p.s.s.o., k. 1. Alternate rows as before.

Neck opening.—Each side of front begins and finishes with 1 patt. of 14 sts. with the 2 over for edge. The following shaping applies only to the neck opening.

Left side *. **1st Patt. Row :** Patt. 14, k. 5, k. 2 tog., p. 6, turn. **2nd Row :** K. 6, p. 6, finish as usual. **3rd Patt. Row :** Patt. 14, k. 6, p. 6, turn. **4th Row :** As row 2. **5th Patt. Row :** Patt. 14, k. 4, k. 2 tog., p. 6, turn. **6th Row :** K. 6, p. 5, finish as usual. **7th Patt. Row :** Patt. 14, k. 5, p. 6, turn. **8th Row :** As row 6. **9th Patt. Row :** Patt. 14, k. 3, k. 2 tog., p. 5, turn. **10th Row :** k. 6, p. 4, finish as usual. **11th Patt. Row :** Patt. 14, k. 4, p. 6, turn. **12th Row :** As row 10. Rep. from last * once more, making the 3 decreasings and allowing for them.

Shoulder.—Continue with 1st row of next patt. as follows : Patt. 13, p. 2 tog.,

FOR AFTERNOON

p. 6, turn. **2nd Row :** K. 8, finish as usual. **3rd Patt. Row :** Patt. 14, p. 6, turn, k. 6, turn, p. 6. **4th Row :** K. 6, finish as usual. Complete patt. in this order, knitting border sts. twice to each row of patt. Cast off 14 on wrong side. Place the remaining 8 sts. for border on a safety-pin.

Right side.—With right side of work in front of you, join wool in at neck opening, leaving a long end. **1st Patt. Row :** P. 6, s. 1, k. 1, p.s.s.o., k. 5, Patt. 14. **2nd (Return) Row :** As usual.

Finish in this order to correspond to left side of front.

Back.—With No. 9 needles, cast on 82 sts. K. off from back of loop. Change to No. 11 needles. K. 1, p. 1 for 5 inches, then k. 1 row and p. 1 row. Change to No. 9 needles. There are 5 sts. at beginning and end of each row, worked in rib of k. 1, p. 1, k. 1, p. 1, k. 1 ; these are not referred to again until under-arms are reached. Rep. patt. on the intermediate 72 sts. until 4 are completed. At beginning of 1st patt. row of 5th pattern, cast off 5 for under-arm, and again at the beginning of return row. (*Continued on page* 41)

Man's Pull-Over designed by Honor Tuite

MATERIALS REQUIRED : 6 ounces of Templeton's "Ayrlream" Soft Knitting Wool, 4-ply, in white ; also 2 ounces of the same wool in navy blue ; 1 pair of No. 8 and 1 pair of No. 12 Stratnoid knitting needles.

TENSION : Approx. 5½ sts. to 1 inch in width when ribbing is stretched out, when garment will fit a 38-inch chest measurement.

ABBREVIA-TIONS : k. = knit ; p. = purl ; sts. = stitches ; tog. = together ; dec. = decrease.

The Back

With white wool and No. 8 needles, cast on 108 sts., then work in the following fancy ribbing :—

1st row.—k. 1, p. 1 to end.

2nd row.— Purl all sts.

These 2 rows form the pattern and are repeated throughout.

Continue until work measures 1 inch, ending at completion of a purl row, then join on navy wool and work 6 rows in navy, rejoin white wool, and work 6 rows white, then another 6 rows navy. Fasten off navy wool and continue in white only until work measures 14 inches from beginning, then shape armholes by casting off 4 sts. at beginning of the next 4 rows, then k. 2 sts. tog. at beginning and end of the next 2 rows.

From here, work straight until armhole measures 9 inches, then shape shoulders by casting off 8 sts. at beginning of the next 8 rows. Cast off remaining sts. for back of neck.

The Front

Work exactly the same as back until work measures 13 inches, ending at completion of a purl row.

Next row.—k. 1, p. 1 over 54 sts. Turn, leaving remainder of sts. on a stitch-holder until first side has been completed.

(*Continued on page* 41)

Any out-door man would appreciate a jumper of this style

Man's Pull-Over

Working over the group of 54 sts. just worked, shape neck by taking 2 sts. tog. (always keeping continuity of ribbing) at beginning of the next row, then every following *4th row* (3 rows without decrease between each decrease row), but when side seam measures 14 inches from beginning, shape armhole by casting off 4 sts. at beginning of the next 2 rows starting from armhole edge. then take 2 sts. tog. at armhole edge on the next 2 rows. Working armhole edge straight from here, continue to decrease every *4th row* at neck edge, until sts. are reduced to 32. Then work straight until armhole measures 9½ inches all round edge, then shape shoulder by casting off 8 sts. at beginning of the next 4 rows, starting from armhole edge.

Join wool to neck edge at other side, and work this to match the first.

To Complete Pull-Over

With blue wool and No. 12 needles pick up

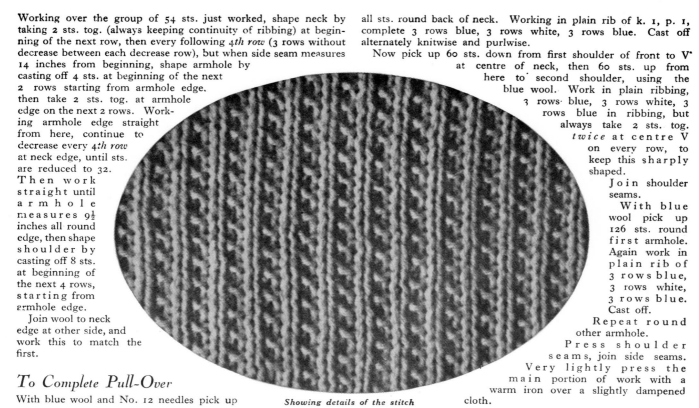

Showing details of the stitch

all sts. round back of neck. Working in plain rib of k. 1, p. 1, complete 3 rows blue, 3 rows white, 3 rows blue. Cast off alternately knitwise and purlwise.

Now pick up 60 sts. down from first shoulder of front to V at centre of neck, then 60 sts. up from here to second shoulder, using the blue wool. Work in plain ribbing, 3 rows blue, 3 rows white, 3 rows blue in ribbing, but always take 2 sts. tog. *twice* at centre V on every row, to keep this sharply shaped.

Join shoulder seams.

With blue wool pick up 126 sts. round first armhole. Again work in plain rib of 3 rows blue, 3 rows white, 3 rows blue. Cast off.

Repeat round other armhole. Press shoulder seams, join side seams. Very lightly press the main portion of work with a warm iron over a slightly dampened cloth.

A JUMPER FOR AFTERNOON

(Continued from page 39)

Top of Back.—After the casting off, every patt. row begins and ends with k. 2 and every alternate row begins and ends with p. 2. Work 2 more complete patts. In the 12th row of 3rd patt. leave 3 sts. on left needles for shoulder shaping. **Turn for 1st Patt. Row :** K. 1, patt. to within 3 sts. of end. Turn. Work 2nd row, leaving 6 sts. **3rd. Patt. Row :** K. 2, w.fd., patt. to within 6, turn. Work 4th row, leaving 9 sts. **5th Patt. Row :** K. 4, patt. to within 9, turn. Work 6th row leaving 15. **7th Patt. Row :** K. 5, k. 2 tog., patt. to within 15, turn. Begin 8th row by k. 2 tog. Finish row leaving 15 as before. **9th Patt. Row :** S. 1, k. 2 tog., p.s.s.o., patt. to within 15, then k. 15. **10th Row :** P. 15, finish row to within 15, then k. 2, p. 13. **11th Row :** Cast off 15 for right shoulder. K. 42 for back of neck, cast off 15 for left shoulder. Join wool in on wrong side and cast off 42. Join shoulders of back and front tog.

Neck.—On the 8 stocking-sts. of border, at present on safety-pins each side of neck front, knit sufficient to reach to centre back of neck. Join tog. and sew to jumper, taking edge sts. only. Thread a needle with the length of wool left at neck opening, place buckle with centre bar across front and cross-st. in position. The border rolls back from opening of front and back of neck.

Sleeves.—Crochet 62 double crochet around arm-holes.

On No. 9 needles pick up centre 16 sts. from wrong side. K. off from back of loops. At the beginning of each successive row, pick up two more stitches from the edge. All these are knitted or purled off from back of loops. **2nd Row :** Pick up

2, s. 1, p. 15. Continue to pick up 2 stitches at beginning of all following rows, though not mentioned. **3rd Row :** s. 1, k. 17. **4th Row :** S. 1, p. 19. **5th Row :** S. 1, k. 3, p. 2, k. 2, w.fd., k. 1, w.fd., k. 1, s. 1, k. 1, p.s.s.o., k. 3, k. 2 tog., k. 1, p. 2, k. 3. **6th Row :** S. 1, p. 2, k. 2, p. 12, k. 2, p. 5. **7th Row :** S. 1, k. 4, p. 2, k. 2, w.fd., k. 3. w.fd., k. 1, s. 1, k. 1, p.s.s.o., k. 1, k. 2 tog., k. 1, p. 2, k. 5. **8th Row :** S. 1, p. 4, k. 2, p. 12, k. 2, p. 7. **9th Row :** S. 1, k. 6, p. 2, k. 2, w.fd., k. 5, w.fd., k. 1, s. 1, k. 2 tog., p.s.s.o., k. 1, p. 2, k. 7. **10th Row :** S. 1, p. 6, k. 2, p. 12, k. 2, p. 9. **11th Row :** S. 1, k. 8, p. 2, s. 1, k. 1, p.s.s.o., k. 3, k. 2 tog., k. 1, w.fd., k. 1, w.fd., k. 3, p. 2, k. 9. **12th Row :** S. 1, p. 8, k. 2, p. 12, k. 2, p. 11. **13th Row :** S. 1, k. 10, p. 2, s. 1, k. 1, p.s.s.o., k. 1, k. 2 tog., k. 1, w.fd., k. 3, w.fd., k. 3, p. 2, k. 11. **14th Row :** S. 1, p. 10, k. 2, p. 12, k. 2, p. 13. **15th Row :** S. 1, k. 12, p. 2, s. 1, k. 2 tog., p.s.s.o., k. 1, w.fd., k. 5, w.fd., k. 3, p. 2, k. 13. **16th Row :** S. 1, p. 12, k. 2, p. 12, k. 2, p. 15.

Continue picking up 2 sts. at the beginning of every row, until there are 62 on the needle. The next row begins the 1st patt. each side of centre one and of course the 1st patt. row of 2nd patt. in centre = 44 sts. The 9 sts. at the beginning and end of the rows are in stocking-stitch = 62 sts.

At beginning of 1st, 3rd, 5th, 7th, 9th and 11th rows of the 3rd patt. s. 1, k. 2 tog., and at the end of the same rows, s. 1, k. 1, p.s.s.o., k. 1 = 50. Cast off on right side. Seam up under-arms and sleeve seams. Crochet 1 D.C. around sleeves.

The sleeves can be made any length and worked in in this way, fit tidily and do not show any ugly " sewing in."

Smart

Hubby's sleeveless pullover is in a simple squared pattern.

A MAN'S SLEEVELESS PULLOVER

MATERIALS

Nine ounces of Sirdar " Supreme " Wool in fawn (shade 71), and a pair each of Nos. 7 and 10 Stratnoid knitting pins.

MEASUREMENTS

Length, 21 ins. ; round chest, unstretched, 34 ins., stretching to 38 ins.

TENSION

Five stitches and 8 rows to 1 in.

THE *Back*.—Cast on 96 sts. with No. 10 needles and work in k. 1, p. 1 rib for 4 ins. Change to No. 7 needles and work the pattern as follows :

1st row : * K. 4, p. 1, then twist the next 2 sts. as follows, miss the next st. on the left needle, k. the next st., but do not slip it off the left needle, now k. the st. on the left needle which was previously passed over, and slip both these sts. off the left needle, p. 1, k. 4. Repeat from * to end of row.

2nd row : * P. 4, k. 1, p. 2, k. 1, p. 4. Repeat from * to end of row.

Repeat the 1st and 2nd rows 3 more times.

9th row : * P. 5, twist the next 2 sts. as before, p. 5. Repeat from * to end of row.

10th row : * K. 5, p. 2, k. 5. Repeat from * to end of row.

Repeat these 10 rows until the work measures 12½ ins. from the cast-on edge, then shape the armholes.

Cast off 4 sts. at the beginning of the next 2 rows, then cast off 2 sts. on every following row until 72 sts. remain. Continue in the pattern until the work measures 20 ins.

Shape the shoulders by casting off 8 sts. at the beginning of each of the next 6 rows.

Change to No. 10 needles and work 8 rows of k. 1, p. 1 rib on the remaining sts. Cast off loosely.

The Front.—Work as for the back to the armhole.

Next row : Cast off 4, work in pattern over 44 sts., leave the remaining 48 sts. on a holder for the right side and continue in pattern as follows :

Next row : Without shaping.

Next row · Cast off 2 sts. for the armhole, work in pattern 'till 2 sts. remain, dec.

Continue to shape the armhole by casting off 2 sts. at the beginning of every row commencing at the armhole edge, until 12 sts. in all have been cast off, and at the same time dec. at the neck edge of every 4th row until there are 12 decs. altogether at the neck edge. Continue on the remaining 24 sts. until the front is the same length as the back, to the shoulder.

Cast off 8 sts. at the beginning of every row commencing at the armhole edge until all the sts. are cast off.

Join the wool to the neck edge of the other side and work to correspond.

The Neck Border.—Along one side of the neck opening pick up and k. 62 sts. with No. 10 needles. Work 8 rows of k. 1, p. 1 rib, and dec. in every row at the lower end of the opening. Cast off loosely, and work a similar border on the other side of the front. Join the two edges of this ribbing at the lower end.

The Armhole Borders.—Join the shoulder seams. With No. 10 needles pick up and k. 120 sts. along one armhole edge. Work 8 rows of k. 1, p. 1 rib, and dec. at both ends of every row. Cast off loosely.

Work the other armhole border in the same way.

TO COMPLETE.—Press the knitting, with the exception of the ribbing, lightly on the wrong side, under a damp cloth. Join the side seams and press them.

A-CYCLING WE WILL GO!

He's sporting the woollen lumber jacket with handy zipp fastener which his wife's clever fingers have knitted for him.   Design by

Finella

MATERIALS

Twelve ounces of Sirdar Kasha Wool in fawn ; a pair each of Nos. 10 and 12 "Aero" knitting pins ; a No. 15 Abel Morrall's crochet hook ; a zipp fastener 19 ins. long, and 4 buttons.

MEASUREMENTS

Length, 22½ ins. ; round chest, 38 ins. ; sleeve seam, 23½ ins., including cuff.

TENSION

Six and a half stitches to 1 in. in width and 10 rows to 1 in. in depth.

THE *Back.*—Using No. 12 pins cast on 120 sts. and work in k. 1, p. 1 rib for 4 ins.   Change to No. 10 pins and the following pattern :

1st row : Moss-st. 6 (starting with k. 1, p. 1), * k. 2, p. 2, k. 2, moss-st. 11 ; repeat from * to last 12 sts., k. 2, p. 2, k. 2, moss-st. 6.

2nd row : Moss-st. 6, p. 2, k. 2, p. 2, * moss-st. 11, p. 2, k. 2, p. 2 ; repeat from * till 6 sts. remain, moss-st. 6.

Repeat these 2 rows 6 times more.

15th row : K.   *16th and 17th rows :* P.   *18th and 19th rows :* K.   *20th row :* P. These 20 rows form the pattern.   Continue thus until the work measures 14 ins. from the beginning, then shape the armhole.

Cast off 4 sts. at the beginning of the next 4 rows, then dec. at each end of the following 6 alternate rows.   Continue without further shaping till work measures 22 ins. from the beginning, then shape the shoulders by casting off 8 sts. at the beginning of the next 8 rows.   Cast off.

The Left Front.—Using No. 12 pins cast on 60 sts. and work in k. 1, p. 1 rib for 4 ins.   Change to No. 10 pins and work in the following pattern :

1st row : Moss-st. 6, * k. 2, p. 2, k. 2, moss-st. 11 ; repeat from * to last 3 sts., k. 2, p. 1.

2nd row : K. 1, p. 2, * moss-st. 11, p. 2, k. 2, p. 2 ; repeat from * to last 6 sts., moss-st. 6.

Repeat these 2 rows 6 times.

15th row : K.   *16th and 17th rows :* P. *18th and 19th rows :* K.   *20th row :* P.

These 20 rows form the pattern.   Work 1 more complete pattern, then work a pocket as follows :

Next row : (Starting on right side of work) Work in pattern over 23 sts., cast off 23, work in pattern to end.

Leave this part of the work for the present, cast on 23 sts. on No. 10 pins, and work in st.-st. for 4 ins.

Now work in pattern over the 14 end sts. of the main part, work in pattern over the 23 st-st. sts. of the pocket underpart, and then work in pattern over the remaining 23 sts.   Continue in pattern on these sts. till work measures 14 ins. from the beginning.

Now shape the armhole by casting off 4 sts. at the beginning of the next 2 rows, beginning at the armhole end of the work (right side of work), and then by decreasing at the beginning of the following 3 rows commencing at this edge. Work 10 more rows in pattern.

On the following row, beginning at the same edge, work in pattern over 12 sts., cast off 23, and work in pattern to the end.   Work the pocket underpart as before, then continue in pattern till work measures 19 ins. from the beginning. On the next row beginning at the centre front, cast off 10 sts., work in pattern to the end.

Dec. at the neck edge of the following 4 rows and then dec. at the neck edge of the following 4 alternate rows.   Continue without further shaping till work measures 22 ins. from the beginning.

Shape the shoulders by casting off 8 sts. at the beginning of the next 3 rows commencing at the armhole edge.   Cast off.

The Right Front.—Using No. 12 pins cast on 60 sts. and work in k. 1, p. 1 rib for 4 ins.   Change to No. 10 pins and work in the following pattern :

1st row : P. 1, k. 2, * moss-st. 11, k. 2, p. 2, k. 2 ; repeat from * till 6 sts. remain, moss-st. 6.

2nd row : Moss-st. 6, * p. 2, k. 2, p. 2, moss-st. 11 ; repeat from * till 3 sts. remain, p. 2, k. 1.

Repeat these 2 rows 6 times.

15th row : K.   *16th and 17th rows :* P. *18th and 19th rows :* K.   *20th row :* P.

These 20 rows form the pattern.   Now continue to work this side to match the left with the pocket positions and all shapings reversed.

The Sleeves.—Using No. 12 pins cast on 52 sts. and work in k. 1, p. 1 rib for 4 ins.   Change to No. 10 pins and work in the pattern used for the back (starting with moss-st. 6), increasing at each end of every 6th row till there are 110 sts. on the pin.   Continue in pattern till sleeve measures 23½ ins.   Shape the top of the sleeve by casting off 4 sts. at the beginning of the next 4 rows, then decreasing at each end of the following 6 alternate rows.   From here dec. at each end of every row until 16 sts. remain. Cast off.

Work another sleeve to match.

Pocket Flaps.—With the right side of the work towards you and the shoulder nearest [CONTINUED ON PAGE 45]

THIS SUMMER—IT'S LACY COTTONS

A Design to Knit Now and Wear All the Season

Cool and light for the hottest days, and a lace pattern specially shaped in such an easy way that beginners need not be afraid to work it.

Materials

Three balls (50 grams each) of ANCHOR *Tricoton, a pair of No. 10 and No. 8 Stratnoid knitting pins.*

Tension and Measurements

Worked at a tension of 6 sts. to the inch in width on the plain knitting with No. 8 pins, the

Imagine this jumper knitted in a soft pastel colour for your cruising outfit.

following measurements are attained after light pressing : Round the bust, 36 inches ; length from shoulder seam to lower edge, 19 inches ; side seam, 13 inches ; short sleeve seam, 8½ inches with the turned-back cuff. (Bear in mind that the open stitch in the lace pattern allows expansion to a larger size.)

Abbreviations

K., knit ; p., purl ; tog., together ; st., stitch ; m., make (by bringing the wool to the front of the pin) ; single rib is k. 1 and p. 1 alternately (directions in brackets are worked the number of times stated after the brackets) ; s.s., stocking-st. (k. on the right side and p. back).

To Work the Back : Begin at the lower edge and, using No. 10 pins, cast on 96 sts. Work 30 rows of single rib. [*Continued overleaf.*

The lacy pattern is quite simple to work.

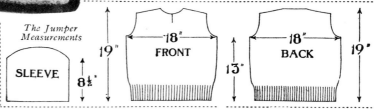

The Jumper Measurements

SLEEVE 8½"

FRONT 18" 19"

BACK 18" 19"

13"

Change to No. 8 pins and work as follows :

1st row : * K. 1, m. 1, k. 2 tog. ; repeat from * to the end of the row.

2nd row : * K. 1, m. 1, k. 2 tog. ; repeat from * to the end of the row.

3rd row : All k.

4th row : All p.

These 4 rows form one pattern.

Work 16 patterns more to the armhole.

To Shape the Armholes : Cast off 3 sts. at the beginning of the next 6 rows (78 sts.). Finish the pattern with one k. row and one p. row, when the yoke-line will be reached.

Now shape the yoke as follows :

1st row : (K. 1, m. 1, k. 2 tog.) 6 times, k. 42 ; repeat brackets 6 times.

2nd row : (K. 1, m. 1, k. 2 tog.) 6 times, p. 42 ; repeat brackets 6 times.

3rd row : All k.

4th row : All p.

Repeat these 4 rows 3 times more.

17th row : (K. 1, m. 1, k. 2 tog.) 3 times, k. 60 ; repeat brackets 3 times.

18th row : (K. 1, m. 1, k. 2 tog.) 3 times, p. 60 ; repeat brackets 3 times.

19th row : All k.

20th row : All p.

Repeat from the 17th to the 20th row 3 times more.

To Slope the Shoulders : Cast off 8 sts. at the beginning of the next 6 rows, then cast off all the remaining sts.

THE FRONT.—Work exactly as on the back until 16 rows of the yoke are finished.

Now divide the sts. in half for the neck opening.

THE LEFT SHOULDER.—*1st row :* (K.1, m. 1, k. 2 tog.) 3 times, k. 30. Pass the remaining 39 sts. on a stitch-holder for the right shoulder.

2nd row : P. 30, * k. 1, m. 1, k. 2 tog. ; repeat from * to the end of the row.

3rd row : All k.

4th row : All p.

Repeat these 4 rows 3 times more.

To Shape the Neck-line : Cast off 3 sts. at the beginning of the next 2 alternate rows, that begin at the neck edge, after which cast off 8 sts. at the beginning of every alternate row (arm-hole end) and 3 sts. at the beginning of alternate rows (neck end) until all are worked off.

THE RIGHT FRONT.—Join the cotton to the centre front and work as follows :

1st row : K. 30, * k. 1, m. 1, k. 2 tog. ; repeat from * to the end of the row.

2nd row : * K. 1, m. 1, k. 2 tog. ; repeat from * twice more, p. 30.

3rd row : All k.

4th row : All p.

Repeat these 4 rows 3 times more, then shape the neck and shoulder-line as on the left shoulder.

THE SLEEVES.—Cast on 6 sts. and p. one row for the wrong side of the work.

1st row of Increase Pattern : Cast on 3, (k. 1, m. 1, k. 2 tog.) 3 times.

2nd row : Cast on 3 sts., (k. 1, m. 1, k. 2 tog.) 4 times.

3rd row : Cast on 3 sts. and k. plain to the end, always working through the back of the cast-on sts. to make a neat edge.

4th row : Cast on 3 sts. and p. to end.

5th row : Cast on 3, k. 6, (k. 1, m. 1, k. 2 tog.) 4 times, k. 3.

6th row : Cast on 3 and p. 6, (k. 1, m. 1, k. 2 tog.) 4 times, p. 6.

7th row : Cast on 3, and k. to end of row.

8th row : Cast on 3, and p. to end of row.

9th row : Cast on 3, and k. 12, (k. 1, m. 1, k. 2 tog.) 4 times, k. to end of row.

10th row : Cast on 3, p. 12, (k. 1, m. 1, k. 2 tog.) 4 times, p. to end of row.

11th row : Cast on 3, and k. plain across the row.

12th row : Cast on 3, and p. across the row.

There are now 42 sts. on.

Repeat from the 9th to the 12th row once more, then the 9th and 10th row again, but note that there will be 3 sts. more to k. plain on the repetition of the 9th row, before the item in brackets ; and there will also be 3 sts. more to purl on each repetition of the 10th row before working the item in brackets. At the end of these 6 extra rows there should be 60 sts. on.

Work a k. row and a p. row to complete the pattern, after which work 48 rows more, keeping s.s. on each side of the 12 sts. of open pattern in the centre of the sleeve. Cast off loosely.

FOR LONG SLEEVES. — Work as directed for the top of the sleeve until there are 60 sts., then work 2 inches more on these sts. Slope the sleeve seam by knitting 2 tog. at each end of every 8th row, that is on the 1st row of every alternate pattern, taking care to keep the centre open work pattern correct on the 12 sts. (the decreases being made on the s.s. only) until the width of sleeve required for the forearm is attained.

Continue on these sts. for the length of sleeve required, less about 2 inches for a ribbed cuff to match the waistband.

THE COLLAR.—Cast on 71 sts. with No. 8 pins. Work the 4 pattern rows 4 times, but remember that there will be one extra st. at the beginning and end of the row, which k. plain. On the 4th row of each pattern, which is usually all purl, k. 2 sts. at each end.

THE BOW.—With No. 8 pins cast on 17 sts. and work 27 patterns as described for the collar and cast off.

THE CUFFS.—Cast on 62 sts. with No. 8 pins and work 3 patterns as described on the collar. K. 2 rows plain and cast off.

TO MAKE UP THE JUMPER.—Press on the wrong side with a thick blanket underneath and make up.

A-CYCLING WE WILL GO!

[CONTINUED FROM PAGE 43]

you, pick up and k. through 23 sts. across the top of the pocket underpart. P. 1 row and, regarding this as the 16th pattern row, continue straight in pattern (following on the section of the pattern in the main part of the work) for 6 more rows. Now continue in pattern, but dec. at each end of the next and following 2 alternate rows.

Next row : Work in pattern over 7 sts., cast off 3, work in pattern to end.

Next row : Dec. then work in pattern till the position of the cast-off sts. is reached, cast on 3, work in pattern to last 2 sts., k. 2 tog. Work 2 more rows, decreasing at each end of the second of these. Cast off.

The Collar.—Join the shoulder seams, then with No. 8 pins and the right side of the work facing you, pick up and k. through 131 sts. round the neck. Work in k. 1, p. 1 rib, increasing at each end of every 4th row until 6 such increase rows have been worked. Work 3 more rows in rib. Cast off.

TO MAKE UP

Sew the sleeves into the armholes and press the work on the wrong side with a hot iron and a damp cloth. Join the side and sleeve seams. Sew the pocket underparts in position. Sew buttons on the fronts to meet the buttonholes on the pocket flaps and sew the zipp fastener in position. Work 1 row of d.c. round each pocket flap.

THE END

A comfortable, well-built sidecar for one toddler can be bought for less than £4.

The softly falling, round collar is very becoming.

FRILLY NECK TO MELT The Heart !

A Very Feminine Affair

2nd row : K. 1, p. 2, * k. 2, p. 2; repeat from *, ending with k. 1.

Repeat these 2 rows until 30 rows have been worked.

Next row (right side) : K. 2, * inc., k. 5 ; repeat from *, which gives 121 sts. on the row.

With No. 9 pins, p. 1 row, then work in pattern as follows :

1st row (right side) : All k.

2nd row : K. 1, sl. 1 knitwise, k. 1, p. 3, * k. 1, (sl. 1, k. 1) twice, p. 3 ; repeat from * until 3 remain, k. 1, sl. 1, k. 1.

3rd row : All k.

4th row : All p.

To work this jumper in wool use 6 ozs. of 3-ply Super Fingering and the same pins. For long sleeves you will need an extra 2 ozs.

THE round frilly collar is a charming feature of this pretty jumper.

MATERIALS : *Three balls (50 grams each) of ANCHOR Tricoton, and a pair of " Aero " knitting pins, No. 9 and No. 12.*

TENSION AND MEASUREMENTS : *Worked at a tension of 6½ sts. to the inch in width the following measurements are attained after light pressing : Round the bust, 37 inches ; front length from shoulder seam to lower edge, 20 inches ; back length, 18½ inches ; side seam, 13 inches ; sleeve seam, 6 inches.*

ABBREVIATIONS : *K., knit ; p., purl ; tog., together ; inc., increase (by working into the back and front of the same st.) ; st., stitch ; m., make (by bringing the wool to the front of the needle) ; rib is k. 2 and p. 2 alternately ; sl., slip. Directions in brackets are worked the number of times stated after the brackets.*

Short sleeves or long ones—whichever you like better —can be made for this pretty jumper.

To Work the Back

WITH No. 12 pins cast on 104 sts. for the lower edge.

1st row (right side) : P. 1, k. 2, * p. 2, k. 2 ; repeat from *, ending with p. 1.

FRILLY NECK to MELT the HEART

Continued

5th row : All k.

6th row : P. 2, * k. 1, (sl. 1, k. 1) twice, p. 3 ; repeat from *, ending the last repeat with p. 2.

7th row : All k.

8th row : All p.

Repeat these 8 rows 7 times more, then 6 rows of the next pattern, to the armhole.

To Shape the Armhole: Cast off 2 sts. at the beginning of the next 16 rows, which leaves 89 sts.

Work 34 rows in pattern to the shoulder line. Cast off 6 sts. at the beginning of the next 8 rows, then cast off the remaining sts.

The Front

WORK the same as the back until the armhole decreases have been completed and there are 89 sts. left.

Work 23 rows to the neckline.

Next row (wrong side): Pattern 39 for the right shoulder, cast off 11, leaving 1 st. on pin, and pattern 38 more for the left shoulder.

THE LEFT SHOULDER: Continue in pattern, casting off 2 sts. at the beginning of alternate rows (neck end) 4 times, then work 2 sts. tog. at the beginning of alternate rows (neck end) for 2 decreases, which leaves 29 sts.

Work 8 rows to the shoulder-line.

To Slope the Shoulder : Cast off 7 sts. at the beginning of the next row, and every following alternate row (armhole end) until 1 st. remains, draw wool through and fasten off.

THE RIGHT SHOULDER: Join to the neck end of the right shoulder sts. and work 2 rows. Continue as on the left shoulder, the neck decreases beginning on the next row.

The Sleeves

WITH No. 9 pins, cast on 25 sts. for the top of the sleeve and p. one row.

Now work in increase pattern as follows :

1st row (right side): Inc. k. until 1 st. remains, inc.

2nd row : Inc. p. until 1 st. remains, inc.

3rd row : As 1st row.

4th row : Inc., k. 1, (sl. 1, k. 1) twice, * p. 3, k. 1, (sl. 1, k. 1) twice ; repeat from * until 1 st. remains, inc.

Repeat these 4 rows 4 times more.

The stitch used for the jumper is specially charming.

21st row : Cast on 3 sts. and k. until 1 st. remains, inc.

22nd row : Cast on 3 sts. and p. until 1 st. remains, inc.

23rd row : As 21st row.

24th row : Cast on 3 sts., k. 3, * p. 3, k. 1, (sl. 1, k. 1) twice ; repeat from * until 2 remain, k. 1, inc. This gives 81 sts.

Work in the straight pattern, beginning with the 3rd row, until 30 rows have been worked. Take 2 sts. tog. at the end of last row, which gives 80 sts.

With No. 12 pins work 15 rows in rib, then cast off.

Work the second sleeve in the same manner.

The Collar

WITH No. 9 pins cast on 129 sts. for the neck edge.

K. 1 row and p. 1 row 3 times.

7th row : * K. 8, m. 1 ; repeat from *, ending with k. 1.

8th row and every wrong side row : All p.

9th row : * K. 9, m. 1 ; repeat from *, ending with k. 1.

11th row : * K. 10, m. 1 ; repeat from *, ending with k. 1.

13th row : * K. 11, m. 1 ; repeat from *, ending with k. 1.

15th row : * K. 12, m. 1 ; repeat from *, ending with k. 1.

17th row : * K. 6, p. 2, k. 5, m. 1 ; repeat from *, ending with k. 1.

19th row : * K. 14, m. 1 ; repeat from *, ending with k. 1.

21st row : * K. 15, m. 1 ; repeat from *, ending with k. 1.

22nd row : P. 5, * into next st., k. 1, m. 1, k. 1, m. 1, k. 1, p. 1, making a tuft of 6 sts. out of 1 st., turn and p. 6, again turn and p. 3 tog. twice, slip the first st. over the second one, p. 7 ; repeat from *, ending the last repeat with p. 3.

23rd row : * K. 16, m. 1 ; repeat from *, ending with k. 1.

25th row : * K. 17, m. 1 ; repeat from *, ending with k. 1.

K. 2 rows and cast off loosely.

To Make Up the Jumper: Press all pieces with a hot iron and a damp cloth over the wrong side of the work. Sew the shoulder seams and sleeves to armholes and press these seams while the work is open. Join collar seams and sew the collar to the right side of the neck edge. Sew the sleeve and side seams and press. A length of thin cord elastic threaded through the neck will give a neat fit.

THE END.

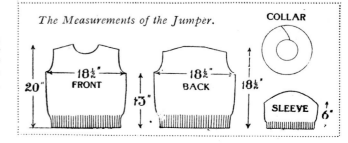

The Measurements of the Jumper.

COLLAR

FRONT — 18½" — 20"

BACK — 18½" — 18½"

3"

SLEEVE — 6"

The cowl is held down in front with a buckle.

YOU WILL LOSE YOUR HEART TO IT!

A Feminine Little Affair in a Charming Lacy Stitch

ments are attained after light pressing: Round the bust, 38 inches ; shoulder seam to lower edge, 21 inches ; side seam, 15 inches ; sleeve seam, 6 inches.

Abbreviations

K., knit ; p., purl ; st., stitch ; tog., together ; inc., increase (by working into the back and front of the same st.) ; rib is k. 2 and p. 2 alternately ; m., make (by bringing the wool forward and over the top of needle). Directions in brackets are worked the number of times stated after the brackets. S.s., stocking-stitch (k. on the right side and p. back).

THIS little jumper will be one of the delights of your knitted wardrobe. With the open pattern worked in a light-weight wool, it is just right for this time of the year.

Materials

Four ounces of "Greenock" 2-ply Super Fingering (obtainable only at any of the branches of the Scotch Wool & Hosiery Stores) ; a pair of No. 8 and No. 11 Stratnoid knitting-pins ; a buckle or clip.

Tension and Measurements

Worked at a tension of 7 sts. to the inch in width on the No. 8 pins, the following measure-

To Work the Back

With No. 11 pins cast on 116 sts. for the lower edge. *1st row :* (Right side) P. 1, k. 2, *p. 2, k. 2 ; repeat from *, ending the row with p. 1.

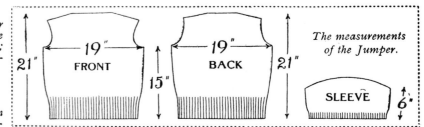

The measurements of the Jumper.

NOTE *the* PRETTY NECK-LINE

Knit It for Tennis in White or a Pretty Pastel Shade

2nd row : K. 1, p. 2, * k. 2, p. 2 ; repeat from *, ending the row with k. 1.

Repeat these 2 rows until 50 rows have been worked.

Next row : (Right side) K. 9, inc., (k. 15, inc.) 6 times, k. 10.

There are now 123 sts.

With No. 8 pins work 3 rows in s.-s., beginning with a p. row ; then work in pattern as follows :

1st, 2nd and 3rd rows : K. 2, m. 1, k. 2 tog., k. 4, * (m. 1, k. 2 tog.) twice, k. 4 ; repeat from * until 3 sts. remain, m. 1, k. 2 tog. k. 1.

Quite pretty enough for any occasion. Knit it in a soft pastel colour.

Detail of Lace pattern

4th row : All p.

5th row : All k.

6th row : All p.

7th, 8th and 9th rows : * K. 4, (m. 1, k. 2 tog.) twice ; repeat from *, ending the row with k. 3.

Work 3 rows in s.-s., beginning with a p. row.

Repeat these 12 rows 5 times more, then 4 rows more, when the armhole will be reached.

TO SHAPE THE ARMHOLE.—*1st row :* Cast off 2 and k. to end.

2nd row : Cast off 2 and p. to end.

3rd row : Cast off 2, k. 1 (2 sts. on pin), m. 1, k. 2 tog., * k. 4, (m. 1, k. 2 tog.) twice ; repeat from *, ending with k. 1.

4th row : Cast off 2 sts., k. 1 (2 on pin), m. 1, k. 2 tog., * k. 4, (m. 1, k. 2 tog.) twice ; repeat from *, ending the last repeat with m. 1, k. 2 tog., k. 1.

(Continued on page 50)

YOU WILL LOSE
YOUR HEART TO IT!

Continued

5th row : Cast off 2, k. 5 (6 on pin), * (m. 1, k. 2 tog.) twice, k. 4 ; repeat from *, ending the last repeat with m. 1, k. 2 tog., k. 1.

6th, 7th and 8th rows : Work in s.-s., casting off 2 sts. at the beginning of each row.

9th row : Cast off 2, k. 5 (6 on pin), * (m. 1, k. 2 tog.) twice, k. 4 ; repeat from *, ending the row with m. 1, k. 2 tog., k. 1.

10th row : Cast off 2 sts., k. 5 (6 on pin), * (m. 1, k. 2 tog.) twice, k. 4 ; repeat from *, ending the last repeat with k. 5.

11th row : Cast off 2, k. 3 (4 on pin), * (m. 1, k. 2 tog.) twice, k. 4 ; repeat from *, ending the last repeat with k. 5.

Work 3 rows in s.-s., casting off 2 sts. at the beginning of each row.

15th row : Cast off 2, k. 3 (4 on pin), * (m. 1, k. 2 tog.) twice, k. 4 ; repeat from *, ending the last repeat with k. 5.

16th row : Cast off 2, k. 3 (4 on pin), * (m. 1, k. 2 tog.) twice, k. 4 ; repeat from *, ending the last repeat with k. 3.

There are now 91 sts., on which work straight in pattern, beginning with the **9th** row, until 38 rows have been worked, ending with the 10th row at the shoulder line.

To Slope the Shoulders.—Cast off 7 sts. at the beginning of the next 2 rows.

3rd back shoulder row : Cast off 7 sts., k. 1 (2 on pin), (m. 1, k. 2 tog.) twice, * k. 4, (m. 1, k. 2 tog.) twice ; repeat from * to end.

4th row : Cast off 7 sts., k. 1 (2 on pin), (m. 1, k. 2 tog.) twice, * k. 4, (m. 1 k. 2 tog.) twice ; repeat from *, ending, the row with k. 1.

5th row : Cast off 7, k. 2 (3 on pin), (m. 1, k. 2 tog.) twice, * k. 4, (m. 1, k. 2 tog.) twice ; repeat from *, ending the row with k. 1.

Work the next 3 rows in s.-s., casting off 7 sts. at the beginning of each row. With No. 11 pins, k. 5 rows and cast off loosely.

The Front

Work the same as the back until the armhole decreases have been completed and 91 sts. remain on the row.

Work 8 rows in straight pattern, beginning with the 9th and ending with the 4th row.

Next row : Inc. at each end of the row. P. 1 row.

Next 3 rows : K. 5, * (m. 1, k. 2 tog.) twice, k. 4 ; repeat from *, ending with k. 4. P. 1 row (93 sts.).

Inc. at each end of the next row (95 sts.). P. 1 row.

Next 3 rows : K. 2, * (m. 1, k. 2 tog.) twice, k. 4 ; repeat from *, ending the last repeat with k. 1. P. 1 row.

Inc. at each end of the next row (97 sts.). P. 1 row.

Next 3 rows : K. 7, * (m. 1, k. 2 tog.)

twice, k. 4 ; repeat from *, ending the last repeat with k. 6. P. 1 row.

Inc. at each end of the next row (99 sts.). P. 1 row.

Next 3 rows : * K. 4, (m. 1, k. 2 tog.) twice ; repeat from *, ending the row with k. 3. P. 1 row.

Inc. at each end of the next row (101 sts.). P. 1 row.

Next 3 rows : K. 1, * (m. 1, k. 2 tog.) twice, k. 4 ; repeat from *, ending with the bracketed item. P. 1 row.

Inc. at each end of the next row (103 sts.). P. 1 row.

Next 3 rows : K. 6, * (m. 1, k. 2 tog.) twice, k. 4 ; repeat from *, ending the last repeat with k. 5. P. 1 row.

To Slope the Front Shoulders.—** Work the next 2 rows in s.-s., casting off 4 sts. at the beginning of each row.

3rd row : Cast off 4 sts., k. 1 (2 on pin), * (m. 1, k. 2 tog.) twice, k. 4 ; repeat from *, ending the last repeat with k. 5.

4th row : Cast off 4, k. 1 (2 on pin), * (m. 1, k. 2 tog.) twice, k. 4 ; repeat from *, ending the last repeat with k. 1.

5th row : Cast off 4, k. 5 (6 on pin), * (m. 1, k. 2 tog.) twice, k. 4 ; repeat from *, ending the last repeat with k. 1.

6th row : Cast off 4 sts., p. to end.

Repeat these 6 rows from ** once more.

With No. 11 pins, k. 5 rows and cast off loosely.

The Sleeves

With No. 8 pins, cast on 25 sts. and p. 1 row.

Continue in inc. pattern as follows :

1st row : (Right side) Cast on 3, k. until 1 st. remains, inc.

2nd row : Cast on 3, p. until 1 st. remains, inc.

3rd row : Cast on 3, k. 4, m. 1, k. 2 tog., k. 4, * (m. 1, k. 2 tog.) twice, k. 4 ; repeat from * until 2 remain, m. 1, k. 2.

4th row : Cast on 3, k. 3, (m. 1, k. 2 tog.) twice, * k. 4, (m. 1, k. 2 tog.) twice ; repeat from * until 1 st. remains, inc.

5th row : Cast on 3, k. 6, (m. 1, k. 2 tog.) twice, * k. 4, (m. 1, k. 2 tog.) twice ; repeat from * until 2 remain, k. 1, inc.

6th row : Cast on 3, p. until 1 st. remains, inc.

Repeat these 6 rows until there are 105 sts.

Work in straight pattern as follows :

1st, 2nd and 3rd rows : K. 1, m. 1, k. 2 tog., k. 4, * (m. 1, k. 2 tog.) twice, k. 4 repeat from * until 2 remain, m. 1, k. 2 tog.

4th, 5th and 6th rows : Work in s.-s.

7th, 8th and 9th rows : K. 3, * (m. 1, k. 2 tog.) twice, k. 4 ; repeat from *, ending the last repeat with k. 2.

10th, 11th and 12th rows : Work in s.-s.

Repeat these 12 straight rows twice more, then 6 rows more.

Next row : Change to No. 11 pins. K. 4, k. 2 tog., * k. 1, k. 2 tog. ; repeat from * until 3 sts. remain, k. 3 (72 sts.).

With No. 11 pins, rib 10 rows and cast off loosely. Now make up the jumper.

First press all pieces, putting a damp cloth over the wrong side of the work. Sew the shoulder-seams, then sew the sleeves to the armholes and press these seams while the work is open. Sew the sleeve and side seams, and press. Fold the centre-front neck in three downward tucks and tack in place.

The Sash : With No. 8 pins, cast on 18 sts.

Next row : P. 2, * k. 2, p. 2 ; repeat from * to the end.

Repeat this row for length required and cast off.

Make a buckle strap by working 12 rows of the sash pattern on 18 sts. Cast off, then draw this through the buckle and sew to front neck.

❊   ❊   ❊

The sleeveless waistcoat is just the thing to wear for holiday walks.

A USEFUL ODD SKIRT

A TRIM knitted skirt is a useful addition to one's wardrobe. It is delightfully lightweight for walking, is almost uncrushable—a fact which makes it ideal for wearing in the car—and rolls up to next-to-nothing in the suit-case should one be off to enjoy a week-end visit.

The particular skirt illustrated and described is knitted entirely in stocking stitch, so it should take only a short time to make.

MATERIALS REQUIRED.—15 ozs. Copley's 4-ply " Clarion " Marl, 30 ins. petersham, 3 hooks and eyes and 3 press studs, a short length of binding, a pair No. 9 knitting needles, a No. 13 Stratnoid crochet hook.

MEASUREMENTS AFTER PRESSING.—Length, 32 ins.; round lower edge, 56 ins.; round waist, 27 ins.

TENSION.—Work to produce 7 sts. to 1 in. Unless this instruction is followed exactly, the measurements of the garment will not work out correctly.

FOUR PANELS

The skirt is worked in four panels.

Begin at the lower edge by casting on 98 sts.

Working into the back of the sts. on the first row only, work 20 rows in smooth fabric (1 row knit, 1 row purl).

Decrease as follows :—

1st row.—Slip 1, K.2 tog., knit to the last 3 sts., slip 1, K.1, pass the slipped st. over the knitted one, K.1.

Continue to decrease in this way on every following 16th row, until 76 sts. remain on the needle.

Now decrease in the same way but on every following 6th row, until 46 sts. remain.

Caption: Notice the becoming slight fullness at the hem, and the well-shaped hip-line

Knitted in Flecked Wool, it has a Pleasing Tweed Effect

Work 5 rows straight.

Cast off.

Make two more panels in exactly the same way.

Make a 4th panel in the same way until 62 sts. remain. Purl the next row.

Next row.—K.31 sts., turn and cast on 11 sts. for the plaquet.

Work on these 42 sts. only, working the 11 cast-on sts. in K.1, P.1 rib and decreasing at the side edge on every 6th row until 34 sts. remain.

Work 5 rows straight.

Cast off.

Join the wool to the inner edge of the panel and work the opposite side to match, but without the extra ribbing.

TO COMPLETE

Sew up the seams all but the plaquet seam, taking care not to pucker the work.

Press out the work on the wrong side and then on the right side with a hot iron over a damp cloth. It should measure 32 ins. long.

Sew up the remaining seam.

Holding the right side of the work towards you, work a row of d.c. all round the lower edge, working st. into st.

Join by a slip st., then work 1 more row and fasten off.

Sew the cast on edge of the ribbing down in position.

Sew the binding to the wrap-over side.

Stitch the petersham to the top of the skirt.

Sew the hooks and eyes and press studs in position.

Press again where necessary.

It is the instinct of chivalry, dating from the far-off past, that makes a man give you the only vacant seat in a Tube, for instance.

SIMPLE—BUT SO ATTRACTIVE!

And It Is Easy Enough For Beginners

MATERIALS

*N*INE ounces of " Sirdar " 3-ply Super Shetland Wool ; a pair each of " Aero " knitting pins No. 9 and No. 13.

TENSION AND MEASUREMENTS

*W*ORKED at a tension of 7 sts. to the inch in width on No. 9 pins, the following measurements are attained after light pressing : Round the bust, 35 inches ; front length from shoulder seam to lower edge, 20 inches ; back length, 19 inches ; side seam, 13 inches ; sleeve seam, 19 inches.

ABBREVIATIONS

K., KNIT ; p., purl ; st., stitch ; tog., together ; inc., increase (by working into the back and front of the same stitch) ; dec., decrease. Single rib is k. 1 and p. 1 alternately ; directions in brackets are worked the number of times stated immediately after the brackets.

THE BACK

*W*ITH No. 13 pins cast on 100 sts. and work 33 rows in single rib.
    INCREASE ROW : * Rib 4, inc. ; repeat from * to end (120 sts.).
Change to No. 9 pins and continue in pattern as follows :
1ST ROW : * K. 2, p. 2 ; repeat from * to end.
Repeat this row 10 times more.
12TH ROW : All purl.
13TH ROW : All knit.
14TH ROW : * P. 2, k. 2 ; repeat from * to end.
Repeat this row 10 times more.
25TH ROW : All knit.
26TH ROW : All purl.
These 26 rows complete 1 pattern.
Repeat the 26 pattern rows twice more, then 10 rows of the next pattern to armholes.
TO SHAPE THE ARMHOLES : Continue in pattern, casting off 3 sts. at the beginning of each of the next 6 rows, then work 2 sts. tog. at the beginning of each of the following 10 rows, when 92 sts. will remain.
Continue straight in pattern on these sts. for 40 rows more.
Cast off straight across.

THE FRONT

*W*ORK exactly the same as the back until the armhole shaping is finished and 92 sts. remain.
Work 16 rows straight on these sts. to neck.

TO SHAPE THE NECK

*N*EXT ROW : Pattern 42 sts. and slip these on to a stitch-holder until needed for the Left Front Shoulder, cast off 8, pattern to end (42 sts. for Right Front Shoulder).
THE RIGHT FRONT SHOULDER.—Continue in pattern as now set, taking 2 sts. tog. at the neck end of every row until 28 sts. remain. Work 19 rows straight on these sts. Cast off straight across.
THE LEFT FRONT SHOULDER.—Slip a No. 9 pin through the 42 Left Front Shoulder sts. with point towards the neck end. Work exactly the same as the Right Front Shoulder.

THE LONG SLEEVES

*W*ITH No. 13 pins cast on 56 sts. and work 34 rows in single rib.
    Change to No. 9 pins and work 9 rows in pattern, as on back.
Continue in pattern, increasing 1 st. at both ends of the next row and every following 10th row, working the increase sts. in the rib pattern as they are added, until there are 76 sts on the pins.
Work 36 rows straight on these sts., or for length of sleeve seam desired.
TO SHAPE THE SLEEVE TOP.—Continue in pattern, taking 2 sts. tog. at both ends of every row until 8 sts. remain. Cast off.
Work a second sleeve in the same manner.
FOR SHORT SLEEVES.—With the No. 13 pins cast on 76 sts. and work 1 inch in single rib. Change to No. 9 pins and work 1 pattern of 26 sts. as at the beginning of the back, then shape the top of the sleeve as on the long sleeves.

THE COLLAR

*B*EGIN at the back and with No. 9 pins cast on 80 sts. and work 10 rows plain.
    Continue in pattern as follows :
1ST ROW : All knit.
2ND ROW : K. 8, p. until 8 remain, k. 8.
3RD ROW : As 2nd row.
4TH ROW : As 1st row.
Repeat the 4 pattern rows 9 times more, then 2 rows of next pattern to neck.
TO SHAPE THE NECK.—Work 22 sts. in pattern and slip these on a stitch-holder until needed for the Right Shoulder, cast off 36 sts. for the back of the neck and work in pattern to end (22 sts. for Left Shoulder).
THE LEFT SHOULDER.—Work straight on these 22 sts. for 25 rows, then continue in pattern, increasing 1 st. at the neck end of every row until there are 36 sts. on the pins. Slip these sts. on to a spare pin for the moment.
Pass the Right Shoulder sts. on a No. 9 pin (point towards the neck end) and work exactly the same as the Left Shoulder until there are 36 sts. on the row. Cast on 8 sts., and then on to the same pin work the 36 Left Shoulder sts. (80 sts. now on).
Work 30 rows in pattern, then knit 10 rows plain and cast off.

A close-up of the stitch in which the main part of the jumper is worked.

Isn't the square collar becoming? It is worked in stripes of plain and purl.

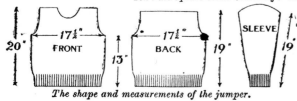

The shape and measurements of the jumper.

TO MAKE UP THE JUMPER

FIRST press all pieces lightly on the wrong side with a hot iron over a damp cloth. Join the shoulder seams, beginning at the armhole end and taking 1 st. from each side at a time. Stitch the collar to neck, matching the shaped edges. Set the sleeves into armholes and press these seams while the work is open. Join the sleeve and side seams in one long line and press.

Notice the perfect set of the Raglan shoulders.

EVERY LITTLE DETAIL SPELLS PERFECTION

Here is a Jumper That is Easy to Knit and Yet Has a Sophisticated Charm. The Polo Collar with the Point in Front is New and Becoming

THIS charming jumper is knitted in a simple ribbing stitch, and is made with Raglan shoulders.

Materials

Eight ounces of Jaeger J.S. " Superspun," 3-ply ; a pair each of " Aero " knitting pins, No. 8 and No. 11.

Abbreviations

K., knit ; p., purl ; st., stitch ; tog., together ; inc., increase (by working into the back and front of the same stitch). Directions in brackets are worked the number of times stated immediately after the brackets.

To Work the Back

Begin at the lower edge and, using No. 11 pins, cast on 127 sts. and work in pattern as follows :

Tension and Measurements

Worked at a tension of 7½ sts. to the inch in width on No. 8 pins and without stretching the rib the following measurements are attained after light pressing : round the bust, 34 inches (but bear in mind that this pattern will stretch to fit a 36-inch bust measurement) ; side seam, 15 inches ; sleeve seam, 19 inches ; length from top of shoulder fold to lower edge, 21 inches.

The Simple Ribbed Pattern

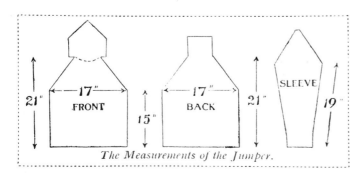

The Measurements of the Jumper.

1st row : (Right side facing) P. 1, * k. 2, p. 1 ; repeat from * to end.

2nd row : K. 1 * p. 2, k. 1 ; repeat from * to end.

Repeat these 2 rows until 60 rows have been worked. Change to No. 8 pins, and work in same rib for 68 rows more to armholes.

To Shape the Armholes.—Continue

(Continued on page 56)

The snug polo-collar is just right worn with a trim, tailored skirt. The simple ribbed pattern is an added attraction.

EVERY LITTLE DETAIL
SPELLS PERFECTION

Continued

in pattern taking 2 sts. tog. at both ends of each of the next 15 rows (97 sts.). Then take 2 sts. tog. at each end of every alternate row (every right side row) 13 times more, when 71 sts. will remain. Finally work 2 sts. tog. at both ends of each of the following 19 rows, when 33 sts. will remain.

Next row : (Right side facing) Change to No. 11 pins ; k. 4, (inc. k. 3) 7 times, k. 1 (40 sts. now on).

Still using No. 11 pins, work 18 rows in single rib. Then work 24 rows in rib as on jumper back and cast off loosely.

(NOTE.—This rib is reversed so that the upper half of the collar can be turned over the single rib with the right side in wear.)

THE FRONT.—This is worked exactly the same as the back until the armhole decreases are begun and there are 71 sts. on the row.

Continue in the same rib, taking 2 sts. tog. at both ends of each of the next 6 rows (59 sts.).

On the next row the sts. are divided for the neck. With the wrong side facing, p. 2 tog., rib 25 and leave these 26 sts. on a spare pin for the Right Front Shoulder, cast off 5 sts. (1 st. on pin), rib until 2 remain, p. 2 tog. which gives 26 sts. for Left Front Shoulder.

The Left Front Shoulder.—Continue in same rib pattern, taking 2 sts. tog. at each end of every row until all are worked off.

The Right Front Shoulder.—Join the wool to the neck end of Right Front Shoulder sts. and continue in rib pattern, taking 2 sts. tog. at each end of every row until all are worked off.

THE SLEEVES.—Begin at the top and, using No. 8 pins, cast on 7 sts.

1st row : (Right side facing) P. 1, * k. 2, p. 1 ; repeat from * to end.

2nd row : K. 1, * p. 2, k. 1 ; repeat from * to end.

3rd row : Inc., k. 2, * p. 1, k. 2, (repeat from * in following patterns) until 1 remains, inc.

4th row : P. 1, k. 1, * p. 2, k. 1 ; repeat from * until 1 remains, p. 1.

5th row : Inc., p. 1, * k. 2, p. 1 ; repeat from * until 1 remains, inc.

6th row : P. 2, * k. 1, p. 2 ; repeat from * to end.

7th row : Inc., k. 1, p. 1, * k. 2, p. 1 ; repeat from * until 2 remain, k. 1, inc.

8th row : K. 1, * p. 2, k. 1 ; repeat from * to end.

Repeat from the 3rd to the 8th row until there are 61 sts. altogether, ending with a right side row.

Continue in same rib inc. at each end of every row until there are 85 sts. Work 7 rows straight in rib pattern, then continue in same pattern, taking 2 sts. tog. at each end of next row and every following 8th row until 53 sts. remain. Work 3 rows more.

Next row : Change to No. 11 pins and work 2 sts. tog at each end of the row (51 sts.).

Work 33 rows more in same rib and cast off.

Work a second sleeve in the same manner. Sew the top edge of each sleeve to matching edges of shoulders.

THE FRONT COLLAR.—With No. 11 pins and right side of work facing, pick up and k. 79 sts. from the edge of front neck and shoulder part of sleeves.

Work 18 rows in single rib, then work the two rib pattern rows (as on back waist) until 24 rows more have been worked.

Next row : (Right side of collar facing) Cast off 3, pattern to end.

Next row : Cast off 4, p. 1 (2 sts. on pin), inc., * p. 2, inc. Repeat from * until 3 remain, p. 1, p. 2 tog.

Next row : K. 2 tog., p. 2, * k. 2, p. 2 ; repeat from * until 2 remain, k. 2 tog.

Continue in k. 2 and p. 2 rib as set on last row, taking 2 sts. tog. at each end of every row until 2 sts. remain ; slip 1 st. over the other and fasten off.

THE BELT.—With No. 11 pins cast on 220 sts. and k. 1 row.

Next row : K. until 2 remain, inc., k. 1.

Repeat these 2 rows for 3 times more. K. 2 rows straight.

Next row : K. 1, k. 2 tog. (mitre end), k. to end.

K. 1 row.

Repeat these 2 rows until the 4th decrease row has been worked. Cast off loosely.

TO MAKE UP THE JUMPER.—First press all pieces with a hot iron and a damp cloth over the wrong side of the work. Join the sleeve tops to back of jumper, and stitch the seams of back and front collars. Press these seams while the work is open. Join the sleeve and side seams in one long line and press.

CONSTANCE, LADY MOON

She HUNTED *big game —*
and FOUND *a new way to Beauty*

In TUFT-STITCH— A TRIUMPH!

An Interesting Knitted Dress—Quite the Latest Design

F OR everyday and all day long this knitted dress is perfect. Choose one of the three lovely colour schemes.

MATERIALS : 15 *ounces of Jaeger " Feather-Fleck " 3-ply wool ; a pair of " Aero " knitting pins, No.* 9 *and No.* 11 *;* 4 *buttons.*

TENSION AND MEASUREMENTS : *Worked at a tension of 7 sts. to the inch in width on No.* 9 *pins, the following measurements are attained after light pressing : Across the back at the underarms,* 19 *inches ; across each front at the same place,* 11 *inches (making a total bust measurement of* 39 *inches when fastened) ; round hips,* 42 *inches ; length from the fold of shoulder strap to hem,* 46 *inches ; side seam,* 40 *inches ; sleeve seam,* 19 *inches.*

ABBREVIATIONS : *K. knit ; p., purl ; st., stitch ; tog., together ; inc., increase (by working into the back and front of the same stitch) ; dec., decrease (by knitting or purling 2 tog. according to the pattern except where directed otherwise) ; s.s., stocking-stitch (knit on the right side and purl back) ; single rib is k. 1 and p. 1 alternately.*

Directions in brackets are worked the number of times stated after the brackets.

'In Jaegar
" Feather-Fleck :"

*Brushwood is
Blend No.* 9

*Granite is
Blend No.* 25

*Maize is
Blend No.* 11

The measurements for the dress.

FRONT 11'
45'

BACK 19'
40'

SLEEVE 19'

The tufts are quite easy to do. Cast on a few sts. and practise them before beginning to make the dress.

TOP-SKIRT ALL-IN-ONE

And Wear a Gay Knotted Scarf Tucked In at the Neckline !

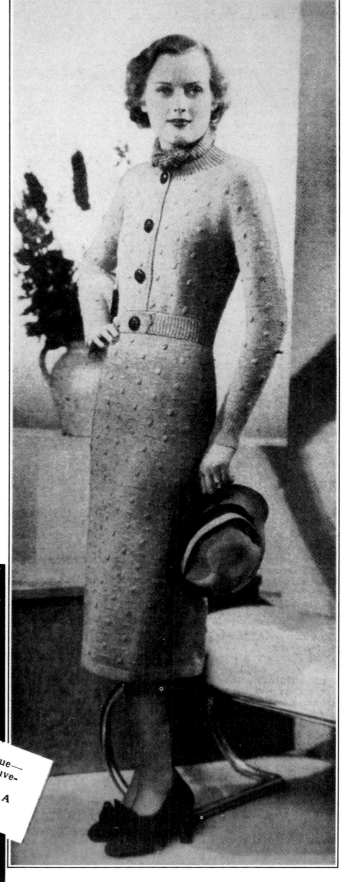

A " Tuft " is worked as follows : * knit into next st., and without slipping the original st. off the pin replace the new st. on the left-hand pin as if casting on, knit into the new st. and slip this off the left-hand pin, still leaving the original st. on the left-hand pin. Repeat from * 4 times more, when there will be 5 extra sts. on the right-hand pin. Drop the original st. from the left-hand pin, ** draw the second st. from the point of the righthand pin over the end st., and repeat from ** 3 times more. When the tuft is completed let it slip through to the other side of the work, as the tufts are worked on the wrong side.

To Work the Back

WITH No. 9 pins cast on 155 sts. for the lower edge.

Change to No. 11 pins and knit 12 rows plain.

Return to No. 9 pins and continue in pattern as follows :

1st row (right side facing) : All knit.

2nd row : All purl.

Repeat these 2 rows until 9 rows have been worked.

10th row (wrong side facing) : P. 5, k. 5, * p. 7, tuft, p. 7, k. 5 ; repeat from * until 5 remain, p. 5.

Work 9 rows in s.s.

20th row : P. 7, tuft, p. 7, * k. 5, p. 7, tuft, p. 7 ; repeat from * to end. The last 20 rows form one pattern.

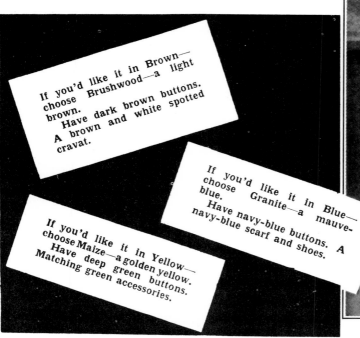

If you'd like it in Brown—choose Brushwood—a light brown.
Have dark brown buttons. A brown and white spotted cravat.

If you'd like it in Blue—choose Granite—a mauve-blue.
Have navy-blue buttons. A navy-blue scarf and shoes.

If you'd like it in Yellow—choose Maize—a golden yellow.
Have deep green buttons. Matching green accessories.

Repeat from the 1st to the 10th row, which gives 30 rows on No. 9 pins.

Decrease row: K. 2, sl. 1, k. 1, pass the slipped stitch over, k. until 4 remain, k. 2 tog., k. 2.

Work 23 rows in pattern, then repeat the decrease row until the 7th decrease row has been worked with 141 sts. Continue in same pattern, decreasing in the same way on every 6th row until 14 decrease rows more have been worked, and there are 113 sts. on the row.

(Remember to keep the pattern correct after decreasing, but this is so plainly seen that it will be quite simple to follow.)

Work 15 rows straight on these sts. to the waistline.

Increase row (right side facing) : Inc., (k. 6, inc.) 7 times, k. 13, inc., (k. 6, inc.) 7 times. (129 sts. now on.)

Work 4 rows straight in s.s.

Next row: P. 2, k. 5, * p. 7, tuft, p. 7, k. 5 ; repeat from * until 2 remain, p. 2.

Work 68 rows more in pattern as now set (73 rows above the waist increase row) to armholes.

To Shape the Armholes : Continue in pattern, casting off 3 sts. at the beginning of each of the next 2 rows, then cast off 2 sts. at the beginning of each of the following 16 rows when 91 sts. will remain.

Work 36 rows on these sts. to shoulders.

To Slope the Shoulders : Cast off 6 sts. at the beginning of each of the next 6 rows. Cast off the remaining sts.

The Front

WITH No. 9 pins cast on 155 sts. Change to No. 11 pins and knit 12 rows plain.

Return to No. 9 pins and work 9 rows in s.s., beginning with a knit row.

10th row: P. 7, tuft, p. 7, * k. 5, p. 7, tuft, p. 7 ; repeat from * to end.

Work 9 rows in s.s.

20th row (wrong side facing) : P. 5, k. 5, * p. 7, tuft, p. 7, k. 5 ; repeat from * until 5 remain, p. 5.

Continue in pattern as now set, and work decrease rows exactly as on the back, until the waist increase row has been worked and there are 129 sts. on the pins.

On the next row the sts. are divided for the two fronts as follows : with the wrong side facing, p. 69, k. 3, (72 sts. for Right Front), slip the remaining 57 sts. on to a stitch-holder until needed for the Left Front.

The Right Front

WORK 3 rows in s.s. with a k. 3 border at the front end of every row.

Next row (wrong side facing) : P. 4, tuft, * p. 7, k. 5, p. 7, tuft, ; repeat from * until 7 remain, p. 4, k. 3.

Work 29 rows in pattern as now set,

keeping the k. 3 border at the front end of every row.

1st buttonhole row : (4th tuft row above the waist increase), pattern until 11 remain, cast off 4, k. 2, p. 2, k. 3.

2nd buttonhole row : All in pattern casting on 4 sts. over those cast off to complete the buttonhole.

Work 38 rows more in pattern to armhole. (74 rows above the waist inc.)

To Shape the Armhole.—Next row : Cast off 3, pattern until 11 remain, cast off 4 for buttonhole, k. 2, p. 2, k. 3.

Next row : Work in pattern casting on 4 sts. over those cast off to complete the buttonhole.

Continue in pattern, casting off 2 sts. at the beginning of the next row and every following alternate row (armhole end) 8 times, when 53 sts. will remain.

Work 20 rows straight on these sts. to neck.

** *To Shape the Neck :* Cast off 12 sts. at the beginning of the next row (neck end), then cast off 3 sts. at the beginning of alternate rows (neck end) for 3 decreases, finally cast off 2 sts. at the beginning of alternate rows (neck end), 3 times when 26 sts. will remain. Work 2 rows more to shoulder.

To Slope the Shoulder : Cast off 6 sts. at the beginning of the next row (armhole end), and work 2 sts. tog. at the beginning of following row (neck end). Cast off 6 sts. at the beginning of next row (armhole end) and every following alternate row until 1 st. remains, draw wool through and fasten off.

The Left Front

JOIN the wool to the front end of Left Front sts. and cast on 15. (72 sts. now on.)

Work 4 rows in s.s. with a k. 3 border at the front end of every row.

Next row : K. 3, p. 4, tuft, * p. 7, k. 5, p. 7, tuft ; repeat from * until 4 remain, p. 4.

Work 68 rows more in pattern as now set. (73 rows above the waist increase row) to armhole.

To Shape the Armhole : Cast off 3 sts. at the beginning of next row, then cast off 2 sts. at the beginning of alternate rows (armhole end) 8 times, when 53 sts. will remain.

Work 20 rows straight on these sts. to neck.

Continue as from ** on Right Front.

The Sleeves

BEGIN at the neck edge of the shoulder-strap and with No. 9 pins cast on 11 sts.

Work 9 rows in s.s. with a k. 1 border at each end.

10th row : K. 1, p. 4, tuft, p. 4, k. 1. S.s. 9 rows with k. 1 border.

20th row : K. 1, p. 2, k. 5, p. 2, k. 1. S.s. 8 rows with k. 1 border.

29th row : Cast on 7, k. to end.

30th row : Cast on 7, k. 5, p. 7, tuft, p. 7, k. 3, inc.

Work 9 rows in s.s. inc. at both ends of every row.

40th row : Inc., k. 3, p. 7, tuft, p. 7, * k. 5, p. 7, tuft, p. 7, in following patterns, repeat from * until 4 remain, k. 3, inc.

Repeat the 31st to 40th rows twice more when there will be 85 sts. on the pins.

Work 6 rows straight on these sts.

Continue in pattern as now set, taking 2 sts. tog. at both ends of next row and every following 8th row until 53 sts. remain.

Work 11 rows in pattern to wrist. Change to No. 11 pins and work 32 rows in single rib. Cast off.

Work a second sleeve in same manner.

The Belt

WITH No. 11 pins cast on 221 sts.

1st row : (right side facing) : K. 2, p. 1, * k. 1, p. 1 ; repeat from * until 2 remain, k. 2.

2nd row : K. 1, * p. 1, k. 1 ; repeat from * to end.

Repeat these 2 rows until 9 rows have been worked.

1st buttonhole row : Rib until 17 remain, cast off 5, rib 12.

2nd buttonhole row : Work in rib as usual, casting on 5 sts. over those cast off to complete the buttonhole.

Rib 9 rows more and cast off loosely.

To Make Up the Dress

FIRST stitch the sleeve tops to back and front shoulders and press.

The Neck Band : With No. 11 pins and right side of work facing, pick up and k. 139 sts. from all round the neck edge.

1st row (wrong side facing) : K. 4, p. 1, * k. 1, p. 1 ; repeat from * until 4 remain, k. 4.

2nd row : K. 5, p. 1, * k. 1, p. 1 ; repeat from * until 5 remain, k. 5.

Repeat these 2 rows once more.

1st buttonhole row : Pattern until 13 remain, cast off 5, pattern to end.

2nd buttonhole row : Work in pattern casting on 5 sts. over those cast off to complete the buttonhole.

Work 10 rows more and cast off.

Press all pieces with a hot iron over a damp cloth and a thick blanket underneath. Set the curved edges of the sleeves to armholes, and join the sleeve and side seams in one long line. Press all seams, then sew buttons in position.

The jumper is knitted in a simple rib pattern, with deep ribbing at the waist and wrists.

A COLLAR *with* SOFT LITTLE FRILLS

A Jumper Cleverly Designed for the Larger Figure

Now continue in the main rib pattern as follows :

1st row : (Right side facing), k. 3, * p. 1, k. 1, p. 1, k. 5 ; repeat from *, ending the last repeat with k. 3 instead of k. 5.

2nd row : P. 3, * k. 1, p. 1, k. 1, p. 5 ; repeat from * ending the last repeat with p. 3.

3rd row : K. 3, * p. 3, k. 5 ; repeat from *, ending the last repeat with k. 3.

Repeat the 2nd row, 1st row, and 2nd row in this order.

7th row : K. 2, * p. 2, k. 1, p. 2, k. 3 ; repeat from *, ending the last repeat with k. 2.

8th row : As 2nd row.

Repeat these 8 rows 8 times more, then 4 rows of next pattern to armholes.

To Shape the Armholes.—Continue in pattern, casting off 3 sts. at the beginning of each of the next 10 rows, then cast off 2 sts. at the beginning of each of the following 8 rows, which leaves 99 sts.

The stitch used for the jumper is shown actual size.

THIS charming jumper is specially planned for the not-so-slender.

MATERIALS : 10 ounces of Patons' Super (or Beehive), Scotch Fingering, 3-ply ; a pair each of No. 8 and No. 11 knitting pins.

TENSION AND MEASUREMENTS : Worked at a tension of 7 sts. to the inch in width on No. 8 pins the following measurements are attained after light pressing : Round the bust (without stretching the rib), 42 inches ; front length from shoulder seam to lower edge, 23 inches ; back length, 21 inches ; side seam, 15 inches ; sleeve seam with cuff, 20 inches.

ABBREVIATIONS : K., knit ; p., purl ; tog., together ; inc., increase (by working into the back and front of the same stitch) ; st., stitch ; dec., decrease. Directions in brackets are worked the number of times stated immediately after the brackets.

To Work the Back

BEGIN at the back, and, using No. 11 pins, cast on 126 sts. for the lower edge. Work in rib as follows :

1st row : (Right side facing), (p. 1, k. 1) 3 times, * p. 2, k. 1, (p. 1, k. 1) twice ; repeat from * until 1 remains, p. 1.

2nd row : (K. 1, p. 1) 3 times, * k. 2, p. 1, (k. 1, p. 1) twice ; repeat from * until 1 remains, k. 1.

Repeat these 2 rows until 50 rows have been worked

Increase row : (Right side facing) inc * rib 6, inc. in next st., repeat from * until 6 remain, rib 5, inc. (145 sts.).

Next row : Change to No. 8 pins and p. 3, * k. 1, p. 1, k. 1, p. 5 ; repeat from * ending the last repeat with p. 3 instead of p. 5.

The soft collar with two frills is very becoming to the older woman.

Work 36 rows straight in pattern to shoulders.

To Slope the Shoulders.—Cast off 6 sts. at the beginning of each of the next 10 rows, then cast off the remaining sts.

To Work the Front

With No. 11 pins cast on 133 sts. for the lower edge and work in rib exactly as for the back, but after the increase row there will be 153 sts. Continue in pattern as on the back until

(*Continued on page* 62)

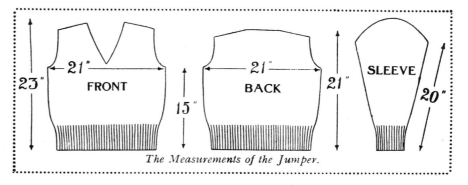

The Measurements of the Jumper.

A COLLAR *with* SOFT LITTLE FRILLS

(Continued from page 61.)

(Continued from page 61.)

the 8 pattern rows have been worked 10 times.

On the next row the armhole shaping is begun.

Next row : Cast off 3 and work in pattern to end.

Next row : (Wrong side facing), cast off 3 (1 st. on needle), pattern 72, and darn these 73 sts. on an odd length of wool for the right front shoulder, cast off 1 st., in centre front, then work in pattern to end, making 73 sts. for the left front.

THE LEFT FRONT.—Continue in pattern, shaping at both ends as follows : Cast off 3 sts. at the beginning of next row and every alternate row (armhole end) 4 times, then cast off 2 sts. at the beginning of following 4 alternate rows (armhole end), after which continue straight at this end. At the same time take 2 sts. tog. at the neck end of the 5th, 7th and 1st pattern rows (that is 3 decreases at the neck end in every 8 pattern rows) until 33 sts. remain. Work 11 rows straight in pattern to shoulder.

TO SLOPE THE SHOULDER.—Cast off 7 sts. at the beginning of next row and every following alternate row 3 times, then cast off 6 sts. at the beginning of the two following alternate rows. Fasten off.

THE RIGHT FRONT SHOULDER.—Join the wool to the neck end of the spare pin sts. and work as for Left Front Shoulder until 33 sts. remain. Work 12 rows in pattern to shoulder, then slope the shoulder as on Left Front.

The Sleeves

WITH No. 8 pins cast on 25 sts.
Next row : (Wrong side facing), p. 1, * k. 1, p. 5, k. 1, p. 1 ; repeat from * to end.

Continue in increase pattern as follows :

1st row : (Right side facing), inc., p. 1, k. 5, p. 1, * k. 1, p. 1, k. 5, p. 1 ; repeat from * until 1 remains, inc.

2nd row : Inc., p. 1, * k. 1, p. 5, k. 1, p. 1 ; repeat from * until 1 remains, inc.

3rd row : Inc., p. 3, * k. 5, p. 3 ; repeat from * until 1 remains, inc.

4th row : Inc., (p. 1, k. 1) twice, * p. 5, k. 1, p. 1, k. 1 ; repeat from * until 2 remain, p. 1, inc.

5th row : Inc., k. 2, p. 1, k. 1, p. 1, * k. 5, p. 1, k. 1, p. 1 ; repeat from * until 3 remain, k. 2, inc.

6th row : Inc., p. 3, k. 1, p. 1, k. 1, * p. 5, k. 1, p. 1, k. 1 ; repeat from * until 4 remain, p. 3, inc.

7th row : Inc., k. 3, * p. 2, k. 1, p. 2, k. 3 ; repeat from * until 1 remains, inc.

8th row : Inc., p. 5, * k. 1, p. 1, k. 1 p. 5 ; repeat from * until 1 remains, inc.

Repeat these 8 rows until there are 95 sts. on the row, ending with the 3rd row.

Work 7 rows straight in pattern as on back, beginning with the 4th row, but each row will begin and end with 1 st. less than given.

Now slope the sleeve seam by taking 2 sts. tog. at each end of next row and every following 8th row (always on the "k. 5, p. 3" row) until 65 sts. remain. Work 7 rows straight in pattern.

Next row : (Right side facing). With No. 11 pins p. 1, k. 1, p. 1, k. 2 tog., * (k. 1, p. 1) 3 times, k. 2 tog. ; repeat from * 6 times more, (k. 1, p. 1) twice.

There are now 57 sts. on which work in rib as follows :

1st row : K. 1, p. 1, k. 1, p. 2, * k. 1, (p. 1, k. 1) twice, p. 2 ; repeat from * until 3 remain, k. 1, p. 1, k. 1.

2nd row : P. 1, k. 1, p. 1, k. 2, * p. 1 (k. 1, p. 1) twice, k. 2 ; repeat from * until 3 remain, p. 1, k. 1, p. 1.

Repeat these 2 rows until 49 rows have been worked. Cast off.

Work a second sleeve in the same manner.

The Collar

WITH No. 11 pins cast on 60 sts.
1st row : (Right side facing), k. 4, p. 4, * k. 2, p. 4 ; repeat from * until 4 remain, k. 4.

2nd row : K. 2, p. 2, * k. 4, p. 2 ; repeat from * until 2 remain, k. 2.

Repeat these 2 rows until 10 rows have been worked.

Next row : (Right side facing), k. 2, k. 2 tog., (p. 1, k. 2 tog.) twice, * (p. 2 tog.) twice, k. 2 tog., (p. 1, k. 2 tog.) twice ; repeat from * until 2 remain, k. 2 (37 sts. left).

** *Next row :* (Wrong side facing), k. 2, * p. 1, (k. 1, p. 1) twice, k. 2 ; repeat from * to end.

Next row : K. 3, (p. 1, k. 1) twice, * p. 2, k. 1, (p. 1, k. 1) twice ; repeat from * until 2 remain, k. 2.

Repeat these 2 rows from ** until 82 rows more have been worked. Cast off. Work a second piece in the same manner.

THE COLLAR ENDS.—With No. 11 pins, cast on 72 sts. and work as given for the collar until the decrease row has been worked with 44 sts.

Work 23 rows straight and cast off.

To Make Up the Jumper

FIRST press all pieces with a hot iron and a damp cloth over the wrong side of the work. Join the shoulder seams beginning at the armhole end, and taking 1 st. from each side at a time.

Join the cast-off edges of the long parts of the collar, for the centre back of neck. Sew the cast-off edges of the collar ends to the first row of the long part of the collar, just under the frill.

Set the sleeves into the armholes and press these seams while the work is open. Place the seam of the collar to the centre back of neck and sew from that point towards the front on each half. Join the sleeve and side seams in one line and press.

THE END

A Ribbed Cardigan

FATHER WILL LIKE TO WEAR THIS UNDER HIS JACKET IN VERY COLD WEATHER. INSTRUCTIONS ARE GIVEN FOR MAKING IT WITH AND WITHOUT SLEEVES

MATERIALS

Use 9 oz. of Charles Sykes' Tulip Non-Shrink Wool for sleeveless cardigan or 15 oz. for cardigan with sleeves, a pair each of Nos. 10 and 9 Stratnoid knitting pins, and 5 buttons.

MEASUREMENTS

Round chest 40 in., length from shoulder 21 in. ; length of sleeve seam 20 in.

TENSION

The tension is 7 sts. and 9 rows to 1 in.

THE BACK.—With No. 10 pins cast on 120 sts. and work in k. 1, p. 1 rib for 20 rows.

Change to No. 9 pins and on the next row * p. 5, p. twice into next st. ; repeat from * to end (140 sts.). Now commence the pattern.

1st row : * K. 5, p. 2, k. 1, p. 2 ; repeat from * to end.

2nd row : P.

Repeat these 2 rows till work measures 12 in. from beginning.

Cast off 10 sts. at beginning of next 2 rows and dec. 1 st. at each end of the next 5 rows, then at each end of the following 5 alternate rows (100 sts.).

Continue without shaping till work measures 20 in. from beginning.

Cast off 6 sts. at beginning of every row till 40 sts. remain. Cast off these sts.

THE LEFT FRONT.—First make the pocket as follows :

Cast on 30 sts. and work in pattern, starting with p. 2, k. 1, p. 2, k. 5, for 4 in. Finish on a pattern row. Break wool and slip sts. to a spare pin.

With No. 10 pins cast on 70 sts. and work in k. 1, p. 1 rib for 9 rows.

Next row : Rib to last 6 sts., wool over pin twice (work into only one of these loops on next row), k. 2 tog., rib to end. A buttonhole is made in this way on every 22nd row until there are 5 buttonholes in all.

Work 10 more rows in rib, then change to No. 9 pins and on the next row (k. 1, p. 1) 5 times, * p. 4, p. twice into next st. ; repeat from * to end (82 sts.). Now commence the pattern,

1st row : K. 2, * p. 2, k. 1, p. 2, k. 5 ; repeat from * to last 10 sts. Rib these sts.

2nd row : (K. 1, p. 1) 5 times, p. to end.

Repeat these 2 rows till work measures 5 in. from beginning, finishing at side edge. Now commence the pocket top.

Next row : Work 22 sts. in pattern (p. 1, k. 1) 15 times, and complete the row as usual.

Next row : (K. 1, p. 1) 5 times, p. 20 (p. 1, k. 1) 15 times, p. 22.

Repeat these 2 rows 4 times.

Next row : Work 22 sts., cast off 30, and complete the row.

Next row : (K. 1, p. 1) 5 times, p. 20, p. across 30 sts. of pocket, p. to end.

Now continue in pattern, still working buttonholes at the correct intervals till the work measures 10 in., finishing at the side edge.

Next row : Work in pattern to last 12 sts., k. 2 tog., rib to end. Dec. in this way on every following 4th row (working the fifth buttonhole in the ribbing border when the correct position is reached). When the work measures 12 in., finishing at side edge, continue the front decs., and shape the armhole by casting off 10 sts. on next row, then dec. at the same edge of the next 5 rows, then on the following 5 alternate rows. Now keep the armhole edge straight and continue the front decs. till 40 sts. remain.

Continue on these sts. till the work measures 20½ in. from the beginning, finishing at side edge. Shape the shoulder by casting off 6 sts. on every row beginning at this edge till 10 sts. remain. Work in rib on these sts. for 5 in. Cast off.

THE RIGHT FRONT.—Work this to match the left front with all shapings at opposite edges and without buttonholes. The pattern for the pocket and front (within the ribbing border) will begin with k. 5, p. 2, k. 1, p. 2. Do not continue the ribbing after completing the shoulder shaping, but cast off the 10 border sts. after the last group of 6 sts.

THE ARMHOLE BANDS.—With No. 10 pins cast on 12 sts. and work in k. 1, p. 1 rib for 21 in. Cast off. Work another band in the same way.

THE SLEEVES.—With No. 10 pins cast on 66 sts. and work in k. 1, p. 1 rib for 4 in.

Change to No. 9 pins and work in main pattern, increasing at both ends of next and every following 6th row till there are 108 sts., being careful to keep the pattern correct.

Continue straight till sleeve measures 20 in. from beginning (or longer if necessary).

Now dec. at each end of every row till 46 sts. remain. Cast off loosely. Work another sleeve in the same way.

TO MAKE UP

JOIN shoulder seams and sew the ribbing band to back of neck. Sew on sleeve bands or sew in sleeves. Now press all parts well under damp cloth, then sew down pockets. Sew up side and sleeve seams and press. Sew on buttons to match buttonholes.

A jumper your daughter would be proud to wear

The "Beatrice" Jumper

Designed by

Edna Powell

THIS style and size is suitable for a well-made girl of about fourteen to sixteen years of age.

MATERIALS REQUIRED : 3 ounces of Baldwin & Walker's 2-ply Ladyship Scotch Fingering or Ladyship Lacilla Wool in blue, 1½ ounces in nigger ; 1 pair of Stratnoid No. 11 knitting needles ; 1 buckle ; 20 buttons.

MEASUREMENTS : Length from shoulders, 20 inches ; width all round at under-arm, 31 inches ; sleeve seam, 8 inches.

TENSION : 8 stitches to the inch.

ABBREVIATIONS : k. = knit ; p. = purl ; s. = slip ; tog. = together ; st. = stitch ; m.s. = moss stitch ; ch. = chain ; inc. = increase ; dec. = decrease.

Pattern

1st row.—Using brown wool, purl all along row.

2nd row.—Using blue wool, k. 7, s. 1, alternately to last **7** sts., k. 7.

3rd row.—Using blue wool, p. 7, slip the brown stitch slipped in the previous row alternately to last 7 sts., p. 7.

Repeat 2nd and 3rd rows twice.

8th row.—Leave blue wool hanging, and with brown wool knit to end.

9th row.—Using brown wool, purl to end.

10th row.—Leave brown wool hanging, and with blue wool k. 3, * s. 1, k. 7. Repeat from * to last 4 sts., s. 1, k. 3.

11th row.—Using blue wool, p. 3, * s. 1, p. 7. Repeat from * to last 4 sts., s. 1, p. 4.

Repeat 10th and 11th rows twice.

16th row.—Leave blue wool hanging, and with brown wool knit to end.

These 16 rows make the pattern.

The Back

Commence at the bottom of the back by casting on 127 sts. in brown wool. Knit the first row into the back of the cast-on sts., then work in pattern until the work measures about 14 inches from the beginning. Now shape the armholes by casting off 6 sts. at the beginning of the next 2 rows, and dec. at each end of every alternate row until 103 sts. remain. Continue in pattern without further shaping until the armhole measures 6 inches on the straight, then cast off 8 sts. at the beginning of every row until 40 sts. are cast off for each shoulder. Cast off the remaining sts.

The Front

Work exactly the same as for the back until the work measures about 10 inches from the beginning, finishing on a 1st row of pattern, then commence the yoke.

1st row.—Blue, (k. 7, s. 1, 6 times), k. 31, (s. 1, k. 7, 6 times).

2nd row.—Blue, (p. 7, s. 1, 6 times), m.s. 31, (s. 1, p. 7, 6 times).

3rd row.—Blue, (k. 7, s. 1, 6 times), m.s. 31, (s. 1, k. 7, 6 times).

Repeat the 2nd and 3rd rows once, then the 2nd row once more.

7th row.—Brown, k. 48. Join on a fresh ball of blue and m.s. 31 ; brown, k. 48.

8th row.—Brown, p. 48 ; blue, m.s. 31 ; brown, p. 48.

9th row.—Blue, k. 3, (s. 1, k. 7, 5 times), s. 1, k. 3, s. 1, m.s. 14, k. 2 tog. Turn, leaving the remaining sts. on a spare needle.

(Continued on page 67)

FOR THE FIFTEEN YEAR OLD

❖

A simple knitted jumper with stripes worked in two directions

Materials : 7 oz. Sirdar "Silcro" Wool, in wine colour, 2 oz. in saxe blue. 1 pair "Stratnoid" Knitting Needles No. 8. 2 Button Moulds. 1 Belt. **Measurements :** All round underarms, 28 inches. Length from shoulder to lower edge, 21 inches. **Tension :** 6 stitches and 9 rows equal 1 inch. **Note :** It is very important that the garment is worked at this tension, in order to produce the same measurements. If the No. 8 needles do not produce this tension, try other sizes until it is obtained. **Abbreviations :** K., knit ; P., purl ; sts., stitches ; tog., together ; m. = make a stitch.

Back.—Using the wine wool, commence at the side edge by casting on 88 sts. **Row 1.**—Working into the back of the sts. to produce a firm edge, knit to end of row. **Row 2.**—Purl. **Row 3.**—Knit. **Row 4.**—Purl. **Rows 5 and 6.**—With the blue wool, knit 1 row, purl 1 row. Change back to wine colour and continue working in stripes as follows : 8 rows wine, 2 rows blue. Proceed until there are 11 blue stripes, then work 4 rows more in wine. Cast off.

Front.—Work exactly as given for Back.

Back Yoke.—Holding the work with the right side towards you and using the blue wool, pick up and knit 84 sts. along one side of the piece you have knitted for the Back. **N.B.**—The stripes of the lower parts of Back and Front should be vertical, that is why the stitches are picked up from the side. Working in stripes of 2 rows blue, 8 rows wine, K. 2 tog. at each end of every knit row, until 28 sts. remain on the needle. Cast off.

Right Front of Yoke.—Holding the work with the right side towards you, and using the blue wool, pick up and knit 45 sts. along the edge of the second half of Front, commencing in the second stitch

of the middle blue stripe. Proceed as follows : **Row 2.**—P. to the last 2 sts., K. 2. **Row 3.**—K. 2 blue, K. in wine to the last 2 sts., K. 2 tog. **Row 4.**—P. in wine to the last 2 sts., K. 2 blue. Repeat the 3rd and 4th rows 3 times more. **Row 11.**—K. 2 blue, cast off the next 5 sts. for a buttonhole, K. to the last 2 sts. in blue, K. 2 tog. **Row 12.**—Blue, P. to the cast off sts., cast on 5 sts. K. 2. Proceed in the stripes to match the Back Yoke, K. 2 tog. at the end of every knit row, until the 4th wine stripe is complete, still continuing to knit 2 sts. in blue at the front edge in each row. On the next 2 rows, make a buttonhole as before. Proceed in the stripes, still K. 2 tog. at the end of every knit row, until 17 sts. remain. Cast off.

Left Front of Yoke.—Holding the work with the right side towards you and using the blue wool, pick up and knit 39 sts. along the left half of the Front, then with the same needle, pick up and knit 6 sts. at the back of the corresponding sts. of Right Yoke Front. Working in the stripes, K. 2 tog. at the beginning of every knit row, until 17 sts. remain. Cast off.

Sleeves (both alike).—Using the wine wool, commence at the top by casting on 2 sts. Working in stocking st., increase in each of these 2 sts., then increase at each end of every row until there are 22 sts. on the needle, thus finishing with a purl row. Leave this piece of work on a spare needle, and work another piece in the same manner. Join on the blue wool and work as follows : Make 1 by knitting twice into the first st., knit to the last 2 sts., K. 2 tog., take the piece of work left on spare needle, and continuing with the blue wool, K. 2 tog., knit to the last st., make 1. **Next Row.**—Make 1 in the first st., purl to the last st., m. 1. Join on the wine wool.

Next Row.—Make 1 in the first st., knit to within 2 sts. of the centre, K. 2 tog., twice knit to the last st., m. 1. **Next Row.**—M. 1 in the first st., purl to the last st., m. 1. Continue repeating the last 2 rows, working in the stripes to match body of jumper, until there are 4 blue stripes worked from the commencement. Using the wine wool, cast on 6 sts. at the beginning of each of the next 2 rows. There are now 88 sts. on the needle. Now increase at each end of every knit row only, still continuing to decrease in the centre as before, until there are 2 more wine stripes completed. Continuing in the stripes, still decreasing in the centre, cast off 4 sts. at the beginning of every row, until 8 sts. remain. Cast off.

Cuffs.—Using the wine wool, cast on 24 sts. Work in stripes to match the body of jumper, until there are 9 blue stripes in all and the cuff measures 11½ ins. Cast off.

Collar.—Using the blue wool, cast on 28 sts. **Row 1.**—K. into the back of the cast on sts. **Row 2.**—K. 26 wine, 2 blue. **Row 3.**—K. 2 blue, P. 26 wine. Proceed in the stripes to match the body of jumper, keeping the 2 sts. in blue at the one edge in each row, until there are 15 blue stripes in all. Cast off.

Covers for Button Moulds.—Using the blue wool, cast on 12 sts. Work 12 rows in stocking stitch. Cast off. Work another cover in the same manner.

To Make Up the Garment.—Press on the wrong side under a damp cloth, with a hot iron. Join the side seams. Sew in the raglan sleeves, matching the stripes. Join the sleeve seam. Fold the cuffs double and sew to edge of sleeve. Sew on the collar, easing in any fullness at back. Hem up 1 inch of the bottom of jumper to prevent rolling. Cover the button moulds. Sew the buttons to left front. Work over the buttonholes with the blue wool.

A Becoming Fair Isle Cardigan

MATERIALS

Use 8 oz. of Paton's Real Shetland Wool, 2-ply, in fawn, 1 oz. each of "misty" green, strawberry, red, and blue, a pair of No. 10 "Aero" knitting pins, and 9 buttons.

MEASUREMENTS

Length from shoulder to lower edge 24½ in., length of sleeve seam 20 in. The cardigan will fit a 36-38-in. bust.

TENSION

The tension is 6½ sts. and 9 rows to 1 in.

THE BACK.—Cast on 121 sts. and work in moss-st. for 10 rows, working into the backs of the sts. on the first row, then work 6 rows in st.-st. Now, still continuing in st.-st., work the Fair Isle pattern.

1st row : 3 fawn, * 3 blue, 5 fawn ; repeat from * all across, finishing 3 blue, 3 fawn.

2nd row : 2 fawn, * 1 blue, 3 fawn ; repeat from *, finishing 1 blue, 2 fawn.

3rd row : 2 blue, * 5 fawn, 3 blue ; repeat from *, finishing 5 fawn, 2 blue.

4th row : All in fawn.

5th row : 3 fawn, * 3 red, 5 fawn ; repeat from *, finishing 3 red, 3 fawn.

6th row : 2 fawn, * 1 red, 3 strawberry, 1 red, 3 fawn ; repeat from *, finishing 1 red, 3 strawberry, 1 red, 2 fawn.

7th row : * 1 fawn, 1 red, 5 strawberry, 1 red ; repeat from *, finishing 1 fawn.

8th row : * 1 red, 1 strawberry, 1 green, 3 strawberry, 1 green, 1 strawberry ; repeat from *, finishing 1 red.

9th row : * 1 red, 2 strawberry, 1 green, 1 strawberry, 1 green, 2 strawberry ; repeat from *, finishing 1 red.

10th row : * 1 red, 3 strawberry, 1 green, 3 strawberry ; repeat from *, finishing 1 red.

Now work backwards from the 9th to the 1st row inclusive. These 19 rows complete the Fair Isle pattern.

Continue in st.-st. in fawn and dec. 1 st. at each end of every 8th row until there are 111 sts. on the pin.

Proceed in st.-st. until work measures 16 in. from the commencement, ending with a p. row.

Shape the armholes by casting off 4 sts. at the beginning of the next 4 rows, and dec. 1 st. at each end of the next and following 4 alternate rows (85 sts.).

Continue without further shaping until the work measures 7½ in. from the commencement of the armhole decreasing, then shape the shoulders.

Next row : K. to within 9 sts. of the end ; turn.

Next row : P. to within 9 sts. of the end ; turn.

Next row : K. to within 18 sts. of the end ; turn.

Next row : P. to within 18 sts. of the end ; turn.

Next row : K. to within 27 sts. of the end ; turn.

Next row : P. to within 27 sts. of the end ; turn. K. 1 row across all sts., then cast off.

THE RIGHT FRONT.—Cast on 67 sts. and work 4 rows in moss-st. On the next row moss-st. 3, then cast off 3 sts. (for a buttonhole) and finish the row in moss-st.

Next row : Work in moss-st. and cast on 3 sts. over the 3 cast off. Work 4 more rows in moss-st. (10 altogether).

Now proceed in st.-st. for 6 rows, but keep the 10 sts. at the buttonhole edge in moss-st. and make another buttonhole in the 5th row ; 9 buttonholes in all are made on successive 9th and 10th rows.

When the 2nd buttonhole is completed, work the Fair Isle pattern on the 57 sts. in st.-st., keeping the 10 sts. at the centre front in moss-st. in fawn wool. When the 19 pattern rows have been completed work 3 rows in fawn.

Next row : Commence the pocket top. Moss-st. 10, k. 16, moss-st. 23, k. 18.

Next row : P. 18, moss-st. 23, p. 16, moss-st. 10. Repeat these 2 rows once.

Next row : Moss-st. 10, k. 16, cast off 23. K. to the end of the row decreasing the last 2 sts.

Now make the pocket back. Using a separate ball of wool and a spare needle cast on 23 sts. and work in st.-st. for 3½ in.

Return to main work. P. 18 and, with the purl side of the pocket towards you, p. across the 23 sts. and finish the row.

Continue in st.-st. with moss-st. border at the centre front, and dec. at the side edge of every 8th row as for back until 62 sts. remain on the pin.

Fair Isle knitting is always popular, and this cardigan has a most attractive border pattern. The main work is in stocking-stitch

Keep this edge straight until the 9 buttonholes are made. On the next and every 8th row k. 2 sts. tog. immediately after the moss-st. border.

Continue until the work measures the same as the back to the armhole.

Cast off 4 sts. at the commencement of the next 2 p. rows, then dec. 1 st. at the commencement of the next 5 p. rows.

Continue, keeping the armhole edge straight, but dec. at the front until 37 sts. remain on the pin.

Proceed without further dec. until the work measures 7½ in. from the commencement of the armhole dec.

Next row : With the k. side of work towards you, moss-st. the first 10 sts., k. to within 9 sts. of end ; turn, and work back.

Next row : Moss-st. 10, k. to withn 18 sts. of end ; turn, and work back.

Next row : Work across all sts., then cast off.

A BECOMING FAIR ISLE CARDIGAN

THE LEFT FRONT.—Work to match the right front with the moss-st. border at the end of k. rows and without buttonholes. The pocket is commenced as follows :

K. 18, moss-st. 23, k. 16, moss-st. 10.

Next row : Moss-st. 10, p. 16, moss-st. 23, p. 18.

Commence the armhole shaping on k. rows and the shoulder shaping on p. rows.

When 1 row has been worked across all shoulder sts., cast off 27 sts. and continue working on the moss-st. border for 5¼ in. Cast off.

THE SLEEVES.—Cast on 55 sts. and work in moss-st. for 10 rows, then work 6 rows st.-st., increasing 1 st. at each end of the 6th row.

Work the Fair Isle pattern, p. 1 row, then continue in st.-st. and inc. 1 st. at each end of the next and every 8th row until there are 77 sts. on the needle. Now inc. at each end of every following 6th row until there are 91 sts., p. 1 row, then cast off 4 sts. at the commencement of the next 4 rows, and then dec. 1 st. at each end of every row until 25 sts. remain. Cast off. Make the other sleeve in the same way.

TO MAKE UP

PRESS all pieces with a hot iron over a damp cloth. Sew up the shoulder, side and sleeve seams and sew in the sleeves. Stitch the moss-st. strip to the back of the neck. Stitch the pockets down and sew the buttons to the left front.

The "Beatrice" Jumper

(*Continued from page* 64)

10th row.—Blue, m.s. 15, s. 1, p. 3, (s. 1, p. 7, 5 times), s. 1, p. 3.

11th row.—Blue, k. 3, (s. 1, k. 7, 5 times), s. 1, k. 3, m.s. 15.

Repeat the 10th and 11th rows, then the 10th row once more.

15th row.—Brown, k. 48 ; blue, m.s. 15.

16th row.—Blue, m.s. 4, cast off 3, m.s. 7 ; brown, p. 48.

17th row.—Blue, (k. 7, s. 1, 6 times), m.s. 8, cast on 3, m.s. 4.

18th row.—Blue, m.s. 15, (s. 1, p. 7, 6 times).

19th row.—Blue, (k. 7, s. 1, 6 times), m.s. 15.

Repeat the 18th and 19th rows twice, then the 18th row once.

25th row.—Brown, k. 48 ; blue, m.s. 15.

26th row.—Blue, m.s. 15 ; brown, p. 48.

Continue in pattern with a border of 15 m.s. in blue, making a buttonhole every 2 inches and making the armhole as on the back ; dec. at the armhole edge until 51 sts. remain, then work without further shaping until the armhole measures 4½ inches on the straight. Now shape the neck by casting off 8 sts. and dec. at the same edge on the 3 next alternate rows (40 sts.). Now continue in pattern for another 1½ inches, then shape the shoulders as on the back.

Work the other side of the front to correspond with the first, always remembering to slip the first st. next to m.s. to make a straight line of brown.

The Sleeves

Cast on 51 sts. in blue and work in m.s. for 1¼ inches.

1st row.—Blue, m.s. 11 ; brown, knit to end.

2nd row.—Brown, purl to last 11 ; blue, m.s. 11.

3rd row.—Blue, m.s. 3, cast off 2, m.s. 5, (s. 1. k. 7 to end).

4th row.—Blue, p. 7, s. 1, alternately to border, m.s. 6, cast on 2, m.s. 3.

5th row.—Blue, m.s. 11, (s. 1, k. 7 to end).

6th row.—Blue, p. 7, s. 1, alternately to border, m.s. 11.

Repeat the 5th and 6th rows once, then the 1st and 2nd rows once.

11th row.—Blue, m.s. 11, s. 1, k. 3, * s. 1, k. 7. Repeat from * to last 4 sts., s. 1, k. 3.

12th row.—Blue, p. 3, s. 1, * p. 7, s. 1. Repeat from * to last 15 sts., k. 3, s. 1, m.s. 11.

13th, 14th, 15th and 16th rows.—As 11th and 12th rows.

Repeat these 16 rows twice, then slip the sts. on a spare needle and work another piece exactly the same except for the m.s. border, which now comes on the opposite side of the work ; be sure always to slip the st. nearest the border. Now place both sides together on one needle with the two borders in the centre. Continue in pattern, inc. 1 st. in the centre of the 1st row to make the pattern come right, then continue without further shaping until the work measures 7 inches from the beginning, then dec. at each end of each alternate row until 47 sts. remain. Cast off.

Make another sleeve in the same manner.

The Collar

Cast on 151 sts. in blue wool and work in m.s. for 2½ inches.

Next row.—* m.s. 8, k. 3 tog., m.s. 8, p. 3 tog. Repeat from *, ending m.s. 9.

Work 3 more rows in m.s., then cast off.

Belt

Cast on 15 sts. in blue and work in m.s. until the work measures 26 inches *when stretched*. Now take 2 sts. tog. at each end of every other row until 3 sts. remain. Cast off.

Making Up

Press all parts carefully with a damp cloth and a warm iron. Join all seams and insert sleeves. Attach the collar and belt, stitching the buckle on the latter. Join the buttons in pairs like links, and slip in position through the buttonholes.

II.

*Could any little girl resist the allure of a cosy dressing-gown
"just like Mummy's"?*

For Mother—and Daughter

Dressing-Gowns which are snug, pretty—and alike

Designed by

D. M. Beckett

of the next 2 rows, then dec. 1 st. at each end of every row until 52 sts. are left. Continue knitting on these until armholes are 5½ inches deep, then shape for the shoulders by casting off 4 sts. at the beg. of every row until 12 sts. are left. Cast off.

The Fronts

Right side front first. Cast on 68 sts. and knit in st.-st. for 6 inches, then dec. 1 st. at beg. of every 6th row on the wrong side. Continue until 27 inches from the start are completed, then shape for the armhole. Cast off 5 sts. at the beg. of the next row with wrong side facing, and dec. 1 st. at beg. of next 5 rows, starting from armhole end. Then knit on the remaining sts. until armhole is 4½ inches deep.

Now shape for the neck. With right side facing you, cast off 16 sts., and work to end. Dec. 1 st. at neck end of work on every other row until 16 sts. are left. To shape for the shoulder cast off 4 sts. at the beg. of every row, starting from the armhole end, until all sts. are worked.

Now knit a left side front to pair. This can be worked from the right front instructions by simply calling the wrong side the right and the right side the wrong, throughout.

Sleeves

Cast on 15 sts.

1st row.—Knit twice into the 1st st., knit to end.

2nd row.—k. 1, p. 1, to end.

3rd row.—As 1st.

4th row.—sl. 1, k. 1, to end.

Repeat these 4 rows three times in all. Then work as follows :—

1st row.—k. 2 tog., knit to end.

2nd row.—k. 1, p. 1, to end.

3rd row.—As 1st row.

MATERIALS

MATERIALS REQUIRED : 30 ounces of James Templeton's "Sestal" Wool in orange and brown for the Mother's dressing-gown ; 16 ounces of the same for the Daughter's dressing-gown ; 1 pair of Stratnoid knitting needles, size 6 ; 7 small brown fancy buttons, and 7 large to match ; a few press studs.

ABBREVIATIONS : k. = knit ; p. = purl ; st. = stitch ; sts. = stitches ; sl. = slip ; tog. = together ; dec. = decrease ; inc. = increase ; beg. = beginning ; st.-st. = stocking-stitch.

TENSION : 4 sts. to 1 inch in width, and about 6 rows in depth.

MEASUREMENTS : MOTHER'S—Length, 52 inches ; sleeve length, 19 inches ; to fit 34–36-inch bust. DAUGHTER'S —Length, 33 inches ; sleeve length, 14 inches : to fit from 26-30-inch chest.

The Daughter's Dressing-Gown

The Back

Cast on 94 sts. and knit in st.-st. for 6 inches. Then dec. 1 st. at each end of every 12th row until work measures 27 inches from the start.

Now shape for the armholes. Cast off 3 sts. at the beg.

For Mother—and Daughter

4th row.—sl. 1, k. 1, to end.

Repeat these 4 rows three times in all.

Now leave these sts. on a needle and work the other half of cuff to pair. With 15 sts. on needle, knit as follows :—

1st row.—Knit to the last st., knit twice into this.

2nd row.—k. 1, p. 1, to end.

3rd row.—As 1st.

4th row.—sl. 1, k. 1, to end.

Repeat these 4 rows three times in all. Then continue as follows :—

1st row.—Knit to the last 2 sts., k. 2 tog.

2nd row.—k. 1, p. 1, to end.

3rd row.—As the 1st row.

4th row.—sl. 1, k. 1, to end.

Repeat these 4 rows until 15 sts. are left.

Join two pieces with the shaped parts meeting, and work right across in st.-st. Inc. 1 st. at each end of every 6th row, until sleeve measures 14 inches from the start. To shape for the top, cast off 3 sts. at the beg. of the next 2 rows, then dec. 1 st. at each end of every row until 12 sts. are left. Cast off.

Work another sleeve to pair.

Collar

Cast on 60 sts. and knit 2 rows in rib of k. 1, p. 1. On the 3rd row (in st.-st.) inc. 1 st. in every 10th st. to end as follows :—k. 5, knit twice into next st., k. 9, knit twice into next st., five times, knit 4 remaining sts.

Continue in pattern, with the 2nd row :—

2nd row.—k. 1, p. 1, to end.

3rd row.—Knit to end (as the 1st row).

4th row.—sl. 1, k. 1, to end.

Repeat these 4 rows once more, then continuing in pattern k. 2 tog. at each end of every 3rd row, making sure to keep sts. in pattern.

Knit until collar is 3½ inches deep. Then cast off loosely and in pattern.

Pocket

Cast on 10 sts. and working in pattern st., inc. 1 st. at each end of every knit row until 16 sts. are on needle. Knit on these until pocket is 5 inches deep. Cast off.

Girdle

Cast on 3 sts. and working in pattern, inc. 1 st. at the end of every knit row until 12 sts. are on needle. Continue on these sts. for 45 inches in length, then dec. 1 st. at beg. of every knit row until no sts. are left. Fasten off.

The Mother's Dressing-Gown

Back

Cast on 120 sts. and working as in the daughter's, dec. 1 st. at each end of every 12th row, until work measures 44 inches from the start. Then shape for the armholes. Cast off 3 sts. at the beg. of the next 2 rows, and dec. 1 st. at each end of the next 7 rows. Continue on these sts. until armholes are 7½ inches deep. To shape for the shoulders, cast off 4 sts. at the beg. of every row until 16 sts. are left. Cast off.

Fronts

Cast on 86 sts. and work as for the front of the daughter's, continuing until work measures 44 inches from the bottom instead of only 27 inches. Then shape for the armhole. Cast off 5 sts. at the beg. of the next row, starting from the shaped or seam side of work. Dec. 1 st. at armhole end on the next 7 rows. Continue until the armhole is 6 inches deep.

Work buttonhole for fastening front as follows :—With right side facing, and front edge at beg. of needle, k. 8, cast off 6 sts., knit to end. On return row cast on 6 sts. over the 6 cast-off sts. in previous row. Then k. 4 more rows.

Now shape for neck. With right side facing, cast off 24 sts., knit to end. Dec. 1 st. at neck end of needle on every row, until 24 sts. are left. Shape shoulder by casting off 4 sts. at the beg. of every row starting from shoulder end, until no sts. remain. Fasten off. Now work a left side front to pair, but with no buttonhole.

The Facings

For the right side front first, with buttonhole.

Cast on 3 sts. and working in st.-st., inc. 1 st. at the beg. of every row when right side facing, until 46 sts. are on needle, and the straight side measures 15 inches from start. Work the buttonhole as follows :—With right side facing, knit to 14 sts. from end, then cast off next 6 sts., knit 8 remaining sts. Cast on 6 sts. over 6 cast-off sts. in previous row on next row, and knit 3 more rows, still inc. at same end as before. Now shape for neck as on front. With wrong side facing, cast off 24 sts., work to end. Dec. 1 st. at neck end on every row, but inc. no more at shaped side. Continue until 6 sts. are left. Cast off.

Work another facing likewise, but with no buttonhole, and making sure the inc. edge of work is at end of row so that both facings pair as do the fronts.

Sleeves

Cast on 20 sts. for each cuff, and knit as in the daughter's. Then join across and continue as before, until the sleeve measures 19 inches from the start. To shape, cast off 5 sts. at the beg. of the next row with right side facing ; work to end. Dec. 1 st. at each end of every row until 16 sts. are left. Cast off.

Work a second sleeve to correspond, and when the 19 inches of sleeve length are worked, cast off 5 sts. at the beg. of the next row with wrong side facing, then continue as in first sleeve.

The Collar

Cast on 84 sts. and work exactly as in the daughter's collar to end. The inc. row (3rd row from beg. of collar) will read, k. 6, knit twice into the next st., k. 7, knit twice into the next st., ten times, knit remaining 6 sts. Finish as in daughter's collar.

The Girdle

Make a girdle as for the daughter's, and inc. until 18 sts. are on needle, instead of 12. Work for length of 54 inches.

The Pocket

Cast on 16 sts. and working as for daughter's pocket, inc. until 24 sts. are on needle. Then work until pocket is 6 inches deep, and cast off.

To Make Up

First pin each part to size and shape on ironing-board and press, using a damp cloth and warm iron. Sew up all seams, and put in sleeves. Pin pockets into position, sew on neatly, and press. Sew on the collars.

Put on facings to the mother's dressing-gown, and work the buttonhole. Hem front edges on both garments, and bottom if needed, to width of 1 inch. Sew on buttons as illustrated, and put on the press studs where needed. Make loops on both garments at waist-line for the belt. Give final light press.

FOR Your SMALL SON or DAUGHTER

Specially Planned to Wear on the Beach

The suit is knitted in a rib pattern, with white stripes going across.

The back view.

rows 3 times more. Change to white wool and work as follows:

9th row : Sl. 1 knitwise, k. to end.

10th row : Sl. 1 knitwise, k. 1, p. 2, k. 2, * p. 5, (k. 2, p. 2) 3 times, k. 2 ; repeat from * once, k. 4.

Repeat these 10 rows three times more.

Change to coloured wool and continue in s.s. (working 1 st. plain at the beginning and 4 sts. plain at the end of every purl row to make front border) for 54 rows, ending with a purl row.

To Shape the Front Neck. — Continue in s.s., taking tog. the 5th and 6th st. at the beginning of next row

(Continued overleaf.)

T HE sun-suit for warm days, worn with the cardigan when it is cooler—this is the perfect wear for the beach.

MATERIALS : *For the cardigan 6 ounces Bairns-Wear Swimwool in any colour preferred and 1 ounce of the same wool in white. For the bathing suit 3 ounces of the same wool in colour and 1 ounce in white. A pair of No. 10 Bairns-Wear knitting pins, and a No. 14 "Aero" crochet hook. 5 buttons.*

TENSION AND MEASUREMENTS : *Worked at a tension of 8 sts. to the inch in width the following measurements are attained after light pressing :* THE CARDIGAN.—*Width all round at underarms, 24 inches ; length from shoulder to lower edge, 15½ inches ; sleeve seam, 10½ inches.* THE BATHING SUIT.—*Width round at waist, 20 inches ; length from shoulder to lower edge, 18 inches ; leg seams, 1 inch.*

ABBREVIATIONS : *K., knit ; p., purl ; tog., together ; st., stitch ; inc., increase (by working into the back and front of the same stitch) ; d.c., double crochet ; sl., slip. Directions in brackets are worked the number of times stated after the brackets.*

To Work the Cardigan

R IGHT FRONT.—Cast on 48 sts. in coloured wool and work as follows : *1st row :* Sl. 1 knitwise, k. 3, * (p. 2, k. 2) 3 times, p. 2, k. 5 ; repeat from * once, p. 2, k. 2, p. 1, k. 1.

2nd row : Sl. 1 knitwise, k. 1, p. 2, k. 2, * p. 5, (k. 2, p. 2) 3 times, k. 2 ; repeat from * once, k. 4.

Repeat these two

The perfect garment for the beach is this unshrinkable sun-suit. There is a cardigan to wear over it when the days are not so warm.

A SUN-SUIT and CARDIGAN

Knit Them for the Summer Holidays

every alternate knit row (every 4th row worked) until 40 sts. remain, ending with a k. row.

To Shape the Armhole.—Continue with front neck decreases as before and also cast off 4 sts. at the beginning of the next row, then k. 2 sts. tog. at armhole end of every alternate row until 30 sts. remain, then keep the armhole edge straight and continue the front neck decreases until 24 sts. remain, finishing at the armhole edge.

To Slope the Shoulder.—Cast off 8 sts. at the beginning of next and every alternate row until all are worked off.

The Left Front

CAST on 48 sts. with coloured wool.

1st row : Sl. 1 knitwise, p. 1, k. 2, p. 2, * k. 5, p. 2, (k. 2, p. 2) 3 times ; repeat from * once, k. 4.

2nd row : Sl. 1 knitwise, k. 3, * k. 2, (p. 2, k. 2) 3 times, p. 5 ; repeat from * once, k. 2, p. 2, k. 2.

This reverses the pattern to match the right front. Continue on these sts. in the same way as for the right front, making the neck decreases at the beginning of every alternate purl row, and the armhole decreases at the beginning of right side rows so that the shaping is reversed.

The Back

CAST on 97 sts. with coloured wool.

1st row : Sl. 1 knitwise, * (p. 2, k. 2) 3 times, p. 2, k. 5 ; repeat from * until 1 remains, k. 1.

2nd row : Sl. 1 knitwise, * p. 5, k. 2, (p. 2, k. 2) 3 times ; repeat from * until 1 remains, k. 1.

Repeat these 2 rows three times more, then change to white wool.

The cardigan is in stocking-stitch and fastens with a button and loop.

9th row : Sl. 1 knitwise, k. to end.

10th row : Sl. 1 knitwise, * p. 5, k. 2, (p. 2, k. 2) 3 times ; repeat from * until 1 remains, k. 1.

Repeat these 10 rows three times more.

Change to coloured wool and work in s.s. for 54 rows, when the armholes will be reached.

To Shape the Armholes.—Cast off 4 sts. at the beginning of each of the next 2 rows, then take 2 sts. tog. at each end of next row, and every following alternate row until 81 sts. remain.

Continue without further shaping for 25 rows more.

To Slope the Shoulders.—Cast off 8 sts. at the beginning of each of the next 6 rows. Cast off the remaining sts.

The Sleeves

CAST on 40 sts. with coloured wool and work 3 inches in single rib.

Continue in s.s., increasing at each end of the next row and every following 8th row until there are 64 sts. on the pins.

To Shape the Top of the Sleeve.—Cast off 2 sts. at the beginning of every row until 40 sts. remain. Cast off.

Work a second sleeve in the same manner.

(Continued on page 72)

FOR Your SMALL SON or DAUGHTER

Continued

The Bathing Suit

BEGIN at the edge of the front leg band and cast on 40 sts. in coloured wool.

1st row : Sl. 1 knitwise, p. 1, * k. 2, p. 2 ; repeat from * until 2 remain, k. 2.

Repeat this row, keeping the rib correct, and increase at the end of every alternate row until there are 44 sts. on the pins, ending at the shaped edge.

Cast off 6 sts. at the beginning of next row and pattern to end. Work one row more, then leave this piece on a spare needle for the present.

Work a second piece in the same manner, ending at the straight edge. K. plain across the row and on to the same pin knit the spare pin sts. (This gives all the sts. on one pin with the shaped edges together.)

Continue in pattern as follows :

1st row : Sl. 1 knitwise, p. 2, * (k. 2, p. 2) 3 times, k. 2, p. 5 ; repeat from * until 16 remain, (k. 2, p. 2) 3 times, k. 2, p. 1, k. 1.

2nd row : Sl. 1 knitwise, k. 1, * (p. 2, k. 2) 3 times, p. 2, k. 5 ; repeat from * until 17 remain, (p. 2, k. 2) 4 times, k. 1.

Repeat these 2 rows twice, then the 1st row once more. Change to white wool.

8th row : Sl. 1 knitwise, k. to end.

9th row : As 1st row.

Change to coloured wool and continue in same pattern, working 8 rows dark and 2 rows light until 80 rows have been worked in striped pattern.

Still keeping to the same pattern work 2 sts. tog. at each end of every alternate row until 60 sts. remain.

Continue straight for 31 rows.

To Shape the Neck.—Pattern 25 and leave these sts. on a spare pin until needed for the right front shoulder, cast off 10 sts., pattern to end. Continue on these 25 sts. for the left front shoulder, taking 2 sts. tog. at the neck edge of every row until 10 sts. remain, then continue without further shaping for 18 rows more. Cast off.

The Right Front Shoulder.—Work on the remaining 25 sts. to match the left front shoulder.

The Back

WORK exactly as given for the front until 70 rows have been worked in striped pattern. Work 10 rows in k. 2 and p. 2 rib, and cast off.

The Straps

CAST on 10 sts. in coloured wool and work 9 inches in single rib.

1st buttonhole row : Rib 4, cast off 2 sts., rib 4.

2nd buttonhole row : Rib 4, cast on 2 over those cast off on previous row, rib 4.

Work in single rib for 1 inch more. Cast off. Work a second strap in the same manner.

To Make Up

PRESS the work with a hot iron and a damp cloth over the wrong side.

Join the shoulder seams of the cardigan, taking 1 st. from each side at a time ; set the sleeves into the armholes and press these seams while the work is open. Join the sleeve and side seams in one long line. Work a row of d.c. all round the sloping edge of the neck. Make a buttonhole loop on the left front, then sew two buttons on the garter-st. borders, as seen in the illustration.

Join the side seams of the suit and the sloping leg seams. Sew the six cast-off stitches of left leg to those of right leg on back and front. Work d.c. all round the top of the suit as on the neck of cardigan, and join the shoulder straps to the front shoulders. Sew two buttons on the back about 1½ inches from each side seam, cross the shoulder straps and fasten to the buttons.

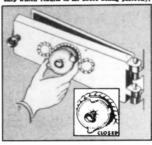
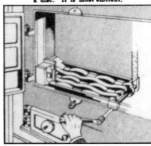

A BLOUSE FOR GIRLIE

LITTLE GIRL'S SMOCKED BLOUSE

(To fit a child of six years)

MATERIALS

Three hanks of Copley's Featherweight Art Silk in yellow; 1 ball of embroidery silk in brown; a pair of No. 10 "Aero" knitting pins, and a small crochet hook.

MEASUREMENTS

Length from shoulder to lower edge, 13 ins.; round chest, 26 ins.

TENSION

Seven stitches to 1 inch.

THE *Back.*—Cast on 102 sts. Do not k. into backs of these, but work 10 rows in st.-st. Now make hem. Turn up the cast-on edge on the wrong side.

11th row : K. each st. on needle tog. with corresponding st. of cast-on edge.

12th row : P.

Work 20 more rows in st.-st., then dec. 1 st. at each end of next and every following 12th row until 94 sts. remain. Work 3 rows st.-st. after last dec.

Now shape for armholes. Cast off 3 sts. at beginning of next 2 rows and dec. 1 st. at each end of next 4 rows. Dec. 1 st. at each end of next 4 *knit* rows (72 sts.). P. 1 row.

Next row : K. 2, * p. 2, k. 1 ; repeat from * till 4 sts. remain, p. 2, k. 2.

Next row : P. 2, * k. 2, p. 1 ; repeat from * till 4 sts. remain, k. 2, p. 2.

Repeat these 2 rows until work measures 5 ins. from commencement of armhole decreasings, finishing on a p. row. Now shape shoulders. Cast off 6 sts. at beginning of next 8 rows. Cast off remaining 24 sts.

The Front.—Work as for back until it measures the same as the back to the yoke ribbing. Continue thus :

1st row : K. 2, (p. 2, k. 1) 8 times, p. 2, k. 2 tog., m. 1, k. 6, put remaining sts. on a holder, turn.

2nd row : P. 8, (k. 2, p. 1) 8 times, k. 2, p. 2.

3rd row : K. 2, (p. 2, k. 1) 8 times, p. 2, k. 8.

Continue in this rib, making an eyelet hole as in the 1st row, in the 7th, 13th and 19th rows. Now commence shaping for neck.

20th row : Cast off 4 sts. Work remainder in pattern.

21st row : Work in pattern.

Now dec. 1 st. at neck edge of next 8 rows. Work 7 more rows without dec., finishing at armhole edge. Shape for shoulder by casting off 6 sts. at the beginning of every k. row until all sts. are cast off.

Pick up sts. from the holder and join on silk at centre of work. Work this side to correspond with the other, all shapings being at opposite edges.

The Collar.—Cast on 90 sts. Work 2 rows in st.-st.

3rd row : * K. 4, k. twice into next st.; repeat from * until 5 sts. remain, k. 5 (107 sts.).

Work 11 more rows in st.-st., then dec. 1 st. at each end of next 8 rows. Cast off.

The Sleeves.— Cast on 75 sts. Work 6 rows in st.-st.

7th row : * K. 1, k. 2 tog.; repeat from * to end of row (50 sts.).

Work k. 1, p. 2 rib for 5 rows.

Next row : K. into back and front of every st. (100 sts.). *Next row :* P. *Next row :* K.

Continue in st.-st. for 1 in., finishing on a p. row, then at beginning of every row cast off 2 sts. until 36 sts. remain. On next row cast off 3 sts. tog. all across. Work another sleeve to match.

Smocking is used with charming effect on the yoke and sleeve edges. The original model was in a lovely sunny shade of yellow, trimmed with brown.

TO MAKE UP.

Press all pieces under a damp cloth with a warm iron. Sew up side, shoulder and sleeve seams, and sew sleeves into place. Sew collar to neck edge.

Using embroidery silk, smock the front and back yokes and round lower edges of sleeves, as in diagram, (page 34), catching the narrow ribs together and leaving 3 rows of knitting between each row of smocking. Round collar, front opening and edge of sleeves work the following edging with embroidery silk and crochet hook : (1 d.c., 3 ch., 1 d.c.) all into first st., * miss a small space, then (1 d.c., 3 ch., 1 d.c.) all into next st., and repeat from * all round.

Make a chain of double embroidery silk and thread through eyelet holes down front of blouse. Thread elastic through hem.

THE END

A Useful Cardigan in an Attractive Fancy Rib

This simple cardigan is made to fit a 32-34 inch bust with Jaegar "Feather-Fleck," and it will only cost you 4/6

MATERIALS REQUIRED : 6 ounces of Jaeger "Feather-Fleck"; 1 pair of No. 8 Jaeger knitting needles; 4 1-inch buttons.

MEASUREMENTS : Width all round under arms when fastened, 32–34 inches; length down centre back, including strapping, 21 inches; length of sleeve seams, including cuffs, 19 inches.

TENSION : 6 sts. to 1 inch in width, and 8 rows to 1 inch in depth.

ABBREVIATIONS : k. = knit; p. = purl; st. = stitch; dec. = decrease; inc. = increase; tog. = together; sl. = slip; p.s.s.o. = pass slipped st. over; fin. = finishing; beg. = beginning; rep. = repeat.

Always work first row into back of all cast-on sts. to procure firm edge.

The Back

Cast on 98 sts. on No. 8 needles, and work thus :

1st row.—k. 2, p. 2 alternately to end, fin. k. 2.

2nd row.—p. 2, k. 2 alternately to end, fin. p. 2.

3rd row.—k. 2, * purl next st.; do not slip off needle, but purl again tog. with next st. (this in future will be called purl double), k. 2. Rep. from * to end.

4th row.—Purl.

These last 2 rows complete pattern. Rep. pattern twice more, then dec. thus :

9th row.—k. 2 tog., work as 3rd row from * to end, fin. sl. 1, k. 1, p.s.s.o. instead of k. 2.

10th row.—Purl.

11th row.—k. 1, work as 3rd row from * to end, fin. k. 1 instead of k. 2.

12th row.—Purl. Rep. last 2 rows once.

15th row.—p. 2 tog., p. 1, k. 2, work as 3rd row from * to last 3 sts., p. 1, p. 2 tog.

16th row.—Purl.

17th row.—As 3rd row from * to last 2 sts., purl double.

18th row.—Purl. Rep. last 2 rows once.

21st row.—p. 2 tog., k. 2, work as 3rd row from * to last 2 sts., p. 2 tog.

22nd row.—Purl.

23rd row.—p. 1, k. 2, work as 3rd row from * to last st., p. 1.

24th row.—Purl. Rep. last 2 rows once.

27th row.—k. 2 tog., k. 1, work as 3rd row from * to end, fin. k. 1, sl. 1, k. 1, p.s.s.o., instead of k. 2.

28th row.—Purl. Rep. 2 pattern rows twice. Rep. from 9th row once more, leaving 82 sts. Rep. 2 pattern rows four more times, then inc. 1 st. each end of next row, and then every 6th row following (keeping continuity of rib in same manner as given for dec.) until there are 98 sts., working 5 rows after last inc. and fin. after purl row.

Shape armholes by dec. 1 st. each end of every row until 74 sts. remain, then continue without dec. until armhole measures 5¾ inches on straight, fin. after purl row.

Shape shoulders by casting off 4 sts. at beg. of every row until 26 sts. remain. Cast off.

A Useful Cardigan in an Attractive Fancy Rib

Continued

The Right Front

Cast on 50 sts. and work first 2 rows as back, then rep. 2 pattern rows three times.

Now continue in pattern, but at same time dec. 1 st. at end of next row, and on this same edge on every 6th row following until 42 sts. remain, working 13 rows after last dec. and fin. after purl row.

Now inc. 1 st. at end of next row and on this same edge on every 6th row following until there are 46 sts., working 5 rows after last inc. and fin. after purl row.

Now beg. front shaping. Dec. 1 st. at beg. and inc. 1 st. at end of next row and then on every 6th row following, another three times, working 5 rows after last row of shaping and fin. after purl row—46 sts.

Now continue dec. on next and every 6th row following for front shaping, but at same time shape armhole by dec. 1 st. at end of next row and on this same edge on next 11 rows, then keep this edge straight and continue dec. on front shaping only until 25 sts. remain, then work without shaping until armhole measures 7 inches on straight, fin. after purl row.

Shape shoulder by casting off 4 sts. at beg. of every purl row until all are cast off.

The Left Front

Work this to match right by reversing all shapings thus :

Dec. for side seams at beg. of 9th row and then on this same edge until 42 sts. remain, then inc. on this same edge until there are 46 sts., working 5 rows after last inc.

For front shaping, inc. 1 st. at beg. and dec. 1 st. at end of next row and then every 6th row another three times, working 5 rows after last shaping, and fin. after purl row.

Now continue dec. on front shaping, but dec. for armhole at beg. of next row and on this edge all through.

Shape shoulder by casting off 4 sts. at beg. of every 3rd pattern row until all are cast off.

The Sleeves

Cast on 42 sts. and rep. first 2 rows of back twelve times, then rep. 2 pattern rows twice. Now continue in pattern, but at same time inc. 1 st. each end of next row and then every 8th row following until there are 74 sts., working 3 rows after last inc.

Shape top by dec. 1 st. at each end of every other row six times, then every row until 14 sts. remain. Cast off.

To Make Up

Press on wrong side with warm iron over damp cloth. Join shoulders. Sew sleeves into armholes. Press seams. Join under-arm and side seams. Now work border thus :

Pick up and knit 3 out of every 4 sts. up right front, then every st. across back of neck, then 3 out of every 4 sts. down left front. Work 1 row of k. 2 and p. 2 rib, taking care to make rib fit to pattern across back of neck.

Next row.—Rib 4 sts., * cast off 5 sts., rib 8 sts. Rep. from * three more times. Rib to end. Now work five more rows of k. 2 and p. 2 rib, casting on 5 sts. in place of those cast off. Cast off in rib.

Press seams and edges. Sew buttons on left front to correspond with buttonholes on right.

★ They're NEW— They're CHIC—

MATERIALS

12 oz. Sirdar "Supreme" Wool.
Abel Morrall's "Aero" knitting pins, two No. 10; two No. 7.
Three buttons.

MEASUREMENTS

Shoulder to lower edge, 19 inches; sleeve seam, 19 inches; to fit a 32-34 inch bust. Always work into back of each cast-on stitch.

Abbreviations.—K., knit; p., purl; tog., together; st., stitch; rep., repeat; rem., remain; inc., increase, by knitting into back as well as front of stitch before slipping it off needle.

Tension of knitting about 6½ stitches and 7½ rows to one inch.

THE BACK

WITH No. 10 needles, commence at lower edge, casting on 100 sts. K. in rib of k. 2, p. 2 for 4 inches, decreasing 1 st. at end of last row (99 sts.). Change to No. 7 needles. **1st row** (above ribbing)—P. 3, then k. 5, p. 3 to end.

2nd row—K. 3, then p. 5, k. 3 to end. Rep. these 2 rows twice. **7th row**—Inc., p. 2, then k. 5, p. 3 until 8 rem., k. 5, p. 2, inc.

8th and each alternate row (unless otherwise directed)—P. the knitted sts. and k. the purled sts. of the previous row.

9th row—P. 4, then k. 5, p. 3, until 1 rem., p. 1. **11th row**—P. 5, then k. 3, p. 5, to end. **12th row**—Inc., k. 4, then p. 3, k. 5, until 8 rem., p. 3, k. 4, inc.

13th row—P. 7, then k. 1, p. 7 to end. **15th row**—P. 3, k. 1, then p. 7, k. 1, until 3 rem., p. 3. **16th row**—Inc., k. 2, then p. 1, k. 7 until 4 rem., p. 1, k. 2, inc.

17th row—P. 3, k. 3, then p. 5, k. 3, until 3 rem., p. 3.

19th row—P. 2, k. 5, then p. 3, k. 5, until 2 rem., p. 2. **21st row**—Inc., p. 1, k. 5, then p. 3, k. 5, until 2 rem., p. 1, inc.

22nd row—As 8th row. Rep. from 5th to 22nd row inclusive once, then from 5th to 15th row inclusive (119 sts.).

52nd row—As 8th row. **53rd row**—P. 2, k. 5, then p. 5, k. 3, until 2 rem., p. 2. **55th row**—P. 1, k. 5, then p. 3, k. 5, until 1 rem., p. 1. Now shape armholes. **57th row**—Cast off 8, p. 1, k. 5, then p. 3, k. 5, until 1 rem., p. 1. **58th row**—Cast off 8, k. 1, then p. 5, k. 3, until 6 rem., p. 5, k. 1.

59th row—K. 2 tog., k. 4, p. 3, then k. 5, p. 3, until 6 rem., k. 4, k. 2 tog. **60th row**—K. 2 tog., k. as 8th row until 2 rem., k. 2 tog. **61st row**—K. 2 tog., k. 2, p. 3, then k. 5, p. 3, until 4 rem., k. 2, k. 2 tog. **62nd row**—As 60th row. **63rd row**—K. 2 tog., p. 3, then k. 5, p. 3, until 2 rem., k. 2 tog. **64th row**—As 60th row. **65th row**—K. 2 tog., p. 2, k. 3, then p. 5, k. 3, until 4 rem., p. 2, k. 2 tog. **66th row**—As 60th row. **67th row**—K. 2 tog., p. 1, k. 1, then p. 7, k. 1, until 3 rem., p. 1, k. 2 tog. **68th row**—As 60th row (83 sts.). **69th row**—P. 5, k. 1, then p. 7, k. 1, until 5 rem., p. 5. **71st row**—P. 4, k. 3, then p. 5, k. 3, until 4 rem., p. 4. **72nd row**—As 8th row. Rep. 1st and 2nd rows 5 times. **83rd row**—As 71st row. **85th row**—As 69th row. **87th row**—P. 1, k. 1, then p. 7, k. 1, until 1 rem., p. 1. **89th row**—K. 3, then p. 5, k. 3, to end. **91st row**—K. 4, p. 3, then k. 5, p. 3, until 4 rem., k. 4. **92nd row**—As 8th row. Rep. last 2 rows 4 times. Rep. 89th, 8th, 87th and 8th rows respectively. Now shape shoulders. **105th row**—Cast off 5, k. 1, then p. 7, k. 1, until 5 rem., p. 5. **106th row**—Cast off 5, p. 1, then k. 7, p. 1, to end. **107th row**—Cast off 5, p. 2, then k. 3, p. 5, until 2 rem., p. 2. **108th row**—Cast off 5, k. as 8th row to end. **109th row**—Cast off 5, k. 1, then p. 3, k. 5, until 1 rem., p. 1. **110th row**—As 108th row. **111th row**—Cast off 5, k. 4, p. 3, then k. 5, p. 3, until 1 rem., k. 1. **112th row**—As 108th row (43 sts.). Cast off.

THE RIGHT FRONT

With No. 10 needles, commence at lower edge, casting on 44 sts. K. in rib of k. 2, p. 2, for 3 rows. Now make buttonhole. **4th row**—K. in rib until 8 rem., cast off 4, k. 2, p. 2. **5th row**—K. 2, p. 2, cast on 4, k. in rib to end. Rib until work measures 2 inches, and make a second buttonhole at the same edge. Make a third buttonhole when work measures 4 inches, finish last row at opposite edge to buttonholes.

Next row—Inc., k. in rib until 1 rem., inc. (46 sts.). Change to No. 7 needles. **1st row** (above ribbing)—K. 3, p. 3, then k. 5, p. 3, to end. **2nd row**—K. 3, then p. 5, k. 3, until 3 rem., p. 3. Rep. these 2 rows twice. **7th row**—K. 3, then p. 3, k. 5, until 3 rem., p. 2, inc.

8th row—As 8th row of back. **9th row**—K. 3, then p. 3, k. 5, until 4 rem., p. 4. **11th row**—K. 2, p. 5, then k. 3, p. 5, to end. **12th row**—Inc., k. 4, then p. 3, k. 5, until 2 rem., p. 2.

13th row—K. 1, p. 7, to end.

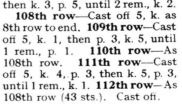

15th row—P. 4, k. 1, then p. 7, k. 1, until 3 rem., p. 3. **16th row**—Inc., k. 2, then p. 1, k. 7, until 5 rem., p. 1, k. 4.

17th row—P. 3, k. 3, then p. 5, k. 3, until 3 rem., p. 3. **19th row**—P. 2, k. 5, then p. 3, k. 5, until 2 rem., p. 2.

21st row—P. 2, k. 5, then p. 3, k. 5, until 2 rem., p. 1, inc. **23rd row**—P. 2, then k. 5, p. 3, to end. **25th row**—P. 2, k. 5, then p. 3, k. 5, until 3 rem., p. 2, inc. **27th row**—P. 2, then k. 5, p. 3, until 1 rem., p. 1. **29th row**—P. 3, then k. 3, p. 5, to end. **30th row**—Inc., k. 4, then p. 3, k. 5, until 6 rem., p. 3, k. 3.

31st row—P. 4, then k. 1, p. 7, to end. **33rd row**—K. 1, then p. 7, k. 1, until 3 rem., p. 3. **34th row**—Inc., k. 2, p. 1, then k. 7, p. 1, to end. **35th row**—K. 2, then p. 5, k. 3, until 3 rem., p. 3. **37th row**—K. 3, then p. 3, k. 5, until 2 rem., p. 2. **39th row**—K. 3, then p. 3, k. 5, until 2 rem., p. 1, inc.

40th row—As 8th row. Rep. from 5th to 15th row inclusive once (56 sts.). **52nd row**—As 8th row.

53rd row—P. 3, k. 3, then p. 5, k. 3, until 2 rem., p. 2. **55th row**—P. 2, k. 5, then p. 3, k. 5, until 1 rem., p. 1.

57th row—As 55th row. Now shape armholes. **58th row**—Cast off 4, p. 2, then k. 3, p. 5, until 2 rem., p. 2.

59th row—K. 2 tog., then k. 5, p. 3, until 2 rem., k. 2. **60th row**—Cast off 4, k. 1, then p. 5, k. 3, until 6 rem., p. 5, k. 1. **61st row**—P. 1, then k. 5, p. 3, until 6 rem., k. 4, k. 2 tog.

62nd row—K. 2 tog., k. as 8th row to end. **63rd row**—K. 2 tog., k. 4, p. 3, then k. 5, p. 3, until 4 rem., k. 2, k. 2 tog.

64th row—As 62nd row.

65th row—P. 1, k. 3, then p. 5, k. 3, until 6 rem., p. 4, k. 2 tog.

66th row—As 62nd row.

67th row—K. 2 tog., k. 1, then p. 7, k. 1, until 5 rem., p. 3, k. 2 tog.

68th row—As 62nd row.

69th row—P. 5, k. 1, then p. 7, k. 1, until 7 rem., p. 5, k. 2 tog.

70th row—As 8th row.

71st row—K. 2 tog., p. 2, then k. 3, p. 5, to end. **73rd row**—P. 2, then k. 5, p. 3, until 1 rem., k. 1. **75th row**—K. 2 tog., then k. 5, p. 3, until 1 rem., k. 1.

77th row—P. 1, then k. 5, p. 3, until 1 rem., k. 1. **79th row**—K. 2 tog., k. 4, p. 3, then k. 5, p. 3, until 1 rem., k. 1.

81st row—K. 5, p. 3, until 1 rem., k. 1. **83rd row**—K. 2 tog., k. 2, p. 5, then k. 3, p. 5 to end. **85th row**—P. 1, k. 1, then p. 7, k. 1, until 6 rem., k. 6.

87th row—K. 2 tog., k. 3, k. 1, then p. 7, k. 1, until 2 rem., p. 2.

89th row—P. 3, k. 3, then p. 5, k. 3, until 1 rem., p. 1. **91st row**—K. 2 tog., k. 5, then p. 3, k. 5, to end.

93rd row—P. 1, k. 5, then p. 3, k. 5, to end. **95th row**—K. 2 tog., k. 4, then p. 3, k. 5, to end. **97th row**—K. 5, then p. 3, k. 5, to end. **99th row**—K. 2 tog., k. 3, then p. 3, k. 5, to end.

101st row—K. 3, then p. 5, k. 3, until 1 rem., p. 1. **103rd row**—K. 2 tog., then p. 7, k. 1, until 2 rem., p. 2.

104th row—As 8th row.

105th row—P. 4, k. 1, p. 7, k. 1, p. 7, k. 1, p. 6. Now shape shoulder. **106th row**—Cast off 5, k. 1, p. 1, k. 7, p. 1, k. 7, p. 1, k. 4. **107th row**—K. 2 tog., p. 1, k. 3, p. 5, k. 3, p. 5, k. 3.

108th row—Cast off 5, k. 3, p. 3, k. 5, p. 3, k. 2. **109th row**—P. 1, k. 5, p. 3, k. 5, p. 2. **110th row**—Cast off 5, p. 2, k. 3, p. 5, k. 1. **111th row**—K. 2 tog., k. 4, p. 3, k. 2. **112th row**—Cast off 5, k. 5. Cast off.

THE LEFT FRONT

K. as directed for right front but omitting the buttonholes. When the pattern rows are reached, work as for right front until 57th row is reached, but working each row backwards, thus the 1st row reads : P. 3, k. 5, until 6 rem., p. 3, k. 3. Now shape armhole.

57th row—Cast off 4, k. 2, then p. 3, k. 5, until 2 rem., p. 2. **58th row**—As 8th row. **59th row**—Cast off 4, p. 1, k. 5, then p. 3, k. 5, until 2 rem., k. 2 tog.

60th row—As 8th row. Rep. from 61st to 104th row inclusive in directions for right front, but working each row backwards. **105th row**—Cast off 5, p. 1, k. 1, p. 7, k. 1, p. 7, k. 1, p. 4.

107th row—Cast off 5, p. 3, k. 3, p. 5, k. 3, p. 1, k. 2 tog.

109th row—Cast off 5, k. 2, p. 3, k. 5, p. 1. **111th row**—Cast off 5, k. 4, k. 2 tog. **112th row**—P. 5. Cast off.

THE SLEEVES (both alike)

With No. 10 needles, commence at lower edge, casting on 48 sts. K. in rib of k. 2, p. 2, for 3½ inches.

Next row—* Inc., k. 11 in rib, rep. from * twice, inc., k. 10 in rib, inc. (53 sts.). Change to No. 7 needles.

1st row (above ribbing)—P. 2, k. 1, then p. 7, k. 1, until 2 rem., p. 2.

2nd and each alternate row (unless otherwise directed)—As 8th row of back.

3rd row—P. 1, k. 3, then p. 5, k. 3, until 1 rem., p. 1. **5th row**—K. 5, then p. 3, k. 5, to end. **6th row**—As 8th row of back. Rep. last 2 rows once.

9th row—As 5th row.

10th row—Inc., p. 4, k. 3, then p. 5, k. 3, until 5 rem., p. 4, inc.

11th row—P. 1, k. 5, then p. 3, k. 5, until 1 rem., p. 1. **13th row**—As 11th row. **15th row**—P. 2, k. 3, then p. 5, k. 3, until 2 rem., p. 2. **17th row**—P. 3, k. 1, then p. 7, k. 1, until 3 rem., p. 3.

19th row—Inc., p. 6, k. 1, then p. 7, k. 1, until 7 rem., p. 6, inc.

21st row—K. 2, p. 5, then k. 3, p. 5, until 2 rem., k. 2. **23rd row**—K. 3, p. 3, then k. 5, p. 3, until 3 rem., k. 3.

25th row—As 23rd row.

27th row—As 23rd row.

28th row—Inc., p. 2, then k. 3, p. 5, until 6 rem., k. 3, p. 2, inc.

29th row—K. 4, p. 3, then k. 5, p. 3, until 4 rem., k. 4. **31st row**—As 29th row. **33rd row**—K. 3, then p. 5, k. 3, to end. **35th row**—P. 1, k. 1, then p. 7, k. 1, until 1 rem., p. 1. **37th row**—Inc., p. 4, k. 1, then p. 7, k. 1, until 5 rem., p. 4, inc. **39th row**—P. 5, then k. 3, p. 5, to end. **41st row**—K. 1, p. 3, then k. 5, p. 3, until 1 rem., k. 1. **43rd row**—As 41st row. **45th row**—As 41st row.

46th row—Inc., then k. 3, p. 5, until 4 rem., k. 3 inc. **47th row**—K. 2, p. 3, then k. 5, p. 3, until 2 rem., k. 2.

48th row—As 2nd row.

49th row—As 47th row.

51st row—K. 1, p. 5, then k. 3, p. 5, until 1 rem., k. 1. **53rd row**—P. 7, then k. 1, p. 7, to end. **55th row**—Inc., p. 2, k. 1, then p. 7, k. 1, until 3 rem., p. 2, inc.

57th row—P. 3, k. 3, then p. 5, k. 3, until 3 rem., p. 3. **59th row**—P. 2, k. 5, then p. 3, k. 5, until 2 rem., p. 2.

61st row—As 59th row.

63rd row—As 59th row.

64th row—Inc., k. 1, then p. 5, k. 3, until 7 rem., p. 5, k. 1, inc.

65th row—P. 3, then k. 5, p. 3, to end. **67th row**—As 65th row.

69th row—P. 4, k. 3, then p. 5, k. 3, until 4 rem., p. 4. **71st row**—P. 5, k. 1, then p. 7, k. 1, until 5 rem., p. 5.

73rd row—Inc., k. 1, then p. 7, k. 1, until 5 rem., inc. **74th row**—As 2nd row. Rep. from 3rd to 48th row inclusive once (79 sts.). Now shape top.

121st row—Cast off 4, p. 1, then k. 5, p. 3, until 2 rem., k. 2. **122nd row**—Cast off 4, k. 1, then work as 2nd row to end. **123rd row**—K. 2 tog., k. 3, then p. 5, k. 3, until 2 rem., k. 2 tog.

124th and every alternate row—K. 2 tog., work as 2nd row until 2 rem., k. 2 tog. **125th row**—K. 2 tog., p. 7, then k. 1, p. 7, until 2 rem., k. 2 tog. **127th row**—K. 2 tog., p. 1, k. 1, then p. 7, k. 1, until 3 rem., p. 1, k. 2 tog. **129th row**—K. 2 tog., k. 1, p. 5, then k. 3, p. 5, until 3 rem., k. 1, k. 2 tog. **131st row**—K. 2 tog., p. 3, then k. 5, p. 3, until 2 rem., k. 2 tog. **133rd row**—K. 2 tog., p. 1, k. 5, then p. 3, k. 5, until 3 rem., p. 1, k. 2 tog. **135th row**—K. 2 tog., k. 4, p. 3, then k. 5, p. 3, until 6 rem., k. 4, k. 2 tog. **137th row**—K. 2 tog., k. 2, p. 3, then k. 5, p. 3, until 4 rem., k. 2, k. 2 tog. **139th row**—As 131st row. **141st row**—P. 2 tog., p. 2, k. 3, then p. 5, k. 3, until 4 rem., p. 2, p. 2 tog. **143rd row**—As 127th row. **145th row**—K. 2 tog., p. 3, k. 1, then p. 7, k. 1, until 5 rem., p. 3, k. 2 tog.

146th row—As 124th row (23 sts.). Cast off.

Using No. 10 needles, cast on 10 sts. for Border.

1st row—* Wool forward, slip 1 purlwise, wool to back, k. 1, rep. from * to end. Rep. this row until band is long enough to reach from bottom of ribbing up to the neck and around to the opposite edge. Cast off.

Pin out each piece and press carefully under a damp cloth with a hot iron. Sew up under-arm, shoulder and sleeve seams. Sew in sleeves, placing seam level with under-arm. Sew border to front edge. Add buttons. Press all seams.

For Baby: A Knitted Robe and Bonnet

By Beryl Grimsby ▼

Continue thus, always working 1 st. less between the decreases on each succeeding row, until only 10 sts. remain.

Next row.—Take 2 sts. tog. all across. *Next row.*—k. 2 tog. twice, k. 1. Break off wool, run end through a darning needle, and catch the 3 sts. tog., fastening off securely.

With a medium-sized crochet hook, work 1 row of d. cr. over the two ends of work (i.e. side edges). Press lightly with a warm iron over a damp cloth. Arrange centre of wide ribbon to centre of bonnet front, holding lace-stitch turn-back over the ribbon, so that the colour shows through the holes of work. Stitch lightly into place, and the bonnet will be complete.

The Robe

Cast on 108 sts. and work 6 rows in garter-stitch, then *** rep. the 6 rows of lace pattern, as given for bonnet.

13th row.—Purl (making a ridge on right side of work).
14th row.—Purl. Continue in stocking-stitch for a further 7 rows.

22nd row.—Knit (making a ridge on right side of work.***

Repeat from *** to *** five times more, then work in stocking-stitch for a further 2 inches.

Next row.—p. 2 tog. all across. *Next row.*—(To form holes at waist edge) k. 1, * m. 1, k. 2 tog., and rep. from * until 1 st. remains, k. 1. *Next row.*—Purl

Work a further 1½ inches in stocking-stitch, then cast off 11 sts. at beginning of the next 2 rows.

Work a further half-inch in stocking-stitch, ending at completion of a purl row. *Next row.*—Knit over half the number of sts., slip these on to a safety-pin or stitch-holder, knit over remaining sts.

Always working over this last set of sts., and knitting the last 4 sts. of every purl row in order to keep a little border of garter-stitch up centre-back, continue until work measures 4 inches from the 11 sts. cast off at armhole.

Cast off. Join wool to neck edge at other side and work this to match the first, making the garter-stitch at beginning, instead of ends, of purl rows.

The Front

Work to match the back until the two sets of 11 sts. have been cast off for armhole, then work 1½ inches in stocking-stitch, ending at completion of a purl row.

Next row.—k. 8, cast off 24, knit remainder.

Working over the last set of 8 sts. only, continue until work measures 4 inches from 11 sts. cast off at armhole edge. Cast off. Join wool to neck edge at other side and work to match the first. Cast off.

The Sleeves

It is necessary to join shoulder seams of back and front before working, then pick up 40 sts. (right side of work towards you) all up the side edges of the rows from the two sets of cast-off sts. at

(*Continued on page* 83)

MATERIALS REQUIRED:

8 ounces "Golden Eagle" Polynit Fingering de Luxe 4-ply Wool in white; 1 pair of No. 8 Stratnoid knitting needles; 2 yards of 1-inch wide double satin ribbon in pink or blue for the waist, 1 yard 2 inches wide to match for the bonnet, and ½ yard of bébé ribbon to match for the back.

ABBREVIATIONS: k. = knit; p. = purl; tog. = together; st. = stitch; sts. = stitches; dec. = decrease; inc. = increase; d. cr. = double crochet; m. = make; rep. = repeat.

TENSION: 6 sts. to the inch in width before pressing.

MEASUREMENTS (before pressing): Length from shoulder to hem, 22½ inches. Width, all round under arms, 18 inches.

The Bonnet

Cast on 60 sts. and work 6 rows in plain knitting, then change to the following fancy pattern:

1st row.—* k. 2 tog. twice, then m. 1 (by throwing wool over needle), k. 1 four times, k. 2 tog. twice, and rep. from * to end.
2nd row.—Purl all sts. *3rd row.*—As 1st row. *4th row.*—As 2nd row. *5th row.*—As 1st row. *6th row.*—As 2nd row.

These six rows form one pattern. Purl the next row in order to make a ridge on right side of work.

Knit the next row (to reverse work), then purl back. Continue in stocking-stitch (i.e. 1 row plain, 1 row purl, alternately) for a further 4 inches, ending at completion of a purl row.

1st row of shaping.—* k. 10, k. 2 tog., and rep. from * to end.
2nd row.—* p. 9, p. 2 tog., and rep. from * to end. *3rd row.*—
* k. 8, k. 2 tog., and rep. from * to end. *4th row.*—* p. 7, p. 2 tog., and rep. from * to end.

A Quickly Knitted Cardigan

For The Outsize Figure—And Just As Smart As You Could Wish !

MATERIALS

SEVENTEEN ounces of Templeton's "Hurricane" Quick Knitting Wool; a pair of Stratnoid knitting pins No. 1 and No. 7; 4 buttons.

TENSION AND MEASUREMENTS

WORKED at a tension of 4½ sts. to the inch in width on No. 1 pins, the measurements given on the diagram are attained after light pressing.

ABBREVIATIONS

KNIT; p., purl; st., stitch; tog., together; inc., increase (by working into the back and front of the same stitch); dec., decrease (by working 2 sts. tog.); w.f., wool forward; w.b., wool back; sl., slip; p.s.s.o., pass the slipped st. over; m., make (by bringing the wool to the front of the pin and over it before working the next stitch); rib is k. 2 and p. 2 alternately. Directions in brackets are worked the number of times stated immediately after the brackets.

THE BACK

WITH No. 7 pins cast on 80 sts. for the lower edge and work in rib as follows :

1ST Row (right side facing) : P. 1, k. 2, * p. 2, k. 2 ; repeat from * until 1 remains, p. 1.

2ND Row : K. 1, p. 2, * k. 2, p. 2 ; repeat from * until 1 remains, k. 1.

Repeat these 2 rows 13 times more, then the first row again. Change to No. 1 pins and purl 1 row.

Continue in main pattern as follows :

1ST Row (right side facing) : K. 1, * w.f., sl. 2 purlwise, w.b., k. 2 ; repeat from *, ending the last repeat with k. 1 instead of k. 2.

2ND Row : All purl.

Repeat these 2 rows twice more.

7TH Row : K. 3, * w.f., sl. 2 purlwise, w.b., k. 2 ; repeat from *, ending the last repeat with k. 3 instead of k. 2.

8TH Row : All purl.

Repeat these 8 rows 5 times more, then 6 rows of the next pattern to armholes.

TO SHAPE THE ARMHOLES.—Continue in pattern, taking 2 sts. tog. at both ends of each of the next 9 rows, then decrease at both ends of following 3 alternate rows, when 56 sts. will remain.

Work 27 rows straight in pattern.

TO SLOPE THE SHOULDERS.—Continue in pattern, casting off 5 sts. at the beginning of each of the next 4 rows. Cast off the remaining sts.

THE LEFT FRONT

WITH No. 7 pins cast on 51 sts. and work in rib as follows :

1ST Row (right side facing) : P. 1, * k. 2, p. 2 ; repeat from * until 6 remain, k. 6, front end.

2ND Row : K. 8, p. 2, * k. 2, p. 2 ; repeat from * until 1 remains, k. 1.

Repeat these 2 rows 13 times more, then the first row again. Change to No. 1 pins.

NEXT Row : K. 6, front end, p. to end.

Continue in pattern as follows :

1ST Row (right side facing) : K. 1, * w.f., sl. 2 purlwise, w.b., k. 2 ; repeat from * until 6 remain, k. 6 (this gives k. 8 at front end, the last 6 forming the garter-st. border).

2ND Row : K. 6, p. to end.

Repeat these 2 rows twice more.

7TH Row : K. 3, * w.f., sl. 2 purlwise, w.b., k. 2 : repeat from * until 4 remain, k. 4 (k. 6 altogether at front end).

8TH Row : As 2nd row.

Repeat these 8 rows 3 times more, then 6 rows of the next pattern.

DECREASE Row (right side facing) : Work in pattern until 7 remain, k. 2 tog., k. 5.

Work 3 rows in pattern with k. 6 border at the front end as before.

Repeat the last 4 rows until the 4th decrease row has been worked and 47 sts. remain.

Work 3 rows.

TO SHAPE THE ARMHOLES.—NEXT Row : Cast off 4 (armhole end), pattern until 7 remain, k. 2 tog., k. 5 (42 sts.).

Work 1 row.

** Continue in pattern, decreasing at the armhole end of each of the next 9 rows, and still working the front slope decreases as before. (31 sts.)

Now decrease at the armhole end of following 3 alternate rows, with front shaping as before. (26 sts.)

Continue straight in pattern, decreasing at the front end of every 4th row until 20 sts. remain.

Work 11 rows.

TO SLOPE THE SHOULDER.—Continue in pattern, casting off 5 sts. at the beginning of next row and following 2 alternate rows, when 5 sts. will remain.

Change to No. 7 pins and work 13 rows plain for half of back neck-band. Cast off.

THE RIGHT FRONT

WITH No. 7 pins cast on 51 sts.

Now work in rib as follows :

1ST Row (right side facing) : K. 6, front end, * p. 2, k. 2 ; repeat from * until 1 remains, p. 1.

2ND Row : K. 1, * p. 2, k. 2 : repeat from * until 6 remain, k. 6 (k. 8 altogether at the front end).

Repeat these 2 rows twice more, then the first row again.

1ST BUTTONHOLE Row : Rib until 6 remain, k. 1, cast off 2, (1 st. on pin) k. 2.

2ND BUTTONHOLE Row : All rib, casting on 2 sts. over those cast off to complete the buttonhole.

Work 18 rows, then repeat the 2 buttonhole rows.

Change to No. 1 pins.

NEXT Row (wrong side facing) : P. until 6 remain, k. 6, front end.

Now work in pattern as follows :

1ST Row (right side facing) : K. 8, front end, * w.f., sl. 2 purlwise, w.b., k. 2 ; repeat from *, ending the last repeat with k. 1 instead of k. 2.

2ND Row : P. until 6 remain, k. 6, front end.

Repeat these 2 rows twice more.

7TH Row : K. 6, front end, * w.f., sl. 2 purlwise, w.b., k. 2 : repeat from *, ending the last repeat with k. 3 instead of k. 2.

8TH Row : As 2nd row.

Repeat from the 1st to the 6th row inclusive.

BUTTONHOLE Row : K. 3, m. 1, k. 2 tog., k. 1, * w.f., sl. 2 purlwise, w.b., k. 2 ; repeat from * ending the last repeat with k. 3 instead of k. 2.

Work 15 rows in pattern.

Repeat the buttonhole row.

Work 7 rows in pattern.

DECREASE Row : K. 5, front end, sl. 1, k. 1, p.s.s.o. pattern to end.

Work 3 rows in pattern.

Repeat the last 4 rows until the 5th decrease row has been worked and 46 sts. remain.

TO SHAPE THE ARMHOLE.—NEXT Row : Cast off 4 (armhole end), pattern to end. (42 sts.)

Continue as from ** on Left Front to end.

THE SLEEVES

WITH No. 1 pins cast on 8 sts. and p. 1 row.

Continue in pattern as follows :

1ST Row (right side facing) : Inc., w.f., sl. 2 purlwise, w.b., * k. 2, w.f., sl. 2 purlwise, w.b., in following patterns repeat from * until 1 remains, inc.

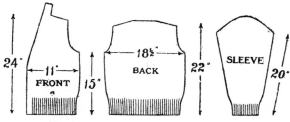

24" ←11"→ FRONT 15" ←18½"→ BACK 22" SLEEVE 20"

The Measurements of the Outsize Cardigan

It is a Perfect All-Purposes Cardigan, Planned to fit the Fuller Figure.

2ND Row (and every wrong side row): Inc., p. until 1 remains, inc.

3RD Row: Inc., k. 2, * w.f., sl. 2 purlwise, w.b., k. 2, repeat from * until 1 remains, inc.

5TH AND 7TH ROWS: As 1st row. 8TH Row: As 2nd row. Repeat these 8 rows until there are 68 sts. on the pins.

Work 4 rows. Continue in pattern, taking 2 sts. tog. at both ends of next row and every following 6th row until 38 sts. remain.

Work 4 rows. Change to No. 7 pins.

DECREASE Row: P. 2 tog., p. until 2 remain, p. 2 tog. (36 sts.) Work 16 rows in rib. Cast off. Work a second sleeve in the same manner.

Make up the Cardigan

The "Robert" Cardigan

Designed by
Edna Powell

until work measures 15½ inches from cast-on edge, then shape armholes by casting off 12 sts. at beg. of next 2 rows and dec. at each end of next 9 rows (106 sts.). Continue without further shaping until work measures 23½ inches from cast-on edge, then shape shoulders by casting off 8 sts. at beg. of next 8 rows. Cast off remaining sts.

The Left Front

Make pocket linings by casting on 30 sts. on No. 11 needles, and working in st.-st. for 4½ inches. Leave sts. on spare needle.

Work another lining in same manner.

Now, using No. 14 needles, cast on 78 sts. and work in k. 1, p. 1 for 1 inch. Make buttonhole by casting off 5th and 6th sts. at beg. of next row, and casting on 2 sts. in their place on next row. Continue in k. 1, p. 1, until work measures 3 inches, then make second buttonhole. Slip first 10 sts. from border edge on to spare needle, then change to No. 11 needles and st.-st. upon remaining 68 sts. until work measures 4½ inches from cast-on edge.

Make pockets thus : (Right side of work) k. 18, cast off 30, knit to end. Next row p. 20, purl across 30 sts. of pocket lining, p. 18. Continue in st.-st. until work measures 13 inches from cast-on edge, then start shaping neck by dec. at front edge of every knit row until armhole is reached. Still dec. at front edge, shape armhole by casting off 12 sts. at beg. of next knit row, and dec. at this same edge on next 9 rows. Continue in st.-st., and dec. at front edge only until sts. are reduced to 32, then continue without further shaping until work measures 23½ inches from cast-on edge.

Shape shoulders by casting off 8 sts. at beg. of next 4 knit rows. Rejoin wool at border sts. and continue in k. 1, p. 1 (using No. 14 needles), making buttonholes at 5, 7, 9, 11 and 13 inches from cast-on edge. Continue in k. 1, p. 1, until border is of sufficient length to go up front edge and half-way across back of neck, when slightly stretched. Leave sts. for grafting.

The Right Front

Work as for left front, but reversing all shapings and omitting buttonholes. Graft border sts. tog. at back of neck.

Oversew border neatly to front edges of cardigan.

(Continued on page 82)

MATERIALS REQUIRED : 10 ounces of Templeton's Ayrbeam Wool, 4-ply ; Stratnoid knitting needles, No. 11 and No. 14 ; 7 buttons.

MEASUREMENTS : Length from shoulder, 24 inches ; width all round at underarm, 41 inches ; sleeve seam, 21 inches.

TENSION : 7 sts. to the inch measured over st.-st. worked with No. 11 needles.

ABBREVIATIONS : st. = stitch ; k. = knit ; p. = purl ; st.-st. = stocking-stitch ; beg. = beginning ; dec. = decrease ; tog. = together.

The Back

Using No. 14 needles, cast on 148 sts. and work in k. 1, p. 1, for 3 inches. Change to No. 11 needles, and continue in st.-st.

POLO STYLE WITH RAGLAN SLEEVES

A Hard-wearing and Well-fitting Garment for Sports Occasions

TO pull on after a game of tennis, to don for the cross-country walk, after rowing or when playing golf, this is an ideal garment. It has the sleeve set in Raglan style, giving particular ease of movement, and it is designed in a pattern that "grows" quickly.

MATERIALS REQUIRED

12oz. of "Anlaby" Lynton wool.
1 pr. "Anlaby" needles No. 8.
1 pr. "Anlaby" needles No. 11.
Measurements.—From shoulder to edge, 22in.; across underarm, 20in.; sleeve length from neck, 30in.

Tension.—13 st. to 2in.

Abbreviations.—K., knit; p., purl; st., stitches; pat., pattern; inc., increase; dec., decrease; beg., beginning; tog., together.

K. into the back of all cast-on st.

BACK AND FRONT (ALIKE)

With No. 11 needles cast on 135 st. and rib in k. 1, p. 1 for 3in. Change to No. 8 needles and the following pat. :—

1st row.—* K. 5, p. 5. Repeat from * to the last 5 st., k. 5.

2nd row.—* K. 1, p. 3, k. 3, p. 1, k. 2. Repeat from * to last 5 st., k. 1, p. 3, k. 1.

3rd row.—* P. 2, k. 1, p. 3, k. 3, p. 1. Repeat from * to last 5 st., p. 2, k. 1, p. 2.

4th row.—As 1st. (These 4 rows complete one pat.).

Continue in pat. until work measures 14in. from the start, then k. 2 tog. every alternate row, each end, until 119 st., then k. 2 tog. each end of every row until 55 st. End with 1st row of pat. and work as follows :—

Neck Shaping.—*1st row.*—K. 2 tog., p. 2, k. 3, p. 1, k. 3, p. 3, k. 3, p. 1, k. 2, cast off 15. K. 1, p. 1, k. 3, p. 3, k. 3, p. 1, k. 3, p. 2, p. 2 tog.

2nd row.—K. 2 tog., p. 3, k. 3, p. 3, k. 1, p. 3, k. 3, p. 1.

3rd row.—Cast off 5, k. 4, p. 5, k. 1, k. 2 tog.

4th row.—K. 2 tog., p. 5, k. 5.

5th row.—Cast off 5. K. 1, p. 1, k. 1, k. 2 tog.

6th row.—K. 2 tog., k. 2, p. 1. Cast off remaining 4 st. Return to 1st 19 st.

1st row. (Join on wool at neck edge.) Cast off 5. P. 1, k. 1, p. 3, k. 3, p. 3, k. 2 tog.

2nd row.—K. 2 tog., k. 1, p. 5, k. 5.

3rd row.—Cast off 5, p. 4, k. 2 tog.

4th row.—K. 2 tog., k. 1, p. 1, k. 2, cast off remaining 5 st.

SLEEVES

With No. 11 needles cast on 65 st. and rib in k. 1, p. 1 for 3in. Change to No. 8 needles and pat., work 2½in., then inc. 1 st. each end of next and every 8th row following until 83 st., and when sleeve measures 20in. from start (with ribbing) k. 2 tog. each end of every alternate row until 35 st. remain, then k. 2 tog. each end of every row until 15 st. remain. Cast off.

COLLAR

With No. 11 needles cast on 140 st. Rib in k. 1, p. 1 for 6in. Change to No. 8 needles, rib 5 rows. Cast off loosely in rib.

To make up.—Press with warm iron and damp cloth. Sew up all seams. Sew in sleeves. Sew on collar. Press seams.

The "Robert" Cardigan

(Continued from page 81)

The Sleeves

Using No. 11 needles, cast on 36 sts. and work in st.-st., casting on 2 sts. at beg. of every row until 116 sts. are on needle. Continue in st.-st. and dec. at each end of every 6th row until 70 sts. remain, then continue without further shaping until sleeve seam measures 17 inches. Change to No. 14 needles, and work in k. 1, p. 1, for 3 inches. Cast off *loosely* in k. 1, p. 1.

Work another sleeve in same manner.

The Pocket Borders

Using No. 14 needles, cast on 10 sts. and work in k. 1, p. 1, for 4½ inches. Cast off.

Making Up

Oversew all seams. Press all parts except ribbing. Slip-stitch pockets to back of garment. Stitch pocket-borders along top of pockets on cast-off edge. Stitch buttons to match buttonholes.

IN THICK WOOL

Neat in Design, This Winter Pullover Will Satisfy Both Knitter and Wearer

HERE is a long-sleeved pullover which would be ideal for sports or motoring or for wear about the farm on really chilly days. The "part-cable" pattern is one of the latest knitting designs and is quite easy to follow.

"Speedwool" is the yarn used, and it fully lives up to its name. You will find that with the heavy wool and thick needles you can knit up the pullover in a very short time.

MATERIALS REQUIRED

15oz. of "Anlaby" Speedwool.

1 pr. "Anlaby" knitting needles. No. 7.

1 pr. "Anlaby" knitting needles, No. 5.

MEASUREMENTS

Length from shoulder to lower edge, 21½in.

Sleeve length from shoulder, 27in.

Across back and front underarms, 19½in.

Tension, 5 st. to 1in.

Abbreviations : K., knit ; p., purl ; dec., decrease ; inc., increase ; tog., together ; pat., pattern ; beg., beginning ; st., stitches.

Knit into backs of all cast on stitches.

BACK

With No. 7 needles cast on 96 st. Rib 3in., k. 1, p. 1. Change to the following pat. and No. 5 needles :

1st row.—K.

2nd row and every alternate row.—*(K. 2, p. 2) 4 times, k. 2, p. 8. Repeat from * twice more. (K. 2, p. 2) 4 times, k. 2.

Repeat these 2 rows 3 times more.

9th row.—*K. 18. Double cable next 8 st. (To double cable, slip 1 st., slip next 2 st. on to a spare needle and place at back of work.) K. next 2 st., then k. the 2 st. from spare needle. (This forms first twist.) Slip next 2 st. on to spare needle and place at *front* of work. K. next 2 st., then k. 2 st. from spare needle. (This forms 2nd twist.) Repeat from * twice more. K. 18.

(This makes three double cables in all.)

10th row.—As 2nd. Continue until work measures 13½in. including welt.

To Shape for Armholes : Cast off 2 st. at the beg. of next 10 rows. Continue on the remaining 76 st. for 5in.

To Shape for Neck : Work 28 st. Cast off 20 st. Work 28 st. Work on each set of 28 st. for 3in. at the same time decreasing 1 st. every row at neck edge until 20 st. remain.

To Shape for Shoulders : Cast off 4 st. every armhole end row 5 times.

FRONT

Work as for the back until 4in. after armhole shaping.

To Shape for Neck : Work 28 st. Cast off 20 st. Work 28 st. Work on each set of 28 st. for 4in. at the same time dec. 1 st. every row at neck edge until 20 st. remain. Shape shoulders as for back.

SLEEVES

With No. 7 needles cast on 44 st. Rib in k. 1, p. 1 for 2in. Change to No. 5 needles and the following pat. :

1st row.—K.

2nd row.—(K. 2, p. 2) 4 times, p. 2, k. 8, (k. 2, p. 2) 4 times, k. 2.

Repeat these two rows three times more.

9th row.—K. 18. Double cable next 8 st., k. 18.

10th row.—As 2nd. Repeat these 10 rows until 6in. from start including ribbing, then inc. one st. each end of every 8th row following until 58 st. and when sleeve measures 20in. from start (including ribbing) cast off 2 st. at the beg. of every row until 12 remain. Cast off.

Note.—Keep increased st. on sleeve in the rib.

RIBBED NECK : FRONT

With No. 7 needles pick up and k. 73 st. Rib 6 rows, k. 1, p. 1. Cast off.

Back as front.

TO MAKE UP

Sew up all seams. Sew in sleeves. Press lightly and carefully with hot iron and damp cloth.

For Baby

(Continued from page 78)

armhole edge, but do NOT pick up the actual sts. cast off. Work 1 row plain.

Next row.—k. 2, * m. 1, k. 2 tog., and rep. from * until 2 sts. remain, k. 2. *3rd row.*—k. 2, purl to within 2 sts. of end, k. 2. *4th row.*—k. 2, * m. 1, k. 2 tog., knit to within 3 sts. of end, m. 1, k. 2 tog., k. 1. Repeat the last 2 rows until you have six holes along each side edge, then purl 1 row.

Next row.—k. 2 tog. once, then work the 1st row of pattern, ending k. 2 tog. once (i.e. three sets of k. 2 tog. at beginning and end of row).

Next row.—Purl dec. by taking 2 sts. together at beginning and end of row.

Work 1st and 2nd rows of pattern twice more ; work 4 rows in garter-stitch, cast off. Work second sleeve exactly the same as the first.

Press work lightly with a warm iron over a damp cloth. Sew up side and sleeve seams. Run ribbon through holes at waist, and tie at one side of front in a smart little bow.

Lace up open back with crossings of the narrow ribbon, pulling it through the knitted border sts. with a bodkin, and tie ends in a bow at back of neck.

Press seams.

With crochet hook, work 1 row of d. cr. evenly round neck edge.

If you'd like it in Green—choose Bright Leaf-Green (Shade No. 256). Have a Green Tweed Skirt. Brown Pigskin Brogues and Gloves. Copper-tone Stockings and a Brown Beret.

★ If you'd like in Scarlet and Grey—choose a Scarlet and Grey Mixture (Shade No. 296). Have a Grey Flannel Skirt. Grey Lizard Shoes. A Wide Scarlet Belt and a Scarlet Bracelet.

★ If you'd like it in Beige—choose Pale Mushroom - Beige (Shade No. 488). Wear a Wine-Red and Beige Mixture Woollen Skirt. Wine Red Shoes and Belt. Amber-tan Stockings.

JUST "TWO-and-TWO" RIB

The Polo Collar and Raglan Sleeves Are Chic Features of This Simple-To-Knit Jumper

Here the sports jumper is shown in speckled wool; on the cover you will see it in a plain colour.

MATERIALS.— 8 ounces of Greenock Super Fingering, 4-ply (obtainable only from branches of SCOTCH WOOL & HOSIERY STORES); a pair of Stratnoid knitting pins, No. 9 and No. 13.

TENSION AND MEASUREMENTS.— Worked at a tension of 9 sts. to the inch in width on No. 9 pins with the ribs closed; the measurements on the diagram are attained, but the ribs will easily expand to a bust measurement of 34 inches.

ABBREVIATIONS.—K., knit; p., purl; st., stitch; tog., together; inc., increase (by working into the back and front of the same stitch); dec., decrease (by working 2 sts. tog.). Rib is k. 2 and p. 2 alternately.

To Work the Back

With No. 13 pins cast on 108 sts. and work 1 row into the back of the sts. to give a neat edge, then work 42 rows in rib.

Change to No. 9 pins and work in same rib, inc. at both ends of the next row and every following 10th row until 6 inc. rows have been worked, and there are 120 sts. on the pins.

Continue straight on these sts. for 19 rows more.

To Shape the Armholes : Continue in rib, casting off 3 sts. at the beginning of each of the next 6 rows (102 sts.), then dec. at both ends of each of the following

6 rows when 90 sts. will remain. Finally dec. at the beginning of every row until 40 sts. remain. Slip these 40 sts. on a stitch-holder until needed for the collar.

The Front

This is worked exactly the same as the back.

(Continued on page 86)

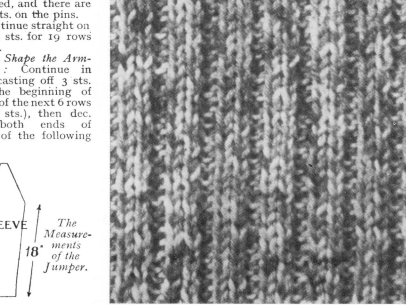

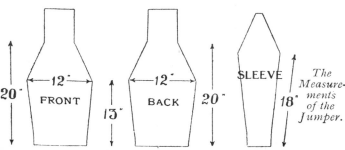

FRONT 12" 20"

BACK 12" 20" 13"

SLEEVE 18"

The Measurements of the Jumper.

JUST TWO-AND-TWO RIB

Continued

The Sleeves

WITH No. 13 pins begin at the wrist and cast on 56 sts. Work 1 row into the back of the sts. to give a neat edge, then work 28 rows in rib.

Change to two No. 9 pins and work 8 rows in rib, then continue in rib, inc. at both ends of the next row and every following 10th row until 12 inc. rows have been worked and there are 80 sts. on the pins. Work 9 rows straight on these sts. (more rows may be worked here if a longer sleeve is desired).

To Shape the Sleeve Top : Continue in rib casting off 3 sts. at the beginning of each of the next 2 rows, then dec. at the beginning of every row until 8 sts. remain. Slip these sts. on a stitch-holder until needed for the collar.

Work a second sleeve in the same manner, leaving the sts. on the pin at the end.

The Collar

WITH the same pin that holds the last sleeve sts. rib the front sts. from the st.-holder, then second sleeve sts., and the back sts., which gives 96 sts. altogether.

Work 50 rows in rib, then cast off in rib.

To MAKE UP THE JUMPER : Do not press the work. Join the sleeve tops to corresponding edges of back and front, then join the sleeve and side seams in one long line, taking 1 st. from each side at a time. Press all seams lightly on the wrong side of the work with the edge of a warm iron.

COLD-PROOF

"*What on earth's all this noise about ?*" Lady Cynthia exclaimed. "*What's wrong with the child ? He seemed such a jolly little fellow yesterday. Well, it's your job, nurse, to keep him cheerful. See to it that he's happy by the time Sir Derrick comes in.*"

A FAIR ISLE CARDIGAN

MATERIALS

Two ounces of Golden Eagle "Polynit" Fingering. de Luxe, 3-ply, in light blue, and 1 oz. each of the same wool in natural, green and red.

A pair of No. 9 Stratnoid knitting pins.

4 red buttons.

MEASUREMENTS

Length, 13 ins.; round chest when buttoned, 23 ins.; sleeve seam, 10½ ins.

TENSION

Seven sts. and 7½ rows to 1 in.

ABBREVIATIONS

B., blue wool; n., natural wool; r., red wool; g., green wool.

NOTE.—When a number of stitches of the same colour occur together, in order to avoid long loops of wool on the wrong side, place the unused wool over the first finger of the left hand. Work the next st. with left finger lowered, so that the working thread is used above the unused thread. Raise the left finger, and work the next st. so that the working thread is used beneath the unused thread. In this way the unused threads are not simply carried along the back, but are woven in the knitted fabric.

CAST on 160 sts. with b. for the lower edge, and work in k. 1, p. 1 rib for 6 rows. Now change to st.-st. and the Fair Isle pattern as follows. In every row repeat the contents of the brackets to the end.

1st and 2nd rows: N.

3rd row: (1 b., 2 n., 4 b., 2 n., 1 b.).

4th row: (1 n., 1 b., 2 n., 2 b., 2 n., 1 b., 1 n.).

5th row: (2 n., 1 b., 4 n., 1 b., 2 n.).

6th row: (1 b., 2 n., 1 b., 2 n., 1 b., 2 n., 1 b.).

7th row: (2 b., 2 n., 2 b., 2 n., 2 b.).

8th – 13th rows: Work the 6th, 5th rows, etc., back to the 1st row. Cut the n.

14th row: B.

15th row: (3 b., 2 r., 2 b., 2 r., 4 b., 3 r., 4 b.).

16th row: (5 b., 2 r., 5 b., 2 r., 2 b., 2 r., 2 b.).

17th row: (1 r., 1 b., 2 r., 1 b., 3 r., 4 b., 3 r., 5 b.).

18th row: (5 b., 4 r., 3 b., 2 r., 1 b., 4 r., 1 b.).

ABBREVIATIONS

St., stitch; k., knit; p., purl; tog., together; dec., decrease by working 2 sts. tog.; inc., increase by working twice into the same st.; st.-st., stocking-stitch (1 row k., 1 row p.).

19th row: (1 b., 5 r., 1 b., 2 r., 1 b., 6 r., 4 b.).

20th row: (4 b., 8 r., 1 b., 6 r., 1 b.).

21st row: (1 b., 9 r., 10 b.).

22nd row: (2 b., 7 r., 2 b., 7 r., 2 b.).

23rd row: (11 b., 5 r., 4 b.).

24th row: (3 r., 1 b., 6 r., 10 b.).

25th row: (10 b., 6 r., 1 b., 3 r.).

26th row: (3 r., 1 b., 6 r., 10 b.).

27th row: (11 b., 5 r., 1 b., 2 r., 1 b.).

28th row: (4 b., 4 r., 12 b.).

29th row: (13 b., 5 r., 2 b.) Cut the r.

30th row: B.

31st–44th rows: As the 1st–14th rows.

45th row: (3 b., 1 g., 1 b., 1 g., 3 b., 1 g.).

46th row: (3 b., 2 g., 1 b., 2 g., 2 b.).

47th row: (1 b., 3 g., 1 b., 3 g., 2 b.).

48th row: (4 b., 3 g., 3 b.).

49th–51st rows: As the 47th, 46th and 45th rows.

52nd row: B.

53rd–66th rows: As the 1st–14th rows.

67th and 68th rows: As the 45th and 46th rows, but with r. instead of g.

The Right Front. Continuing in pattern as the 47th row, but with r. instead of g., dec. at the beginning of the row. There is 1 st. on the right pin, then 2 r., 1 b., 3 r., and continue as the 47th pattern row, until there are 39 sts. on the right pin. These are for the right front. Leave the remaining 120 sts. on a spare pin. Turn.

Now, continuing in pattern to end of 66th row, shape the armhole by casting off 2 sts. at side edge on every alternate row until 10 sts. have been cast off altogether. At the same time, dec. at the front edge on every k. row until 10 such decs. have been made in all. Then continue straight on the remaining 20 sts. and after the completion of the 66th row repeat the 45th–52nd rows. Cut the g. and the b. and change to n.

Next row: K.

Next row: Cast off 10, p. to end.

Next row: K. Cast off the remaining 10 sts.

The Back.—Return to the 120 sts. on the spare pin. Cast off 2, work across the next sts. as the 47th row, but with r. instead of g., until there are 78 sts. on the right pin. These sts. are for the back. Leave the remaining 40 sts. for the left front on a spare pin.

Continue in pattern as for the right front, and cast off 2 sts. at the beginning of every row until 60 sts remain. Work straight in pattern until the back is the same length as the front up to the shoulder.

Cast off 10 sts. at the beginning of each of the next 4 rows. Cast off the remaining sts.

The Left Front.—Return to the 40 sts. on the spare pin. Commence at the under-arm, and cast off 2 sts. Work as the 47th row (with r. instead of g.) until 2 sts. remain, dec. Finish this side to correspond with the right side.

The Sleeves.—Cast on 40 sts. with b. and work 22 rows in k. 1, p. 1, rib. Work in pattern as for the main part of the cardigan, to the end of the 46th row. Now inc. at the beginning of every row to the end of the 68th row. Shape the top by casting off 2 sts. at the beginning of each of the next 20 rows, working in the same pattern as the back, and keeping the pattern correct throughout the shaping. Cast off.

Make the other sleeve to match.

The Front Border.—Cast on 10 sts. with b. * Rib 12 rows, then make a buttonhole as follows:

Next row: Rib 4, cast off 3, rib to the end. Next row: Rib 3, cast on 3, rib to the end.

Repeat the 14 rows from * 3 more times, and after the 4th buttonhole, continue in rib until the strip is long enough for a border for the front and neck edges of the cardigan. Cast off.

TO MAKE UP

Press the Fair Isle knitting on the wrong and the right side under a damp cloth. Join the shoulder seams and the sleeve seams. Sew the border to the front edges, with the buttonholes on the right front for girl and the left front for a boy. Work the buttonholes, and sew the buttons to the other front border. Sew the sleeves in the armholes. Press the seams.

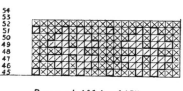

Repeat 1st to 14th rows

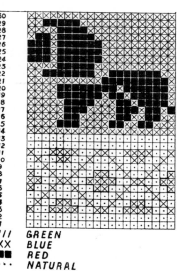

/// GREEN
XX BLUE
■■ RED
··· NATURAL

This diagram will help you in working the Fair Isle Pattern for the little cardigan.

Sunray Neck

·A practical, becoming fashion point, ensuring a perfect fit for the shoulders of this delightful streamline knitted frock. Here's a grand job for black-out evenings.

SO cosy on cold days . . . with the trim-fitting yoke buttoning neatly down the back.

Back and Front Alike

USING No. 9 needles start at lower edge of left side of skirt, cast on 78 sts. and work 8 rows in st.-st. Now work in pattern as follows:
1st row—* K. 3, wool forward, slip 3, wool back, rep. from * to end of row. **2nd row**—Purl. Rep. these 2 rows twice. **7th row**—* W.fd., s. 3, w.b., k. 3, rep. from * to end of row. **8th row**—Purl. Rep. these 2 rows twice. These 12 rows form the pattern which is repeated throughout.

Rep. these 12 rows once, then rep. rows 1-5 inclusive again. **30th row**—P. till 2 sts. remain, p. 2 tog. **31st row**—W.fd., s. 2, w.b., k. 3 * w.fd., s. 3, w.b., k. 3, rep. from * to end of row. **32nd row**—Purl. Rep. last 2 rows once, then rep. 31st row again. **36th row**—As 30th row. **37th row**—K. 1, w.fd., s. 3, w.b. * k. 3, w.fd., s. 3, w.b., rep. from * to end of row. **38th row**—Purl. Rep. last 2 rows once, then rep. 37th row again. **42nd row**—As 30th row. **43rd row**—K. 3 * w.fd., s.3, w.b., k.3, rep. from * to end of row. **44th row**—Purl. Rep. last 2 rows once, then rep. 43rd row again. **48th row**—As 30th row. **49th row**—W.fd., s. 2, w.b. * k. 3, w.fd., s. 3, w.b., rep. from * to end of row. **50th row**—Purl. Rep. last 2 rows once, then rep. 49th row again. **54th row**—As 30th row. **55th row**—K. 1 * w.fd., s. 3, w.b., k. 3, rep. from * to end of row. **56th row**—Purl. Rep. last 2 rows once, then rep. 55th row again. **60th row**—As 30th row. Rep. rows 1 and 2 twice. **65th row**—As 1st row. Rep. rows 30-65 inclusive (66 sts.). Continue in pattern decreasing 1 st. at the end of the next row and every 12th row after till 52 sts. are on needle. Work in pattern till work measures 27 inches from start, finishing with a pattern row. Leave on a spare needle.

For the Right side of skirt use No. 8 needles and cast on 78 sts. Work 8 rows in st.-st. then work rows 1-12 of pattern twice, then rep. rows 1-5 inclusive again.

30th row—P. 2 tog., p. to end of row. **31st row**—* W.fd., s. 3, w.b., k. 3, rep.

MATERIALS

22 ozs. Sirdar Boucle wool. 2 No. 11 and 2 No. 9 Abel Morrall's "Aero" knitting needles. 4 No. 11 knitting needles with double points. Steel crochet hook, No. 12. Linen collar. Belt.

MEASUREMENTS

Length from shoulder to lower edge, 42 inches. To fit a 34-36-inch bust. Sleeve seam, 19 inches. Hips, 38-40 inches.

Tension on No. 9 needles about 5½ stitches and 10 rows to one inch. Always knit into back of cast on stitches.

ABBREVIATIONS

K., knit; p., purl; st., stitch; tog. together; rep., repeat; w.fd., wool forward; s., slip; inc., increase (by knitting twice into stitch); w.b. wool back; d.c., double crochet.

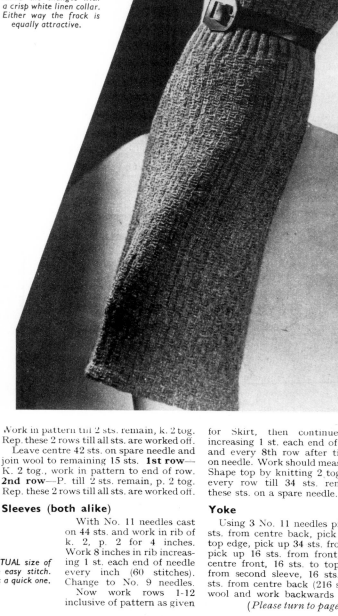

RING the changes with a crisp white linen collar. Either way the frock is equally attractive.

from * till 5 sts. remain, w.fd., s. 3, w.b., k.2. **32nd row**—Purl. Rep. last 2 rows once, then rep. 31st row again. **36th row**—As 30th row. **37th row**—* K. 3, w.fd., s. 3, w.b., rep. from * till 4 sts. remain, k. 4. **38th row**—Purl. Rep. last 2 rows once, then rep. 37th row again. **42nd row**—As 30th row. **43rd row**—* W.fd., s.3., w.b., k.3, rep. from * till 3 sts. remain, w.fd. s.3, w.b. **44th row**—Purl. Rep. last 2 rows once, then rep. 43rd row again. **48th row**—As 30th row. **49th row**—* K. 3, w.fd., s. 3, w.b., rep. from * till 2 sts. remain, k. 2. **50th row**—Purl. Rep. last 2 rows once, then rep. 49th row again. **54th row**—As 30th row. **55th row**—* W.fd., s. 3, w.b., k. 3, rep. from * till 1 st. remains, k. 1. **56th row**—Purl. Rep. last 2 rows once, then rep. 55th row again. **60th row**—As 30th row. Rep. rows 1 and 2 of pattern twice. **65th row**—As 1st row. Rep. rows 30-65 inclusive (66 sts.). Continue in pattern decreasing 1 st. at the beginning of the next row and every 12th row after till 52 sts. remain on needles, ending with a pattern row. **Next row**—P. 3 * p. 2 tog., p. 5, rep. from * to end of row; then work across left side of skirt as follows: * p. 2 tog., p. 5, rep. from * till 3 sts. remain, p. 3. (90 sts.). Straight ends are down centre.

Change to No. 11 needles. **1st row**—K. 2 * p. 2, k. 2, rep. from * to end of row. **2nd row**—P. 2 * k. 2, p. 2, rep. from * to end of row. Rep. these 2 rows for 2 inches.

Now change to No. 9 needles and work rows 1-12 of pattern. Continue in pattern increasing 1 st. each end of the next row and every 12th row after till 100 sts. are on needle. Continue in pattern without shaping till work measures 36½ inches from start. Now shape armholes:

Continue in pattern casting off 6 sts. at the beginning of the next 2 rows and knitting 2 tog. each end of every row till 72 sts. remain. Work 2 rows without shaping.

Now start yoke-shaping. **1st row**—Work in pattern over 15 sts. Leave remaining sts. on spare needle. **2nd row**—P. 2 tog., p. to end of row. **3rd row**—

Work in pattern till 2 sts. remain, k. 2 tog. Rep. these 2 rows till all sts. are worked off.

Leave centre 42 sts. on spare needle and join wool to remaining 15 sts. **1st row**—K. 2 tog., work in pattern to end of row. **2nd row**—P. till 2 sts. remain, p. 2 tog. Rep. these 2 rows till all sts. are worked off.

Sleeves (both alike)

With No. 11 needles cast on 44 sts. and work in rib of k. 2, p. 2 for 4 inches. Work 8 inches in rib increasing 1 st. each end of needle every inch (60 stitches). Change to No. 9 needles.

Now work rows 1-12 inclusive of pattern as given

for Skirt, then continue in pattern increasing 1 st. each end of the next row and every 8th row after till 84 sts. are on needle. Work should measure 19 inches. Shape top by knitting 2 tog. each end of every row till 34 sts. remain. Leave these sts. on a spare needle.

Yoke

Using 3 No. 11 needles pick up last 21 sts. from centre back, pick up 16 sts. to top edge, pick up 34 sts. from one sleeve, pick up 16 sts. from front, 42 sts. from centre front, 16 sts. to top edge, 34 sts. from second sleeve, 16 sts. to back, 21 sts. from centre back (216 sts.). Join on wool and work backwards and forwards

(*Please turn to page* 90)

ACTUAL size of the easy stitch. It's a quick one.

DAINTY AND USEFUL

This Shawl is Easy to Knit and the Pattern is Reversible

IN spite of the variety of bed-jackets and wraps one sees in the shops nowadays, the hand-knitted shawl still holds its own on account of its comfort and convenience.

Elderly folk appreciate the extra warmth across the shoulders which a shawl affords; being more easily slipped on it may be preferable to a sleeved wrap for the invalid who can only sit up for short periods; and in the outfit of the young baby, of course, the shawl is an important item.

Illustrated here is a reversible shawl of an attractive pattern which is easy to knit. To make it you will require:—

15oz. Baldwin and Walker's Ladyship Ripple-sheen.

1 pair knitting needles, No. 6.

Measurement: 45in. square, not including the fringe.

Tension before pressing: 5½ st. to 1in. in width; 4½ ridges to 1in. in depth.

Note.—If the needles stated do not produce this tension, try different sizes until you get it correct.

Alteration in Size.—For a larger shawl, use thicker needles. or a size which produces fewer stitches to the inch. For a smaller shawl, use finer needles, or a size which produces a larger number of stitches to the inch.

Abbreviations.—K., knit; st., stitches; m. 1, make a stitch by bringing the wool forward; tog., together; rep., repeat.

Begin by casting on 192 st. (or any number divisible by 12 if a bigger or smaller square is required) and work in the pattern as follows:—

1st row.—* K. 2 tog., m. 1, k. 10. Rep. from * to end of row.

2nd row.—K. 9, m. 1, k. 2 tog., * k. 10, m. 1, k. 2 tog. Rep. from * to the last st., k. 1.

3rd row.—K. 2, k. 2 tog., m. 1, * k. 10, k. 2 tog., m. 1. Rep. from * to the last 8 st., k. 8.

4th row.—K. 7, m. 1, k. 2 tog., * k. 10, m. 1, k. 2 tog. Rep. from * to the last 3 st., k. 3.

5th row.—K. 4, k. 2 tog., m. 1, * k. 10, k. 2 tog., m. 1. Rep. from * to the last 6 st., k. 6.

6th row.—K. 5, m. 1, k. 2 tog., * k. 10, m. 1, k. 2 tog. Rep. from * to the last 5 st., k. 5.

7th row.—K. 6, k. 2 tog., m. 1, * k. 10, k. 2 tog., m. 1. Rep. from * to the last 4 st., k. 4.

8th row.—K. 3, m. 1, k. 2 tog., * k. 10, m. 1, k. 2 tog. Rep. from * to the last 7 st., k. 7.

9th row.—K. 8, k. 2 tog., m. 1, * k. 10, k. 2 tog., m. 1. Rep. from * to the last 2 st., k. 2.

10th row.—K. 1, m. 1, k. 2 tog., * k. 10, m. 1, k. 2 tog. Rep. from * to the last 9 st., k. 9.

11th row.—* K. 10, k. 2 tog., m. 1. Rep. from * to the last 12 st., k. 12.

12th row.—* K. 11, * m. 1, k. 2 tog., k. 10. Rep. from * to the last 11 st., k. 11.

Repeat these 12 rows of pattern until the shawl measures 45in. square. Cast off.

THE FRINGE

Using a piece of cardboard about 2in. wide, wind the wool around the cardboard, and cut along one edge, making the strands of wool 4in. long. Using a crochet hook, take two of the lengths of wool and double into two, place the crochet hook through a stitch of the knitting along one side, pull the loop through, then pull the ends of wool through the loop, thus forming a knot. Repeat all round the outer edges of shawl.

KNITTED DRESS Continued

on these sts. in rib of k. 2, p. 2 for 3 inches, leaving an opening at centre back. **Next row**—(Right side of work towards you) * K. 2, p. 2 tog., rep. from * to end of row. **Next row**—* K. 1, p. 2, rep. from * to end of row. **Next row**—* K. 2, p. 1, rep. from * to end of row. Rep. these 2 rows for one more inch. **Next row**—* K. 2 tog., p. 1, rep. from * to end of row. Work in rib of k. 1, p. 1 until yoke measures 5¼ inches. Cast off in rib.

Buttons (5 alike)

Using crochet hook, make 3 chain and join in a ring. Work 6 d.c. into ring. **Next round**—2 d.c. into each d.c. **Next round**—D.c. **Next round**—* 1 d.c. miss next d.c., rep. from * to end of round. Fasten off, stuff with wool and stitch up.

To Make Up

Press work lightly. Join side, sleeve and centre seams. Make loops down right side of back opening and sew buttons to left side. Work a row of double crochet round neck edge. Press all seams.

Useful PULLOVER
with V-NECK

row inclusive 5 times, then rep. from 23rd to 28th row inclusive. Now shape shoulders.

209th row—Cast off 5, k. 2, (s. 1, k. 3) to end. **210th row**—Cast off 5, p. 2, (s. 1, p. 3) till 3 rem., **s. 1, p. 2. 211th row**—Cast off 5, k. 1, (s. 1, k. 3) till 3 rem., **s. 1, k. 2. 212th row**—Cast off 5, p. 1, (s. 1, p. 3) till 2 rem., **s. 1, p. 1. Next 2 rows**—Cast off 5, k. to end. Rep. 211th and 212th rows. **217th row**—Cast off 6, (k. 3, s. 1) till 1 rems., k. 1. **218th row**—Cast off 6, p. 3, (s. 1, p. 3) to end.

Next 2 rows—Cast off 6, k. to end. Slip the 31 sts. on to a piece of wool for neck-band.

Front

K. as for back till 119th row is reached. Now shape armholes and divide for neck. **119th row**—Dec., (k. 3, s. 1) 16 times, dec., slip these sts. on to stitch-holder for left side of front, k. 1, s. 1, (k. 3, s. 1) 15 times. k. , dec.

120th row—Dec., p. 2, (s. 1, , till 2 rem., s. 1, p. 1. **121st row**—K. 1, (s. 1, k. 3) till rem., s. 1, k. 1, dec. **122nd row**—Dec., (s. 1, p. 3) till 2 rem., s. 1, p. 1.

123rd row—K. till 2 rem., dec. **124th row**—Dec., k. to end. **125th row**—Dec., k. 1, (s. 1, k. 3) till 2 rem., dec.

126th row—Dec., p. 2, (s. 1, p. 3) till 3 rem., s. 1, p. 2. **127th row**—K. 2, (s. 1, k. 3) till 4 rem., s. 1, k. 1, dec. **128th row**—Dec., (s. 1, p. 3) till 3 rem., s. 1, p. 2. Rep. 123rd and 124th rows. **131st row**—Dec., k. 2, (s. 1, k. 3) till 2 rem., dec. **132nd row**—Dec., p. 2, (s. 1, p. 3) till 2 rem., dec. **133rd row**—(K. 3, s. 1) till 3 rem., k. 1, dec.

134th row—Dec., (s. 1, p. 3) to end. Rep. 123rd and 124th rows. **137th row**—Dec., (k. 3, s. 1) till 5 rem., k. 3, dec. **138th row**—Dec., p. 2, (s. 1, p. 3) till 1 rems., p. 1. (44 sts.). **139th row**—K. 4, (s. 1, k. 3) to end. **140th row**—(P. 3, s. 1) till 4 rem., p. 4. **Next 2 rows**—K. **143rd row**—Dec.,

MATERIALS

8 oz. Copley's "Excelsior" knitting wool, 4-ply.
Double Century knitting pins, 2 No. 9 and 4 No. 12 (double points).
Stitch-holder.

MEASUREMENTS

Shoulder to lower edge, 22 inches; to fit a 36–38-inch chest.

Always work into back of each cast-on stitch.
Tension of knitting, about 7 sts. and 10 rows to one inch.

ck

WITH No. 12 needles commence at lower edge, casting on 134 sts. K. in rib of k. 1, p. 1 for 22 rows, increasing 1 st. at end of last row. (135 sts.) Change to No. 9 needles. **23rd** —K. 1, (s. 1, slip all sts. purlways, k. 3) till 2 rem., s. 1, k. 1. row—P. 1, (s. 1, p. 3) till 2 rem., s. 1, p. 1. Rep. last once. **27th row**—K. **28th row**—K. **29th row**—K. 3, 3) to end. **30th row**—P. 3, (s. 1, p. 3) to end. Rep. ws once. **33rd row**—K. **34th row**—K. Rep. last times more. Now shape armholes. row—Dec., k. 3, (s. 1, k. 3) till 6 rem., s. 1, k. 3, h row—Dec., p. 2, (s. 1, p. 3) till 5 rem., s. 1, p. 2, row—Dec., k. 1, (s. 1, k. 3) till 4 rem., s. 1, k. 1, row—Dec., (s. 1, p. 3) till 3 rem., s. 1, dec. ws—Dec., k. till 2 rem., dec. Rep. last 6 rows p. 119th and 120th rows. (95 sts.) Rep. 29th s. **Next 2 rows**—K. Rep. from 23rd to 34th

V-NECK PULLOVER

(s. 1, k. 3) till 2 rem., s. 1, k. 1. **144th row**—P. 1, (s. 1, p. 3) till 2 rem., s. 1, p. 1. **145th row**—K. 1, (s. 1, k. 3) till 2 rem., s. 1, k. 1. **146th row**—As 144th row. **Next 2 rows**—K.

149th row—Dec., k. 1, (s. 1, k. 3) to end.

150th row—(P. 3, s. 1) till 2 rem., p. 2.

151st row—K. 2, (s. 1, k. 3) to end. **152nd row**—As 150th row. **Next 2 rows**—K. **155th row**—Dec., k. 2, (s. 1, k. 3) till 2 rem., s. 1, k. 1. **156th row**—P. 1, (s. 1, p. 3) to end. **157th row**—(K. 3, s. 1) till 1 rem., k. 1. **158th row**—As 156th row. **Next 2 rows**—K. **161st row**—Dec., k. 3, (s. 1, k. 3) to end. **162nd row**—(P. 3, s. 1) till 4 rem., p. 4.

163rd row—K. 4, (s. 1, k. 3) to end. **164th row**—As 162nd row. **165th row**—K. Rep. last row. Rep. from 143rd to 166th row inclusive, then from 143rd to 158th row inclusive. **207th row**—K. **208th row**—K. **209th row**—As 161st row. (32 sts.) Now shape shoulder.

210th row—Cast off 4, (p. 3, s. 1) till 4 rem., p. 4.

211th row—K. 4, (s. 1, k. 3) to end. **212th row**—As 210th row. **213rd row**—K. **214th row**—Cast off 4, k. to end.

215th row—K. 2, (s. 1, k. 3) till 2 rem., s. 1, k. 1.

216th row—Cast off 4, p. 1, (s. 1, p. 3) till 3 rem., s. 1, p. 2. Rep. last 2 rows once, then rep. 213th and 214th rows. (8 sts.) Cast off. Return to left shoulder, slip sts. from stitch-holder to needle, point toward centre, join on wool. Rep. from 120th to 208th row inclusive in directions for right side of front, but working each row backwards; the 120th row would read

thus :—P. 1, s. 1, (p. 3, s. 1) till 4 rem., p. 2, dec. Now shape shoulder.

209th row—Cast off 4, (k. 3, s. 1) till 5 rem., k. 3, dec. **210th row**—P. 4, (s. 1, p. 3) to end. **211th row**—Cast off 4, (k. 3, s. 1) till 4 rem., k. 4. **212th row**—As 210th row.

213rd row—Cast off 4, k. to end. **214th row**—K.

215th row—Cast off 4, k. 1, (s. 1, k. 3) till 3 rem., s. 1, k. 2. **216th row**—P. 2, (s. 1, p. 3) till 2 rem., s. 1, p. 1. Rep. last 2 rows once, then rep. 213rd and 214th rows. (8 sts.) Cast off.

TO MAKE UP

Pin out each piece and press on wrong side under a damp cloth with a hot iron. Sew up shoulder seams.

Neck-band.—Join wool at centre front, and with No. 12 needles pick up and k. 80 sts. as far as back of neck ; with 2nd needle, k. the back 31 sts. ; with 3rd needle, pick up and k. 80 sts. along other side of neck. (80, 31, 80.)

Next 6 rounds—Dec., k. till 2 rem., dec.

Next 6 rounds—Inc., k. till 1 rems., inc. Cast off.

Sleeve Bands (*both alike*).—With No. 12 needles, pick up and k. 144 sts. along armhole. **2nd row**—P. K. 12 rows st.-st. Cast off.

Press each band, then turn over on to wrong side and hem ; this forms a narrow band of double stocking-stitch. Sew up underarm seams. Press all seams.

Raise yourself, quite slowly, from the waist, until your head is upright, turn the b... sharply to the right, your left hand caressing the top of your head, and bend over to th... your right hand touches the middle of your right leg. You will feel the little " pull" at the...

● a business-like pullover

THIS thin, but warm, pullover will be most useful to slip on under your regulation uniform coat. It is made in 2-ply fingering, and fits neatly round the neck-line of your collar and tie. Special care has been taken to make the instructions simple enough for you to knit in spare moments when you are hanging about on duty. A good knitter will only have to take care at armhole and neck shapings, otherwise she will be able to make the entire garment without giving it other than an occasional glance from time to time.

●

MATERIALS: 6 ozs. Patons Super, or Beehive, Scotch Fingering, 2-ply. Original uses blue, No. 2189. A pair No. 12 and a pair No. 10 "Isis" needles.

MEASUREMENTS: To fit 34–36-inch bust; length from top of shoulders, 19½ inches; sleeve seam, 18½ inches.

TENSION: 7½ stitches to an inch, measured over stocking-stitch, worked on No. 10 needles.

BACK

With No. 12 needles cast on 110 stitches, and work 3½ inches in k. 1, p. 1 rib. Change to No. 10 needles and stocking-stitch, increasing at each end of next and every following 8th row until there are 128 stitches on the needle.

Carry on straight until side edge measures 12 inches. Here shape armholes:—Cast off 6 stitches at beginning of next 2 rows, then k. 2 tog. at each end of every row, eight times. Work straight until back measures 19 inches.

Shape shoulders by casting off 9 stitches at beginning next 6 rows; cast off remaining 46 stitches.

FRONT

rk exactly as for back until work measures 12 inches. shape armholes as for back, and at the same time neck:—Working on first 64 stitches, k. 2 tog. at ge on next and every 3rd row until 27 remain. straight until front measures same length as ape shoulders by casting off 9 at beginning of ernate rows, armhole edge. l to remaining stitches and work to correspond.

SLEEVES

12 needles cast on 54 stitches, and work 1, p. 1 rib. Change to No. 10 needles and increasing at each end of next and every following 6th row until there are 94 stitches on the needle.

Work straight until side edge measures 18½ inches. Shape top by casting off 6 at beginning of next 2 rows, then k. 2 tog. at each end of every alternate row until 30 remain. Cast off.

TO MAKE UP

Press pieces lightly on wrong side under a damp cloth; join right shoulder seam. With No. 12 needles and front of work facing, pick up and knit 160 stitches round neck edge, 60 down each front and 40 across back. Work in k. 1, p. 1 rib, working 2 together, twice, on every 4th row at centre front of neck, twice. Work in rib until it is 1 inch in depth. Cast off loosely in rib.

Sew together side, shoulder and sleeve seams; insert sleeves.

KNITCRAFT

In this article " FINELLA," our knitting expert, gives you some professional tips which should help you to improve the quality of your work

KNITTING is so universally popular nowadays that there must be few who cannot do plain and purl, but alas ! the finished garment is often disappointing in its workmanship, simply because the secrets of knitcraft, as distinct from knitting, are not as well known as they ought to be. Let me try to explain the chief of them.

As with all handwork, it is the attention to detail which will produce best results, and it is a mistake to choose too intricate a design to begin with. After all, the simplest patterns are often the most effective, as my experience in designing for WIFE and HOME has shown me.

It is important to obtain the materials stated. Wool of a different kind, and needles of a different gauge, will produce a garment of a different size from that of the model. The " gauge " of the needle is its size, or thickness, which naturally affects the size of the stitches, but even needles of the same gauge may produce a slightly different stitch if one pair has points which are more tapered than the other pair.

One thing which remains unalterable is the required tension of the knitting. If the instructions state that there are 6 stitches to the inch, it is essential that the knitter should produce this number. Before beginning the work itself, cast on about 24 stitches, and knit in the pattern for about 30 rows. Press this specimen, if the finished garment is to be pressed, and place a ruler across the middle of it. Count the number of stitches to the middle inch. Should there be too many, either knit more loosely or use larger needles. If there are too few stitches, knit more tightly or use smaller needles.

CASTING ON

THE cast-on edge should have the same elasticity as the rest of the work. There is a great tendency for this edge to be too tight, and to overcome this defect it is a good plan to cast on with needles one or two sizes larger than those which will be employed for the beginning of the work.

There are several methods of casting on, and some knitters use double wool to ensure an edge which will withstand strain. The most common method is probably the " knitting " method. Make a slip loop on the left needle for the first stitch. Insert the right needle in it and draw a loop of wool through the stitch on the left needle. Now there is also a stitch on the right needle. Slip it from the right to the left needle. Proceed in this way for the number required. It is advisable to knit one row into the back of these stitches before proceeding with the work, in order to produce a firm and even edge.

A very good, but less known method is as follows. Make the slip loop on the left needle. Cast on the second stitch as in the previous method. Now insert the right needle, from front to back immediately beneath the left needle, and between the two previous stitches. Draw the wool from back to front on the right needle, thus producing a stitch, and place this stitch on the left needle. Cast on the remaining stitches in this way.

A third method is the old-fashioned way of knitting into loops on the left thumb, using one needle only. This is shown in the diagrams on this page. It has the advantage of producing a firm edge, but cannot be used in the middle of a piece of work.

Good knitting should be even, and the rhythm which is attained by continuous knitting will produce a more even tension than the work which is picked up repeatedly for short periods. Avoid joins where they will be seen. Do not begin a row if the wool is insufficient to finish the row, but commence the new ball, having wound the wool very loosely.

Protect the early stages of the work from soil and rubbing by pinning or tacking the knitting in a large handkerchief or some other piece of fabric, and keep the hands as clean as possible. Try to knit quickly and handle the work lightly.

Not everyone knows the neatest method of decreasing. At the beginning of a plain row, knit 2 stitches together, picking up the backs of the stitches. At the end of a similar row, knit 2 stitches together, picking up the fronts. This ensures that the decreases slope in the right way. Another method of decreasing at the beginning of the row is to slip the first of the 2 stitches from left to right needles, without knitting it, to knit the second of the two stitches, and then to pass the slipped stitch over the knitted stitch.

In purl rows, purl 2 stitches together and work into the fronts of the stitches at the beginning of rows, and purl into the backs of stitches at the end of rows.

To increase, first knit (or purl) a stitch into the front of the stitch on the left needle, and then knit another stitch into the back of the same stitch on the left needle. In lace patterns, where the open design needs a hole, a stitch is made by simply passing the wool over the needle. This is usually called " m. 1 " (make one).

Stitches are sometimes dropped accidentally, and they may run down the work. A skilled knitter can pick up such stitches even in lace patterns, without any mistake. A crochet hook is always useful when a stitch is dropped. Plain stitches can be retrieved by working chain stitches up the rows. Purl stitches are picked up in the same way, but the chain is worked on the wrong side.

Beginners are sometimes puzzled directions given for repetition of a part or group of stitches or rows. Groups of stitches in brackets are repeated the number of times stated immediately after the bracket. For example, (k. 7, p. 3) 4 times. An asterisk (*) serves the same purpose as a bracket, directions following the * are repeated the number of times stated.

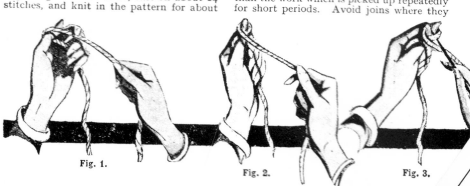

Fig. 1.   Fig. 2.   Fig. 3.

HOW TO CAST ON

Measure off a length of wool about four times as long as the row of knitting is to be. Leave this end loose and at this point hold the thread in the left hand and with the right hand bring the main thread round the front of the left thumb (Fig. 1). Wind the wool once round the left thumb, thus crossing the thread already on the left thumb (Fig. 2). Take a knitting needle in the right hand, also holding the thread from the ball in the right hand, and [...] left thumb (Fig. 3). [...] through, still holding the [...] the left thumb and pull the [...] to the needle. This is the first stit[...] same way. Keep them as even as p[...]

More About Knitcraft

CASTING OFF

A CAST-OFF edge has a tendency to be too tight, and it is advisable to use a larger needle for the process. Work two stitches in the ordinary way, then, using the left needle, pull the first stitch over the second stitch and drop it. Work the next stitch on the left needle, so that there are again two stitches on the right needle. Pass the first over the second and drop it. Continue thus to the end. Draw the end of the wool through the last stitch and darn it in the back of the fabric, for safety.

It sometimes happens that there are two sets of stitches, equal in number, which will have to be joined to form a seam. They may be grafted together in such a way that the join is invisible. Place the two sets of stitches beside each other, with the wrong sides together and the right sides outside, and cut the wool attached to one set of stitches, so that it is about 5 times the length of the seam. Thread it in a wool needle, and hold the work with this end on the right side of the back needle. Pass the wool needle through the first front stitch purlwise without slipping the stitch off the knitting needle. Pass the wool needle through the first back stitch purlwise, without slipping it off the knitting needle.

* Insert wool needle in next stitch of front needle (through the same stitch as the wool needle has already passed purlwise) knitwise. Slip the stitch off the knitting needle. Pass the wool needle through the next stitch of the front row purlwise, but do not slip it off the knitting needle.

Pass the wool needle through the next stitch on the back needle purlwise (through the same stitch as the wool has previously passed) and slip it off the knitting needle. Pass the wool needle through the next stitch of the back row knitwise, but do not slip this stitch off the knitting needle.

Repeat from * to * to the end, and adjust the tension of the grafting thread so that it is the same as that of the knitting. At the end of the row, fasten off by darning the wool in the back of the knitting.

Knitting in which two or more colours are employed is usually known as Fair Isle knitting, although some of these patterns are not Fair Isle designs. The colour not in use may be carried along the back, at an easy tension, so that it does not hold the fabric tightly. This method certainly has the best effect as regards appearance, but there is a risk that the loops of wool at the back may catch on a button or similar object and will then be tightly dragged, thus spoiling the pattern. The alternative is to weave the colour not in use along the back. Place the wool which is required for use over the first finger of the right hand, and the unused colour over the first finger of the left hand. Lower the left finger, and knit the next stitch so that the unused colour is beneath the knitted stitch. Raise the left finger, and knit the next stitch so that the unused colour is above the knitted stitch. Continue in this way, alternately raising and dropping the left finger, so that the stitches are knitted alternately under and over the unused thread. When the pattern needs a change of colour, reverse the two threads on the right and left first fingers. Press the work heavily for some time on the wrong side under a damp cloth.

MAKING UP

W HEN the knitting is completed there still remains the equally important task of making up the garment. The parts should be the correct size to fit the figure. Pressing may stretch the fabric a little. Some knitting, such as ribbing and raised patterns, is best left unpressed. If there be any doubt as to the way to obtain the best effect, try pressing lightly on the wrong side ; and if it improves the appearance, increase the pressure. For really heavy pressing use a damp cloth and a heavy iron. Sometimes really heavy pressing on the right side under a damp cloth will give the best result. This experimental pressing may be carried out on a small sample piece of the knitting. In the case of competition work it is always advisable to knit a sample of the pattern first, and this may be kept for trial pressing.

If the parts of a garment are rather small it may be possible to stretch them sufficiently while pressing. As an alternative method, strips of knitting may be made and neatly let into the garment at the seams.

Should the parts be too large, a tacking thread can be run in the fabric as a guide to the amount of surplus material. Along this line run two rows of hand or machine stitching, without stretching it out of shape. Cut away the excess, leaving $\frac{1}{4}$ inch edge, and work double crochet over the edge.

Necks and armholes which have a tendency to stretch, or which are too large, may be drawn to size by a row of double crochet

Opinions vary as to the best method of making seams. Shoulder edges which have been shaped are probably best joined like a. seam for textiles—with small running stitches and an occasional back-stitch, allowing a narrow single turning on either edge. Straight shoulder edges may be grafted, or the cast-off stitches may be oversewn. Whatever the method, it is essential that this seam be the correct length, which is usually 4 inches for a stock size woman's garment, and from $5\frac{1}{2}$ to 6 inches for a man's. Sleeves may be set in the armholes by either of these two methods. Press each seam as it is finished. Some seams, such as side and sleeve seams, are better if they are free to stretch, otherwise they may break. In such cases, provided the wool be not too thick, it is best to work them in double crochet. This is certainly advisable for underwear.

Any parts which may sag owing to strain, such as front openings, pocket edges, shoulders in heavy garments, should be strengthened by means of strips of tape, ribbon, or similar binding. Should there be any uncertainty as to the position of buttonholes, omit them while knitting, and make them when the garment has been fitted by cutting the wool at the required place, unravelling a few stitches, darning in the ends, and working double crochet into the stitches along the edge.

Ribbing which does not grip the figure as it should, may have a fine elastic threaded along the back, but a better way to overcome this trouble is to join two ends of a waist length of elastic, turn the garment inside out, place the elastic on the ribbing, and work herringbone-stitch over the elastic.

Garments which are in a pattern needing no pressing may have an unfinished appearance when they are completed. In such cases, arrange the garment carefully in shape, place a board on it, and leave it with heavy weights on the top for a day or more.

THE END